Anti-Dumping and Countervailing Action

Limits Imposed by Economic and Legal Theory

Philip Bentley QC

Partner, McDermott Will & Emery Stanbrook, Brussels, Belgium

Aubrey Silberston CBE

Emeritus Professor of Economics, Imperial College, London, UK

Edward Elgar
Cheltenham, UK • Northampton, MA, USA

Published by
Edward Elgar Publishing Limited
Glensanda House
Montpellier Parade
Cheltenham
Glos GL50 1UA
UK

Edward Elgar Publishing, Inc.
William Pratt House
9 Dewey Court
Northampton
Massachusetts 01060
USA

A catalogue record for this book
is available from the British Library

Library of Congress Cataloguing in Publication Data

Bentley, Philip, Q.C.
  Anti-dumping and countervailing action : limits imposed by economic and legal theory / by Philip Bentley, Aubrey Silberston.
    p. cm.
  Includes bibliographical references and index.
  1. Antidumping duties—Law and legislation. 2. Subsidies—Law and legislation. 3. Dumping (International trade)—Law and legislation. 4. Export subsidies. 5. Dumping (International trade)—Government policy. I. Silberston, Aubrey. II. Title.
  K4635.B46 2007
  343′.087—dc22
                                                                    2007000729

ISBN 978 1 84720 344 1

Typeset by Cambrian Typesetters, Camberley, Surrey
Printed and bound in Great Britain by MPG Books Ltd, Bodmin, Cornwall

Contents

Preface

This book has resulted from discussions between a lawyer and an economist, both of whom have worked extensively in this area. Most books on these subjects have the objective of setting out the relevant international agreements and regulations, and examining how these have been interpreted by regulatory authorities, by courts and by World Trade Organisation panels. Our objective has been different. On close examination both the relevant laws and their interpretation give rise to numerous contradictions. In addition, much practice in this area defies economic as well as legal logic. We have therefore tried to explore these questions afresh, and our hope is that we have succeeded in throwing fresh light on many of them. We have concluded by suggesting, in the light of our analysis, a number of changes in law and practice. Even if changes in the relevant agreements and regulations are unlikely in the near future, we hope that practice in these areas will be modified by the arguments and suggestions that we have put forward.

P.B.
A.S.

1. Introduction

1.1 PURPOSE OF THE STUDY

The purpose of this study is to provide an overview of the World Trade Organisation (WTO) rules on countervailing action and dumping. These are based on the implementation of Article VI of the General Agreement on Tariffs and Trade (GATT),[1] and are the rules which determine the circumstances in which the USA, the European Union (EU) and other WTO member countries may adopt countervailing or anti-dumping measures against imports of products from a third country. These measures are imposed on the grounds that the products are either subsidized in the country of origin, or are being dumped, and that their import is causing injury to domestic producers of the like product.

In this study, after some brief introductory remarks about the historical background, and the WTO framework for countervailing action and dumping, these matters are considered in some detail, together with an examination of a number of economic and legal problems that arise in their operation. Many countries now take action under these rules, including a growing number of developing countries, but long experience of such actions by the USA and the EU has given rise to many cases initiated by them, as well as numerous GATT and WTO Panel findings, and judgments of the national courts. This is therefore reflected in many of the cases cited in this study.

We will begin this introduction with some basic terminology. The expression 'anti-dumping action' is used to refer to state measures, usually in the form of additional customs duties, designed specifically to protect that state's own producers of a given product against unfair dumping practices carried on by exporters of the like product in another state. 'Countervailing action' is similar except that the purpose of the additional customs duties is to protect one state's domestic producers of a given product against the unfair trade effects of subsidization of the like product by another state.

This study is about the internationally accepted rules on anti-dumping and countervailing action. These are contained in two international agreements on

---

[1] See Appendix 1.

the implementation of Article VI of the GATT. Pursuant to these rules, anti-dumping or countervailing action measures may be imposed against imported products that are either subsidized in the country of origin or are being dumped, and where it is also demonstrated that their import is causing injury to domestic producers of the like product.

This simple introductory statement raises many questions. Since every state is sovereign in its own territory, one would expect states to have completely unfettered freedom to impose customs duties or quantitative restrictions (quotas) for any purpose whatsoever. And, indeed, they have such freedom. For centuries, kings and emperors have imposed customs duties both as a means of raising revenue and as a means of protecting domestic industry, arts and crafts. It is only in comparatively modern history that we come across serious questioning of whether 'protectionism' is good policy, whether there might not be some practical economic limits to sovereign power to levy import duties and to protect domestic industry. This is one aspect of the present study – the economic limits to anti-dumping and countervailing action in modern trade policy.

When, by the end of the Second World War, it had become widely accepted among trading nations that 'free trade' was good for the world trading order, and 'protectionism' was bad, a multilateral trade agreement was negotiated, the General Agreement on Tariffs and Trade. The text of this agreement was concluded in 1947 and is generally referred to as the GATT 1947.[2] The GATT 1947 set up a mechanism for the 'regulation' of international trade, in a very loose sense of the word 'regulate'. However, this was the opportunity for lawyers to enter on the scene, as rules were developed in more or less binding form, culminating in the setting up of the World Trade Organisation at the end of the Uruguay Round of multilateral trade negotiations in 1995. Thus, in addition to the pragmatic economic limitations on anti-dumping and countervailing action, there came to be 'legal' limits, using the word 'legal' in the broad sense accepted by public international lawyers. It is from this dual point of view, economics and law, that this study will analyse the limits to anti-dumping and countervailing action.

1.2   FREE TRADE VERSUS PROTECTION

It may be helpful to sketch first the historical background to the issues discussed in this study – in particular, the historical background to the conflict between advocates of free trade and advocates of protection. Countervailing

---

[2]   The text, dated 30 October 1947, is annexed to the Final Act Adopted at the Conclusion of the Second Session of the Preparatory Committee of the United Nations Conference on Trade and Employment.

and anti-dumping measures may or may not be regarded as desirable forms of trade protection, depending on one's point of view.

The issue of free trade versus protection has long been at the heart of all trade discussions, including those concerning dumping and subsidies. It is a subject which has preoccupied scholars, and has exercised governments, for many centuries.[3] There are many historical examples of free trade and of protection, especially of the latter. In spite of the founding of the GATT in 1947, and more recently of the WTO, measures in favour of protectionism have persisted strongly to the present day. It may be of interest to study this issue in the context of the British experience over several centuries.

A striking example of protection in British history is that of the Navigation Acts, which dated originally from 1381. Cromwell's famous Act of 1651 (re-enacted in 1660, on the restoration of the monarchy) prohibited all import or export of goods into or from British colonies outside Europe, and all import into England from such colonies, except in ships belonging to British subjects with, moreover, the master and three-quarters of the crew English. However, the free trade movement that followed the Napoleonic wars eventually did away with the Navigation Acts. In the 1820s, two acts were passed relating to navigation. One gave powers to permit goods to be imported or exported in foreign ships, subject to the same duties as goods carried in British ships. Another permitted British ships to go to sea with less than three-quarters of the crew British. Finally, as part of the general free trade movement, the Navigation Acts were repealed, although not until 1849.

The first great reform of the British tariff was carried out in 1825, when a large number of tariffs were consolidated and reduced. The power of retaliation by higher duties was, however, retained against countries which did not make corresponding concessions in favour of British trade. The next great reform was carried out in 1842, by which time free trade ideas, based on the writings of Adam Smith and David Ricardo, had influenced opinion even more strongly. This reform affected 750 of the 1200 articles then dutiable. Gladstone, as President of the Board of Trade, had the task of trying to get tariff concessions from foreign countries to match the reductions in the British tariff. He failed in every case. Foreign protectionist countries were too well informed of the prevailing free trade sentiment in Britain to give compensation for what they regarded as inevitable reductions in British duties. This was a striking early example of the problems involved in negotiating multilateral trade concessions.

Britain remained loyal to free trade throughout the late nineteenth and early twentieth centuries, in spite of growing protectionism in Europe and the

---

[3]   See Aubrey Silberston, 'Free trade versus protection', in *Striking a Balance: the role of the Board of Trade 1786-1986*, HMSO, 1986.

United States of America. The movement back to protectionism in Britain had its origin in the realization, after the outbreak of the First World War, that many of its industries were handicapped by lack of some essential part or material, for the supply of which they had been dependent on countries with which Britain was now at war. Perhaps the most important of these materials was synthetic dyestuffs, formerly supplied by Germany. In 1915, duties of $33^{1}/_{3}$ per cent were consequently imposed on a wide range of imported manufactures and materials, including vehicles, clocks, watches and some scientific instruments. In 1919, imports from Empire countries were given preferential treatment, at two-thirds of the full rate.

Following the economic crisis of 1931, emergency measures were introduced in Britain to introduce a general tariff of 10 per cent *ad valorem* on all goods not already subject to import duty, except for foodstuffs and industrial raw materials. Soon afterwards there was a rise in duties on manufactured goods to 20 per cent or more. Commonwealth products were largely admitted free of duty, and in return most Commonwealth countries granted preferences to imports from the United Kingdom. In contrast to the situation in 1914, Britain entered the war in 1939 with a highly protective tariff, except on imports from Commonwealth countries.

During the 1930s, Britain was by no means the only leading country to become more protectionist. In 1930–33 the Hawley–Smoot tariff in the USA raised average tariffs, on imports subject to duty, from 27 per cent to 53 per cent. France and other European countries had recourse to direct trade controls by quotas, while many countries, including Germany, introduced stringent exchange controls.

The restrictionism of the 1930s, with its prevalence of 'beggar-my-neighbour' policies, was thought by many at the time, and by more as the Second World War progressed, to have led to a diminution in world real income, and to have aggravated the world depression. During the war much thought was given to how the post-war world could avoid the mistakes of the 1930s. Soon after the end of the war, the International Monetary Fund (IMF) and the World Bank were set up in the monetary sphere. As regards trade, the 1948 Havana Charter was drawn up to establish an International Trade Organisation, but this was never ratified by the United States. This was partly because of the US dislike of the British preferential system, which had, in fact, to be abandoned some years later. A less ambitious, but still ground-breaking, substitute was found in the General Agreement on Tariffs and Trade (GATT), which had been drawn up a year earlier, in 1947.[4] Following this, 23 nations

---

[4]   For this reason the original General Agreement on Tariffs and Trade is usually referred to as 'GATT 1947', although it did not enter into force until 1948.

decided to negotiate immediate tariff concessions, and to undertake some of the commercial policy commitments of the Havana Charter. As a result of these developments, free trade had in principle once more gained ascendancy over protectionism.

1.3 THE WTO FRAMEWORK

The GATT 1947 was based on the principle of multilateral trade negotiations in which each negotiating party respected two important conditions. First, the principle of the Most Favoured Nation (MFN). According to this principle any concession made by a negotiating party to another party had to be made to all the other parties. Second, once each negotiating party had agreed his particular offer, of the tariffs available to all other parties on an MFN basis, that offer was to be set out in a Schedule to the GATT 1947 and would be binding on that negotiating party. It is for this reason that one speaks about 'bound tariffs', that is to say, tariffs that a member of the GATT has agreed will be the maximum tariffs imposed by it. A GATT member is always free to impose tariffs lower than those bound in its Schedule, provided that, in accordance with the MFN rule, it grants the lower tariff to all GATT members.

The GATT 1947 recognized that there were certain circumstances in which an exception should be made to the rule of bound tariffs and the MFN principle, including those in which the conditions of competition in trade between two member countries could be characterized as 'unfair'. Subsidization is one of these circumstances. If the exports of a GATT member are subsidized and, as a result, the prices of these exports are so low as to cause injury to the industry of an importing country, the importing country may impose a countervailing duty, of an amount no greater than that necessary to counteract the effect of the subsidy. 'Dumping' is another circumstance in which an exception to the MFN principle and bound tariffs can be made. The basic idea behind anti-dumping action is that an exporter should not be allowed to charge a lower price for his exports than for his domestic sales. If an exporter were allowed to charge lower prices for exports than for domestic sales he would be able to cover his fixed costs by his sales on the domestic market (where he could benefit from tariff protection) and then price his exports on the basis of marginal costs. To prevent such a practice from causing injury to the domestic industry of an importing country, the importing country is entitled to impose an anti-dumping duty, by way of exception to the principle of bound tariffs and MFN treatment.

The GATT 1947 dealt with anti-dumping and countervailing action in Article VI of its text. These provisions were relatively brief but they represented an important start to a process of introducing detailed disciplines into the procedures used by member countries for the adoption of anti-dumping and countervailing action. In particular, Article VI exhorts the contracting parties to condemn dumping (pricing exports below the home market price or below the cost of production) 'if it causes or threatens material injury to an established industry'. However, it left the country of importation to respond to injurious dumping by imposing a duty 'not greater than the margin of dumping'.

These disciplines have been developed in subsequent rounds of multilateral trade negotiations. The Kennedy Round introduced a Code on Anti-dumping action, and the Tokyo Round improved this Code and introduced a Code on Subsidies. The Uruguay Round, which established the World Trade Organisation (WTO) to strengthen the operation of the GATT, took these Codes a lot further, resulting in the Anti-dumping Agreement and the Subsidies and Countervailing Measures Agreement. These two measures are referred to as Agreements rather than Codes because they are subject to the WTO Dispute Settlement Understanding, which was also agreed during the Uruguay Round.

It is no longer a question of member countries agreeing loosely to apply a Code, with no sanction for failure to comply. Failure to comply with one of the Agreements of the Uruguay Round leads to proceedings before the WTO Dispute Settlement Body, whereby an independent panel and, if appealed, the Appellate Body of the WTO, will decide whether a member country has complied with the Anti-dumping Agreement or the Subsidies and Countervailing Measures Agreement. If not, the offending country will be ordered to correct the situation, failing which the injured member country can be authorized to take countermeasures, in the form of increased tariffs (that is, in derogation from the principle of bound tariffs and MFN treatment). As a result of this innovation, the WTO can be a far more effective body than the GATT, which had no teeth, and had to rely solely on exhortation to correct any abuses which it found to be contrary to its free trade principles. However, even the WTO Dispute Settlement Body's powers of enforcement have limits, owing to the fact that the subjects of WTO law are all sovereign powers. This is one of the difficulties of WTO anti-dumping and countervailing law, and is also one of reasons why the subject is so complex, and so interesting.

1.4   THE INTEREST OF THE SUBJECT

The interest comes from the fact, first of all, that the WTO rules were negotiated and drafted by diplomats, not by lawyers. Many of the rules are the result of negotiating compromises. The texts are not precise from a technical point of view. Unlike a Bill that passes through the Westminster Parliament, the texts adopted in Marrakesh at the end of the Uruguay Round have not been subjected to rigorous scrutiny by parliamentary draftsmen. In many cases the texts are open to more than one reading, each delegation having negotiated the compromise as to how it could, in good faith, interpret the text. When certain texts are analysed closely it transpires that their fine sounding phrases are unhelpful. Sometimes the phrases are merely exhortative: 'It is desirable that . . .' or merely acknowledge a general principle: 'It is recognized that . . .'.

Then there are the options. Here the compromise is patent. The text offers WTO members alternatives, each more or less clearly defined. A typical example can be found in the option between imposing anti-dumping duties on a prospective basis, or on a retrospective basis. Then, even when the WTO rule is relatively clear, there remains the fact that this rule has to be transposed into the national legal and administrative order of each WTO member. Legal and administrative traditions vary considerably among WTO member countries, notably in the style of legislative drafting, in the way instructions are communicated within the public administration, in the way administrative investigations are carried out, and lastly, in the way Government exercises political influence over trade policy matters. All this increases the scope for divergent interpretation and application of the WTO rules.

It is true that, with the creation of the WTO, there is, as we have already indicated, a Dispute Settlement Body designed to provide authoritative ruling on disputes over the interpretation of WTO rules, including the rules contained in the Anti-dumping Agreement and the Subsidies and Countervailing Measures Agreement. It would be naïve, however, to think that the Dispute Settlement Body provides a remedy in the same way as a national enforcement agency does. The Dispute Settlement Body ultimately has no powers of enforcement. It simply oversees a method of settlement of trade disputes agreed by the WTO members as sovereign states. If one member country has not complied with its obligations under a WTO text, an aggrieved member country may take the matter before the Dispute Settlement Body. If the Dispute Settlement Body finds that the first member country has not complied with its obligations, the latter must take steps to bring its legislation and administrative practices into conformity with WTO rules.

It is important to understand that this is not a question of punishing the offending member country for past action, but of ensuring that it does not offend in the future. The offending member country is a sovereign state and so is free to choose whether to comply with the ruling of the Dispute Settlement Body or not. If it chooses to comply, that is the end of the matter. If it chooses not to comply, the aggrieved member country may request 'compensation'. Compensation here is not compensation for past wrongdoing, in the sense that a civil court might award damages. It is the granting of additional trade concessions by the offending member country to compensate the aggrieved member country for the denial of benefits of trading concessions which it would have enjoyed if the offending member country had complied with its internationally agreed obligations. The determination of a fair amount of compensation is itself a potentially litigious matter in which the Dispute Settlement Body again acts as arbiter. If, finally, no agreement can be reached, the Dispute Settlement Body may authorize the aggrieved member country to adopt countermeasures, referred to colloquially as retaliatory measures. In other words, the aggrieved member country may impose additional duties on imports of the offending member country's products up to the value of the compensation to which it would be entitled. The purpose of such measures is to encourage the offending member country to comply with its WTO obligations. If the offending member country does not comply, or if the aggrieved member country adopts retaliatory measures in excess of that authorized by the Dispute Settlement Body, the system for regulation of world trade will have failed. The extent to which a member country abides by the WTO rules will depend to a certain extent on its belief in the multilateral trading system and whether it has more to gain by staying within a regulated trading system, or by 'going it alone'.

Thus far we have been talking about WTO member countries. Not all trading countries are members of the WTO, notable exceptions being Russia and the ex-Soviet Union countries. In trading relations between these non-member countries and WTO member countries there are no 'legal' restraints in relation to anti-dumping and countervailing action, but in practice the WTO rules are applied. Many of these non-member countries, being ex-Soviet Union countries, are what are known as 'non-market economies'. It is not necessary for a state to be a market economy country in order to qualify for WTO membership. China is a good example of a non-market economy country which is a WTO member. However, the fact that a WTO member may be classified as a non-market economy country brings added complications in matters of anti-dumping and countervailing action which will be examined later in this study. For the purposes of this introduction it suffices to observe that the WTO rules grant member countries a certain amount of latitude in the way they determine anti-dumping or countervailing action against non-market economy countries, compared with when they are taking action against market economy countries. Different WTO members have used this latitude in different ways, which leads to yet further diversity and interest.

As we have explained, diversity is a prevalent characteristic of the way anti-dumping and countervailing action is taken by different WTO member countries, owing to the way the WTO rules are drafted, and the fact that the parties who are supposed to follow these rules are sovereign states. For these reasons, the 'rule of law' is perhaps not as strong as in domestic legal systems.

At the end of the day, Reason and Common Sense, supported by economics, are more important than legal rules. In this study we will be illustrating how Reason and Common Sense can be used to uncover some of the illogicalities in anti-dumping and countervailing rules, and how economic principles lead us to propose some improvements.

We will begin with two chapters setting out the basic principles of anti-dumping and countervailing action. These chapters are not intended to be comprehensive textbooks on the subject. They are intended merely to give the uninformed reader a basic understanding of the principles so as to be able to follow the later discussion of the problems and the recommendations for improvement. In Chapter 4 we examine the criterion of injury. This is important for a basic understanding of anti-dumping and countervailing action because a condition *sine qua non* for such action is that the dumping practices or subsidization are causing injury to the domestic industry of the importing country. Then, in the next three chapters we enter into the heart of the subject with an examination of some specific problem areas. Chapter 5 discusses a selection of anti-dumping problems. One particular anti-dumping problem, that of so-called 'zeroing', is so complex that we have set aside a separate chapter, Chapter 6, for this. Then, in Chapter 7, we examine problems specific to countervailing action, which are relatively straightforward compared to the problems in the anti-dumping field.

Before commencing with our recommendations, we examine, in Chapter 8, the public policy issues which can influence both anti-dumping and counter-vailing action, and which, because of their inherent political nature, can also be a source of difficulty. Then, in the penultimate chapter, Chapter 9, we examine some alternative approaches in the anti-dumping field before ending, in Chapter 10, with our recommendations for modifications to the rules on anti-dumping and countervailing action. We hope, in this way, to achieve two objectives. On the one hand, we aim to extract the subject of anti-dumping and countervailing action from its arcane rituals, reserved to a few initiated specialists, so that anyone with some spare time and an inclination for reflection will be able to discuss this important subject from an informed point of view. On the other hand, we seek to provide a little intellectual entertainment from the interesting results that can be obtained by taking loosely drafted rules to their logical conclusions. But in the last analysis there is a serious purpose underlying this study, which is to make some sensible suggestions for improvement and refinement of the WTO anti-dumping and countervailing rules, based on a combination of economic reasoning and good sense.

2. Anti-dumping principles

The concept of dumping is defined in Article VI(1) of the GATT 1947. This article has been implemented by WTO member countries on the basis of the WTO Agreement on Implementation of Article VI of the General Agreement on Tariffs and Trade 1994.[1] It is convenient at this stage to provide a brief summary of this Agreement, referred to herein as 'the AD Agreement'.

2.1 PRINCIPLES

An anti-dumping duty may be imposed upon the import of a product to compensate for the amount by which the product is dumped, provided such imports are causing injury to the producers of the like product in the country of import. A product is considered to be dumped if its export price is less than 'normal value'. The normal value is usually taken to be a comparable price for the 'like' product on the domestic market of the exporting country. However, if the price on the domestic market is not reliable for various reasons, which we shall examine, the normal value can be determined as the comparable price of export of the like product when exported to an appropriate third country, or as the constructed normal value, namely the costs of production[2] plus a reasonable amount for administrative, selling and general costs and for profits.

The term 'like product' is interpreted to mean a product which is alike in all respects to the product under consideration or, in the absence of such a product, a product which closely resembles the product.

---

[1]   Article VI of GATT 1947 is reproduced at Appendix 1 and the AD Agreement is reproduced in Appendix 2. It should be noted that, with the establishment of the WTO, a new General Agreement of Tariffs and Trade was entered into called GATT 1994. This incorporates the text of GATT 1947 and certain additional protocols, understandings and notes. The change is of no consequence for the subjects discussed in the present work, save that references to Articles of the GATT should be references to GATT 1994 instead of GATT 1947.

[2]   The AD Agreement uses the term 'costs of production' but the EU uses the term 'costs of manufacture', and reserves the term 'costs of production' to mean 'costs of manufacture' plus 'sales, general and administrative expenses'.

2.2   NORMAL VALUE[3]

Dumping is the practice of selling a product for export at a price below its 'normal value' (or 'fair market value' in US legislation). The normal value shall normally be based on the prices paid or payable, in the ordinary course of trade, by independent customers for a like product in the exporting country. Where the exporter in the exporting country does not produce or sell the like product, the normal value may be established on the basis of prices of other sellers or producers.

Sales of the like product intended for domestic consumption shall normally be used to determine normal value if the volume of such sales constitutes 5 per cent or more of the sales volume of the (imported) product under consideration to the importing Member. When there are no sales, or insufficient sales, of the like product in the ordinary course of trade, the normal value of the like product shall be calculated on the basis of the cost of production in the country of origin, plus a reasonable amount for selling, general and administrative costs and for profits (this basis is often called 'constructed value'). Or it should be calculated on the basis of the export prices, in the ordinary course of trade, to an appropriate third country, provided that these prices are representative. In practice the EU never uses export prices to third countries as a measure of normal value.

Sales of the like product in the domestic market of the exporting country, or export sales to a third country, at prices below unit production costs (fixed and variable), plus selling, general and administrative costs (SG&A), may be treated as not being in the ordinary course of trade, and may be disregarded in determining normal value, provided that such sales are made within an extended period in substantial quantities, and do not provide for the recovery of all costs within a reasonable period of time.

If, however, prices are below costs at the time of sale, but are above weighted average costs for the period of the investigation, such prices shall be considered to provide for recovery of costs within a reasonable period of time.

The extended period of time shall normally be one year, but in no case shall be less than six months. Sales below unit costs shall be considered to be made in substantial quantities when the weighted average selling price is below the weighted average unit cost, or the volume of sales below unit cost is not less than 20 per cent of sales being used to determine normal value.

Costs shall normally be calculated on the basis of accounting records, and any allocation of costs shall have a historical basis. Where costs for part of the period are the result of start-up operations, the average costs for the start-up phase shall be those applicable at the end of such a phase. The amounts for

---

[3]   AD Agreement, Articles 2.1 and 2.2.

selling, general and administrative costs (SG&A) and for profits shall be based on actual data pertaining to production and sales of the like product. When such amounts cannot be determined on this basis, the amounts may be determined on the basis of data relating to other exporters of the like product in respect of production and sales in the domestic market of the country of origin, or of exporters of the same general category of products, or on the basis of any other reasonable method.

A note to Article VI of GATT recognizes that the determination of normal value for exports from non-market economy countries may present difficulties. This note says:

> It is recognised that, in the case of imports from a country which has a complete or substantially complete monopoly of its trade and where all domestic prices are fixed by the State, special difficulties may exist in determining price comparability for the purposes of paragraph 1, and in such cases importing contracting parties may find it necessary to take into account the possibility that a strict comparison with domestic prices in such a country may not always be appropriate.

This note gives member countries plenty of room for manoeuvre. Most member countries, and notably the EU and the US, determine what is called an 'analogue' or 'surrogate' normal value. In the EU the 'analogue' normal value is determined on the basis of the price or constructed value in a market economy third country, or the price from such a third country to other countries, or, where this is not possible, on any other reasonable basis, including the price actually paid or payable in the EU for the like product, adjusted if necessary to include a reasonable margin of profit.

2.3   EXPORT PRICE[4]

The export price shall be the price actually paid or payable for the product when sold for export to the importing country. Where the export price is unreliable, the export price may be constructed on the basis of the price at which the imported products are first resold to an independent buyer. Adjustments shall be made for all costs, including duties and taxes.

A fair comparison shall be made between the export price and the normal value. This comparison shall be made at the same level of trade and in respect of sales made as nearly as possible at the same time. When the normal value and the export price are not on a comparable basis, due allowance, in the form of a number of specified adjustments, may be made.

---

[4]   AD Agreement, Articles 2.3 and 2.4.

2.4   DUMPING MARGIN[5]

The dumping margin shall normally be established by one of three possible methods: a comparison of a weighted average normal value with a weighted average of prices of all export transactions to the importing country, or by a comparison of individual normal values and individual export prices, or by a comparison of a weighted average normal value with the prices of all individual export transactions to the importing country. The last method may be used when there is a pattern of export prices which differs significantly among different purchasers, regions or time periods.

The dumping margin shall be the amount by which the normal value exceeds the export price. Where dumping margins vary, a weighted average dumping margin may be established.

2.5   INJURY[6]

As explained above, the existence of dumping alone does not justify the taking of anti-dumping action. It has to be shown that the dumped imports are causing injury to the producers of the like product in the country of import. Injury is taken to mean material injury to the domestic industry of the importing country, or a threat of material injury to the industry, or material retardation of the establishment of such an industry. A determination of injury shall be based on positive evidence, and shall involve an objective determination of the volume of dumped imports, their effect on prices in the importing country, and the consequent impact of those imports on the domestic industry of the importing country.

The examination of the impact of the dumped imports on the relevant industry shall include an evaluation of all relevant economic factors having a bearing on the state of the industry. A non-exhaustive list of such factors is given in Article 3.4 of the AD Agreement. In addition, known factors other than the dumped imports which are injuring the domestic industry shall also be examined, to ensure that injury caused by these other factors is not attributed to these dumped imports, and Article 3.5 of the AD Agreement provides an illustrative list of such factors.

In making a determination regarding the existence of a threat of material injury, consideration shall be given to a number of specified factors, including a significant rate of increase of dumped imports into the market, free capacity

---

5   AD Agreement, Article 2.4.2.
6   AD Agreement, Article 3.

on the part of the exporter, and whether import prices are likely to depress domestic prices or prevent price increases which would otherwise have occurred.

The determination of injury is examined in greater detail in Chapter 4.

2.6   DOMESTIC INDUSTRY[7]

The term 'domestic industry' refers to the domestic producers as a whole of the like product in the importing country, or to those whose collective output constitutes a major proportion of the total domestic production.

A complaint has to be made by or on behalf of the domestic industry. It shall be considered as having been so made if it is supported by those domestic producers whose collective output constitutes more than 50 per cent of the total production of the like product, produced by that portion of the domestic industry expressing either support for or opposition to the complaint. However, no investigation shall be initiated when the domestic producers supporting the complaint account for less than 25 per cent of the total production of the like product produced by the domestic industry.

Opposition to a complaint is rare. Even if some producers do oppose the complaint, there will be little difficulty in applying the 50 per cent rule because the producers who support the complaint and the producers who oppose it are clearly identified. The investigating authority simply has to verify the production of all these identified producers in order to calculate whether the 50 per cent rule is satisfied or not. The 25 per cent rule can present practical difficulties. The producers who support the complaint will claim that they represent more than 25 per cent of total production, but the other producers may choose not to cooperate. As a result, the investigating authority cannot verify the production of the non-cooperating producers in order to determine total production within the country. Instead, the investigating authority will have to look for reasonable means of estimating such production.

2.7   PROVISIONAL MEASURES[8]

Provisional duties may be imposed if a provisional affirmative determination has been made of dumping and consequent injury to the domestic industry.

The amount of the provisional anti-dumping duty shall not exceed the

---

[7]   AD Agreement, Article 4.
[8]   AD Agreement, Article 7 and Article 10.

margin of dumping as provisionally established but, in the EU, although not the US, case, it should be less than the margin if such lesser duty would be adequate to remove the injury to the Community industry.[9]

Provisional duties are not actually paid at the time of import, but have to be secured by a guarantee, and the release of the products concerned for free circulation is conditional on the provision of such a guarantee.

Provisional duties may normally be imposed for six months and any decision to collect the provisional duties definitively must be taken before the expiry of this period. Investigations have to be concluded, except in special circumstances, within one year, and in no case more than 18 months, after their initiation. In the EU, the usual practice is to impose provisional duties at the end of the first nine months of investigation, so that a decision can be taken to collect them at the end of the definitive investigation, six months later, and not later than 15 months from initiation of the investigation.

2.8   PRICE UNDERTAKINGS[10]

Investigations may be terminated without the imposition of duties provided that satisfactory voluntary undertakings are given by the exporter, to revise its prices or to cease exports at dumped prices. Price increases under such undertakings shall not be higher than necessary to eliminate the margin of dumping, and they should be less than this if such increases would be adequate to remove the injury to the domestic industry. Undertakings shall not be sought or accepted unless dumping and injury have been found provisionally.

If the undertakings are accepted, the investigation of dumping and injury shall normally be completed. Where an undertaking is breached or withdrawn, anti-dumping duties may be imposed on the basis of the best information available.

2.9   DEFINITIVE DUTIES[11]

Where the facts as finally established show that there is dumping and consequent injury, a definitive anti-dumping duty may be imposed, at the discretion of the authorities of the importing Member.

---

[9]   The EU lesser duty regulation is based on Article 9.1 of the GATT AD Agreement: 'It is desirable that the duty be less than the margin if such lesser duty would be adequate to remove the injury to the domestic industry.'
[10]   AD Agreement, Article 8.
[11]   AD Agreement, Article 9.

Proceedings may, however, be terminated where it is determined that the margin of dumping is *de minimis,* that is, less than 2 per cent, expressed as a percentage of the export price. The volume of dumped imports shall normally be regarded as negligible if the volume of dumped imports from a particular country is found to account for less than 3 per cent of imports of the like product in the importing Member, unless countries which individually account for less than 3 per cent of the imports of the like product in the importing Member collectively account for more than 7 per cent of imports of the like product in the importing Member.

Anti-dumping duties may be assessed retrospectively or prospectively. Refunds may be requested for any duties paid in excess of the margin of dumping.

A definitive anti-dumping measure shall expire five years from its imposition. But an expiry review shall be initiated where there is evidence that the expiry of the measures would be likely to result in a continuation or a recurrence of dumping and injury. An interim review is, however, possible where there is evidence that the continuation of the measure is no longer necessary to offset dumping and/or injury.

Anti-dumping duties may be extended to imports from third countries of like products, when circumvention of the measures in force is taking place.[12]

2.10   REVIEWS AND REFUNDS

The principle of anti-dumping action is that the amount of anti-dumping duty imposed shall not be more than the margin of dumping (and it is desirable that it should be less if a lesser duty would suffice to remove injury). Circumstances change, and so do margins of dumping. The AD Agreement therefore requires that review procedures must be possible to deal with such changes. There are basically four kinds of review: an interim review, a newcomer review, an expiry review and a refund procedure (or administrative review).

An interim review is designed to deal with changed circumstances. If, owing to changed circumstances, the margin of dumping is less than the rate of duty imposed, the exporters may ask for a review so that the rate of

---

[12]   The AD Agreement does not provide for anti-circumvention action, nor does it prohibit it. During the Uruguay Round negotiations, the member countries were unable to agree on common provisions regulating anti-circumvention investigations. It was acknowledged, however, that member countries were entitled to take appropriate steps to deal with circumvention of anti-dumping duties, provided such steps were compatible with all WTO obligations, notably those contained in GATT 1947.

collection of duties is reduced. If, on the other hand, the duties are no longer sufficient to compensate for injurious dumping, the domestic industry may request a review so that the rate of collection of duties can be increased. A newcomer review is designed to deal with the case where a 'newcomer' starts to export for the first time and so requires to be brought within the system of collection of anti-dumping duties at a rate appropriate to that company, rather than at the residual or general rate applicable to all companies for whom no specific rate of duty has been specified. Last of all, it is a general principle of the AD Agreement that anti-dumping duties should expire after five years, unless it is determined that their expiry would lead again to injurious dumping. An expiry review is a review that can be opened at the end of the five years, at the request of the domestic industry, to determine whether expiry of the measures would lead again to injurious dumping. If it is so determined, the measures are allowed to continue unchanged, in principle, for another five years, unless modified in the meantime as the result of an interim review.

A refund procedure is a review whereby the importer may obtain reimbursement of anti-dumping duties collected if it can be demonstrated that the rate of duty collected is higher than the margin of dumping. In countries which assess duties on a retrospective basis, such as the US, such a procedure is normally referred to as an administrative review. It involves a determination of the actual margin of dumping over the period under review, as a result of which the importer's liability for duties is finalized. In countries which assess duties on a prospective basis, such as the EU, the procedure is normally referred to as a refund procedure. It enables the importer to obtain reimbursement of all or part of anti-dumping duties if it is determined that the amount of duties collected on the basis of the prospective duty is more than the actual margin of dumping practised.

2.11 PERMISSIVE IMPOSITION OF DUTIES

Article 9.1 of the AD Agreement states that it is desirable that the imposition of anti-dumping duties should 'be permissive in the territory of all Members'. In the case of the EU, this freedom has been embodied in Article 21 – Community Interest – of the EU Anti-dumping Regulation.[13]

A determination by the EU authorities as to whether the Community interest calls for intervention has to be based on an appreciation of all the various interests taken as a whole, including the interests of the domestic industry and

---

[13]   Council Regulation (EC) No 384/96 OJ L56, 6.3.96.

users and consumers. Measures, as determined on the basis of the dumping and injury found, may not be applied where the EU authorities can clearly conclude that it is not in the Community interest to apply such measures.

All parties, including representative users and representative consumer organizations, who may be affected by the measures, may make themselves known to the EU authorities and provide information. The parties may also request a hearing. The balance of views of all the interested parties must be taken into account in deciding whether to terminate the proceedings without measures or whether to impose anti-dumping duties.

2.12   THE US APPROACH

The US anti-dumping regulation ('US AD Regulation'), like that of the EU and of other countries with anti-dumping legislation, is based on Article VI of GATT 1994. As compared with the EU AD Regulation, however, the US AD Regulation does not contain two important provisions.

Article 7(2) of the EU AD Regulation states: 'The amount of the provisional anti-dumping duty shall not exceed the margin of dumping as provisionally established, but it should be less than the margin if such lesser duty would be adequate to remove the injury to the Community industry.' The US AD Regulation does not include this 'lesser duty' provision. In the US case, therefore, the anti-dumping duty is based simply on the established margin of dumping.

In addition, Article 21 of the EU AD Regulation contains provision for considering the Community Interest. There is no equivalent article (which might possibly relate to State or Federal interest) in the US AD Regulation.

These differences are also common to the US legislation regarding subsidies and countervailing duties.

As well as these differences in regulation, there are a number of practices in which the US differs from the EU. One concerns the way in which duties are levied. As has been mentioned, anti-dumping (or countervailing) duties may be imposed prospectively or retrospectively. The EU adopts the former principle, the USA the latter. The implications of this difference in procedure are explored in Chapter 5 below.

A less transparent difference lies in the contrasting US and EU procedures relating to 'zeroing'. This issue arises when an average dumping margin is to be established. Those cases where dumping is established are of course included in the average. The problem arises in cases where no dumping is established, because the export price is above, or equivalent to, the normal value. Should this 'negative dumping' be included in the average, thus reducing the average dumping margin, or not? The US practice has been to express such cases of negative value as of zero value, while the EU, as a general rule, includes them at their actual value, thus allowing a set-off between negative and positive dumping. This practice, which has of course led to relatively larger dumping margins in the case of the USA, has recently been the subject of a WTO ruling, condemning the US procedure. The complex subject of zeroing is discussed fully in Chapter 6 below.

The treatment of imports from non-market economy countries constitutes a further source of difference between EU and US practice. When imports from such countries – notably China – are examined, the EU practice is to examine individual exporting firms, from China for example, to see whether they qualify under market economy rules (explained in Chapter 5 below). If so, they are granted market economy status and, experience suggests, will be found to have smaller dumping margins than if this were not the case.

The US practice, however, is to examine the entire exporting industry concerned, to see whether the industry as a whole qualifies for market economy status or not. The result is, not surprisingly, that this leads to fewer determinations that market economy status exists than under the EU procedure. As a result, dumping margins are likely to be higher for exporting industries as a whole, than for qualified individual firms identified by the EU practice.

3. Anti-subsidy and countervailing principles

The concept of countervailing action is contained in Article VI of GATT 1994 and Part V of the WTO Agreement on Subsidies and Countervailing Measures ('the SCM Agreement'). These provisions are implemented in the EU by the EU AS Regulation.[1]

3.1 PRINCIPLES

Countervailing action is a course of unilateral action that an importing country can take against subsidized imports of product from another country which cause injury to the domestic industry producing the like product in the importing country (in much the same way as it can take anti-dumping action against injurious dumped imports from another country in accordance with the provisions explained in the previous chapter). Unlike dumping, however, subsidization flows directly from state action in the country of export, not just from the exporter's pricing policy. There are potentially two different types of dispute arising out of subsidization by an exporting country.

First, subsidization in an exporting country may cause injury to producers of the like product in an importing country. These producers will want their country, the importing country, to impose additional duties (called countervailing duties) to compensate for the unfair advantage conferred on the subsidized production in the country of export. One could describe this as an 'ad hoc' remedy because it seeks to solve a specific problem suffered by the producers of a particular product as the result of subsidization in another country. An importing WTO member is entitled to take countervailing action in accordance with the procedures laid down by Part V of the SCM Agreement, which we shall examine later below.

Second, in addition to creating problems for a specific industry in the importing WTO member, subsidy schemes can distort competition generally in the multilateral free trading system and so nullify or impair the benefits

---

[1]   Council Regulation (EC) No 2026/97, OJ L288, 21.10.97, as amended.

accruing directly or indirectly to WTO members under GATT 1994, or cause them serious prejudice. For example, a subsidy scheme in WTO member A could result in that country increasing its market share for product X in WTO member B, at the expense not only of the domestic industry in WTO member B but also of the unsubsidized exporters in WTO member C who, until WTO member A started its subsidy scheme, had a substantial share of the market in WTO member B. In this second respect subsidization becomes a matter for dispute settlement action pursuant to the WTO Dispute Settlement Understanding as applied by the SCM Agreement. These remedies against subsidization, countervailing action and dispute settlement, were recognized already in GATT 1947. Article VI of GATT 1947 allows a member country to take countervailing action against subsidized imports that are causing injury to its domestic industry, that is, to the domestic producers of a particular product. Article XVI of GATT 1947 establishes limits within which member countries undertake not to use subsidization. If they exceed these limits they expose themselves to dispute settlement proceedings. The principles behind both these Articles were further developed in the Uruguay Round, and embodied in the Subsidies and Countervailing Measures Agreement (SCM Agreement) at the same time as the mechanism for the settlement of disputes was strengthened by the Dispute Settlement Understanding.

In the present study we are interested principally in the rules laid down by the SCM Agreement for the taking of countervailing action because it is closely related to anti-dumping action. The principle behind anti-dumping action is that an exporter should not be allowed to use the profits he makes on his domestic market in order to subsidize his export price. In the same way, an exporter should not be allowed to subsidize his export price from benefits provided by his country's government. So if either of these practices causes injury to the domestic industry of the like product in the importing country, the latter may impose additional duties: anti-dumping duties in the first case, countervailing duties in the second. Since subsidization also opens up the possibility for the injured WTO member country to bring dispute settlement proceedings before the WTO Dispute Settlement Body, we shall for completeness examine this remedy briefly at the end of this chapter, although, as we have said, our principal interest is in anti-dumping and countervailing action.

3.2 COUNTERVAILING ACTION

A WTO member country may take countervailing action against subsidies by imposing countervailing duties or accepting undertakings to increase prices or remove the subsidy. In such cases it is necessary to show that there is a subsidy which is specific, and that imports of the subsidized product are causing injury to the domestic producers of the like product. The amount of the countervailing duty must not exceed that necessary to remove the effects of subsidization, and it is desirable that the amount of the duty should be less if a lesser duty would suffice to remove the injurious effects of subsidization – the so-called 'lesser duty' rule. The rules on injury and the lesser duty rule are common to both anti-dumping and countervailing action, and are discussed in Chapter 4. In the present chapter we will examine the definition of a subsidy, the rules for determining whether the subsidy is specific, and the criteria for assessing the amount of the subsidy and the corresponding countervailing duty.

3.3   DEFINITION OF A SUBSIDY

The basic notion behind countervailing action is the notion of a 'subsidy'. The SCM Agreement defines a subsidy as a financial contribution by government which confers a benefit.[2] The two aspects, a financial contribution by government, and the conferral of a benefit on an economic operator, are equally important. If there is no financial contribution by government there can be no subsidy. Thus, for example, if a government introduces price control regulations which set minimum prices for certain products, this may be beneficial to the producers of those products, but there is no financial contribution by government and so no subsidy. On the other hand, if government sets up a price support mechanism whereby a government agency will purchase all excess production at a minimum price, this will have the effect of maintaining price levels, thus conferring a benefit on producers. Since this benefit is derived directly from a financial contribution by government to the price support mechanism, there is a subsidy.

Article 1.1 of the SCM Agreement provides five generic examples of subsidies:

(1)   a government practice which involves a direct transfer of funds (for example grants, loans or equity infusion), potential direct transfers of funds or liabilities (for example loan guarantees);

(2)   government revenue, otherwise due, which is forgone or not collected (for example fiscal incentives such as tax credits);

(3)   a government which provides goods or services other than general infrastructure, or purchases goods;

(4)   a government which makes payments to a funding mechanism, or entrusts a private body to carry out one or more of the type of function

---

[2]   Article 1.1.

illustrated in (1) to (3) above, which would normally be vested in the government, and where the practice, in no real sense, differs from practices normally followed by governments;

(5) where there is any form of income or price support in the sense of Article XVI of GATT 1994.

There are many hybrid cases which have to be analysed into their component parts to see how they should be classified. For example, if a loan is granted by a government body on full commercial terms, there is no subsidy, provided those terms are respected. If subsequently the loan is fully 'forgiven', that is, released, by the government body, the transaction becomes a cash grant. One must not allow the analysis to be confused by the fact that the transaction commenced as a loan. Another interesting case is a tax deferral, as opposed to a tax exemption or tax reduction. A tax reduction or exemption would constitute a one-off subsidy payment, but a tax deferral does not exempt the taxpayer from paying the tax; it merely delays the date for payment. Thus the correct analysis is that a tax deferral constitutes an interest-free loan until the date that the tax is paid. The same analysis applies to a reimbursable grant: it is an interest-free loan until reimbursed. If, before the date for reimbursement, the government authority decides not to claim repayment, the amount of the reimbursable grant becomes a definitive cash grant and must be analysed as such.[3] An interesting issue arises in the case of privatization of state enterprises, where the state sells a state-owned enterprise for a fair market price. The question is whether such sale puts an end to any subsidization flowing from the state's intervention prior to the privatization. This issue will be discussed in Chapter 7.

3.4 SPECIFICITY

A subsidy will be *specific* if it can be granted only to an enterprise or to certain enterprises, that is, it is not generally available. The SCM Agreement formulates this principle as follows:[4] 'Where the granting authority, or the legislation pursuant to which the granting authority operates, explicitly limits access to a subsidy to certain enterprises, such subsidy shall be specific.' It should be added that the expression 'certain enterprises' can mean enterprises in a designated region. Thus a subsidy which is limited to certain enterprises situated in

---

[3]   Arguments based on the European Commission Guidelines for the Calculation of the Amount of Subsidy in Countervailing Duty Investigations, OJ C394, 17.12.98, p. 6.

[4]   SCM Agreement, Article 2.1(a).

a designated geographical region will be specific.[5] The counterpart principle, which determines when there is no subsidy, is formulated by the SCM Agreement as follows:[6]

> Where the granting authority, or the legislation pursuant to which the granting authority operates, establishes objective criteria or conditions governing the eligibility for, and the amount of, a subsidy, specificity shall not exist, provided that the eligibility is automatic and that such criteria and conditions are strictly adhered to. The criteria or conditions must be clearly spelled out in law, regulation or other official document, so as to be capable of verification.

This latter criterion is very important because it excludes from the definition of specificity all general regulation of a country's economy and budget, notably generally applicable tax rates,[7] generally applicable rules for determining the tax base, and so on. The dividing line between objective criteria and criteria which favour certain enterprises is not easy to draw. For example, if lower tax rates are applicable to enterprises below a certain size, is that a benefit which is granted in accordance with objective criteria, or is it in fact a measure designed to favour certain sectors of the economy? A footnote to Article 2.1(b) of the SCM Agreement provides the answer: 'Objective criteria or conditions, as used herein, mean criteria or conditions which are neutral, which do not favour certain enterprises over others, and which are economic in nature and horizontal in application, such as number of employees or size of enterprise.'

Thus it is clear that lower tax rates for enterprises with less than a certain number of employees, or below a certain size in terms of balance sheet or turnover, are not specific.

This is not the end of the story, however. The principles examined above lay great importance on the fact that the objective conditions for granting a benefit must be clearly spelled out in law, regulation, or other official document, so as to be capable of verification. The difficulty with this requirement is that, in some countries, the public administration does not pay attention to what is written down in the legal and administrative sources. Or some countries prefer not to lay down any detailed rules in the first place, leaving a wide margin of discretion to the public authorities. Article 2.1 of the SCM Agreement sets out a third principle to deal with this:

---

[5]   SCM Agreement, Article 2.2, first sentence.
[6]   SCM Agreement, Article 2.1(b).
[7]   For the avoidance of doubt, Article 2.2, second sentence, confirms that the setting or change of generally applicable tax rates does not constitute a subsidy.

If, notwithstanding any appearance of non-specificity resulting from the application of the principles laid down in subparagraphs (a) and (b), there are reasons to believe that the subsidy may in fact be specific, other factors may be considered. Such factors are: use of a subsidy programme by a limited number of certain enterprises, predominant use by certain enterprises, the granting of disproportionately large amounts of subsidy to certain enterprises, and the manner in which discretion has been exercised by the granting authority in the decision to grant a subsidy.

Thus the question whether a subsidy is specific is not just a question of applying hard and fast rules: it is a question of examining the factual situation to see whether a subsidy is really available to any enterprise which satisfies certain objective criteria, or whether it is available, in practice, only to certain enterprises. A footnote to section 2.1(c) of the SCM Agreement tells us that 'information on the frequency with which applications are refused or approved and the reasons for such decisions shall be considered'.

Thus, for example, if some applications are refused, it is important to examine whether the reason for refusal was that the applicant did not satisfy the objective qualification criteria, or whether there was some other undisclosed reason, for example that the enterprise was not active in a sector which the granting authority was seeking to promote. The last sentence of Article 2.1(c) says: 'In applying this subparagraph, account shall be taken of the extent of diversification of economic activities within the jurisdiction of the granting authority, as well as of the length of time during which the subsidy programme has been in operation.'

Thus, for example, if a granting authority has jurisdiction only over enterprises in a given sector or region, it would follow that any grant of a subsidy by that authority would be specific to the sector or the region. The length of time during which the subsidy programme has been in operation also enables one to judge the history of the granting of a particular subsidy, in order to determine whether it appears to be given to all enterprises who apply, or whether it is, in fact, limited to enterprises in a given sector or region.

3.5   DEEMED SPECIFICITY OF EXPORT AND DOMESTIC INPUT SUBSIDIES

Export and domestic input subsidies are deemed by the SCM Agreement to be specific. An export subsidy is one which is contingent in law or in fact, whether solely or as one of several other conditions, upon export performance.[8] A subsidy which is not legally contingent on export performance, but

---

[8]   SCM Agreement, Article 3.1(a).

which is in fact tied to actual or anticipated exportation or export earnings, will constitute an export subsidy. However, the SCM Agreement limits the scope of this 'factual contingency' test by providing that the mere fact that a subsidy is granted to enterprises which export shall not for that reason alone be considered to be an export subsidy.[9] Annex I to the SCM Agreement provides an illustrative, that is, non-exhaustive, list of some 12 typical examples of export subsidies. Three of these warrant mention here. First, the list clarifies that a truly neutral value-added tax system does not involve an export subsidy; there will be an export subsidy, on the other hand, if the amount of tax exempted or remitted when goods are exported is more than tax levied in respect of the production and distribution of like products when sold for domestic consumption.[10] Second, the remission or drawback of import charges and duties in excess of those levied on imported inputs that are consumed in the production of the exported product (making normal allowance for waste) constitutes a subsidy. Special rules govern the operation of so-called 'substitution drawback systems' whereby domestic inputs may be substituted for imported inputs.[11] Third, government-funded export credits at rates more favourable than market rates constitute export subsidies. However, export credit practices in accordance with certain international undertakings, notably the OECD Convention on Export Credits, are deemed not to involve export subsidies.[12]

As stated above, a domestic input subsidy is also deemed to be specific. A domestic input subsidy is defined as a subsidy contingent, whether solely, or as one of several other conditions, upon the use of domestic over imported goods.[13] No examples are given in the SCM Agreement. Domestic input subsidies are less common than export subsidies. A typical example would be a state intervention scheme whereby financial benefits are granted when raw materials are supplied by national producers but not when the same raw materials are imported.

3.6 CALCULATION OF THE AMOUNT OF SUBSIDY

Article 14 of the SCM Agreement provides scant guidance on the determination of the amount of a subsidy, although one could argue that this is a matter

---

[9]   SCM Agreement, Article 3.1(b), footnote 4. For a perhaps questionable illustration of the factual contingency test see *Australian subsidies to producers and exporters of automotive leather* – Panel Report WT/DS126/R.

[10]   SCM Agreement, Annex I, paragraph (h) and footnote 60.

[11]   SCM Agreement, Annex I, paragraph (i) and Annexes II and III.

[12]   SCM Agreement, Annex I, paragraph (k).

[13]   SCM Agreement, Article 3.1(b).

of common sense. Article 14 of the SCM Agreement establishes the general principle that the amount of the subsidy shall be calculated as the amount of the benefit to the recipient, thus putting an end to another theory according to which the amount of the subsidy should be the cost to the public body providing the benefit. Article 14 requires that the rules for determining the amount of the subsidy shall be laid down in national legislation or implementing provisions, and their application in individual cases shall be transparent and adequately explained. Article 14 then states four guiding principles, only three of which state explicitly how the amount of the subsidy is to be calculated.

The first principle is that government provision of equity capital shall not be considered as conferring a benefit, unless the investment decision can be regarded as inconsistent with the usual investment practice of private investors in the territory of that member country. This principle does not say how one calculates the amount of the subsidy if the provision of equity capital is inconsistent with usual investment practice. Since there seems to be no half-way measure here, the amount of the subsidy should be taken as the whole of the amount of the equity capital. This is certainly the practice of the EU and the USA.

The second principle is that a loan by government is not considered as conferring a benefit unless the amount that the firm receiving the loan pays in reimbursement of the loan, fees and interest, is less than it would pay on a comparable commercial loan which it could obtain on the market. The amount of the subsidy is the amount by which the repayment amounts on the government loan are less than the repayment amounts on a comparable commercial loan. This is the approach of the EU and the USA.

The third principle is similar to the second. A loan guarantee is not considered as conferring a benefit unless the amount that the firm receiving the guarantee pays in reimbursement of the loan, fees and interest, is less than it would pay on a comparable commercial loan which it could obtain on the market. The amount of the subsidy is the amount by which the repayment amounts, with the benefit of the government loan guarantee, are less than the repayment amounts on a comparable commercial loan without a government guarantee. This is the approach of the EU and the USA.

The fourth principle is that the purchase of goods by a government shall be considered as conferring a benefit if the purchase price is more than an adequate remuneration. Equally, the supply of goods by government for less than an adequate remuneration is also considered as conferring a benefit. The adequacy of the remuneration is determined in relation to prevailing market conditions in the country concerned for the goods or services in question. Clearly, if the government uses a public call for tenders before selling or purchasing, this can be a way of establishing that the remuneration paid is adequate.

Article 19.4 of the SCM Agreement provides that no countervailing duty shall be levied in excess of the amount of the subsidy found to exist, calculated in terms of subsidization per unit of the subsidized exported product. If the amount of the subsidy is less than 1 per cent *ad valorem*, it is considered to be *de minimis* and no countervailing duty should be imposed.[14] In the case of subsidized exports from developing country members of the WTO, the *de minimis* threshold is increased from 1 per cent to 2 per cent.[15] Apart from this, the SCM Agreement provides no other guidance. For example, it does not give any guidance on how or whether one should make a distinction between subsidies granted in the form of a one-off capital grant, and subsidies granted as a function of each individual export transaction. The capital grant will continue to produce its effects for several years, whereas an excess remission of sales tax upon exports will produce its effect at the time of each individual export. It therefore seems logical to suppose that subsidies in the form of a capital grant should be allocated over time in some way. This is the approach of the EU and also of the USA. Thus, for example:

- Recurring subsidies not linked to the acquisition of fixed assets, such as tax incentives, produce their full effects in the year in which they are granted and so are allocated to that year.
- Non-recurring subsidies linked to the acquisition of fixed assets are allocated over the normal depreciation period of the assets. If the asset is not depreciable, the subsidy is treated as an interest free loan.
- Non-recurring subsidies which amount to less than 1 per cent *ad valorem* in the EU (0.5 per cent in the US) are usually expensed in the year.
- Recurring subsidies linked to the acquisition of fixed assets are allocated over the normal depreciation period of the fixed assets, and the respective portions falling within the investigation period are totalled.
- Recurring subsidies granted in large concentrated amounts prior to the investigation period can, in certain circumstances, be allocated over time if it is determined that they are likely to be linked to the purchase of fixed assets, and still confer a benefit during the investigation period.

Application of these principles can be fairly complex. As in anti-dumping investigations, the amount of subsidization is determined by reference to an

---

[14]   SCM Agreement, Article 11.9. The reader may have noticed already the difference between the per unit language of Article 19.4 and the *ad valorem* language of Article 11.9. This will be commented upon in Chapter 7 below.
[15]   SCM Agreement, Article 27.10(a). For the least developed countries, the *de minimis* threshold was 3 per cent until 31 December 2002.

investigation period of, usually, 12 months. The exporter may have acquired assets with the help of subsidies in the year before the investigation period, in the year before that, and so on. If those assets are still being depreciated in the exporter's accounts during the investigation period, a proportion of the subsidy used to acquire that asset will have to be taken into consideration, using the time allocation principles set out above. Table 3.1 will illustrate this, assuming that all the assets purchased have normal depreciation periods of five years.

A remarkable practice of the EU authorities concerns the charging of interest on export subsidies received during the year. For example, if a subsidy scheme is found to involve a benefit of X per cent every time an export is made, the EU authorities add an interest factor over six months, on the theory that, on average, the recipient will have had the benefit for six months of the year. This approach will be criticized in Chapter 7 below.

Table 3.1 Depreciation on investments

	Year 1	Year 2	Year 3	Year 4	Year 5 (Investigation period)
Amount of new investments made in the year, subsidized as to 30%	1 000 000	500 000	300 000	0	100 000
Annual depreciation on investments made in year 1	200 000	200 000	200 000	200 000	200 000
Annual depreciation on investments made in year 2		100 000	100 000	100 000	100 000
Annual depreciation on investments made in year 3			60 000	60 000	60 000
Annual depreciation on investments made in year 4				0	0
Annual depreciation on investments made in year 5					20 000
Total depreciation attributable to the investigation period					380 000
Total subsidy attributable to the investigation period (30%)					114 000

As we have seen, in the case of government purchases or sales of goods, the test is whether the price paid or charged represents an adequate remuneration. The normal test of what is an adequate remuneration is to look at market rates for similar transactions. However, it may not always be possible to find an exact or near equivalent in the market. In such cases an alternative measure of an adequate remuneration has to be found. The EU and the USA use the approach of cost plus a reasonable margin.

Where a subsidy is allocated over sales, it is important to determine which sales are giving rise to the subsidy, and to allocate the subsidy over these. Thus, for example, in the case of an export subsidy, the normal practice should be to determine the total subsidy granted under the subsidy scheme during the reference period and allocate this over all export sales which qualified for the subsidy. With careful thought it can be seen at once that, if a subsidy is not contingent on export performance but is granted in respect of all sales, whether domestic or export, the total amount of subsidy should be allocated over all sales, not just over export sales.

The EU authorities apply the principle that any costs incurred by the exporter in order to obtain the subsidy can be deducted from the total amount of subsidy. Thus, for example, any application fee or other costs necessarily incurred in order to qualify for, or to obtain, the subsidy can be deducted. This provision is rarely of any significant value to an exporter. Equally, in the unlikely event that the exporting country has levied a compensatory tax to neutralize or reduce the effect of the subsidy, the amount of this tax should be deducted in determination of the full amount of the subsidy.[16]

It can be seen that, compared with the calculation of dumping, the calculation of subsidization is different, but just as complex. There is no need to compare domestic prices with costs of production, or export prices with domestic prices, but there is the question of finding the total amount of subsidization from which the exporting company benefited and allocating it correctly to the investigation period.

3.7 THE RELATIONSHIP BETWEEN DUMPED AND SUBSIDIZED EXPORTS

Article VI(5) of GATT 1994 provides as follows: 'No product of the territory of any contracting party imported into the territory of any other contracting

---

[16] Arguments based on on the European Commission Guidelines for the Calculation of the Amount of Subsidy in Countervailing Duty Investigations, OJ C394, 17.12.98, p. 6.

party shall be subject to both anti-dumping and countervailing duties to compensate for the same situation of dumping or export subsidization.'

A concrete example will explain what this means. Suppose that the unit costs of production are 98, and that the unit domestic price is 100 and the unit export price is 96. There is clearly dumping of 4. But the cause of this dumping could in fact be a subsidy which gives the exporter a cost advantage for his export sales, and so encourages him to reduce his export price. Suppose, in this example, there was an export subsidy of 4 per unit. A countervailing duty could be imposed equal to 4 per unit. In addition to neutralizing the subsidy, such a countervailing duty would put an end to dumping because the export price including countervailing duty would be 100, the same as the domestic price. Article VI(5) of GATT 1994 provides that, in such a case, the importing country may not impose an anti-dumping duty in addition to the countervailing duty. If we vary the facts a little, so that the export price reduces to 93, but the level of subsidization stays at 4, the countervailing duty of 4 would bring the export price up to 97 leaving a small dumping margin of 3. So, in addition to the countervailing duty of 4, it would be possible for the importing country to impose an anti-dumping duty of 3.

It can be seen that this approach is based on the theory that export subsidization produces similar effects to dumping, that is, it causes the exporter to reduce his export price without necessarily reducing his domestic price. If the subsidy is not an export subsidy, but a domestic subsidy, that is to say, a subsidy that benefits domestic sales and export sales equally, the rule in Article VI(5) of GATT 1994 has no application. Such a subsidy will affect export and domestic pricing equally and so does not, of itself, tend to give rise to a difference between export prices and domestic prices. Suppose that, in our example, there is a production subsidy of 3 in addition to the export subsidy of 4. The production subsidy benefits all production, whether destined for exports or for the domestic market, and so falls outside the scope of Article VI(5) of GATT 1994. The importing country would find a gross dumping margin of $100 - 93 = 7$. It could impose a countervailing duty of 4 to deal with the export subsidy, and a full anti-dumping duty of 3 to deal with the balance of the dumping margin: $7 - 4 = 3$. In addition, however, it could impose an additional countervailing duty of 3 to deal with the element of domestic subsidization. This latter element is considered to have reduced the export price and the normal value by the same amount. It does not contribute to dumping, but it does contribute to a reduction of prices, and so can be countervailed.

It can be seen from this brief discussion that a determination of whether a subsidy is an export subsidy or a domestic subsidy can be of considerable significance. If an export subsidy were wrongly characterized as a domestic subsidy, the importing country would be able to circumvent Article VI(5) of

GATT 1947 and impose a countervailing duty and an anti-dumping duty, with no set-off for the amount by which dumping was caused by export subsidization.

3.8   MATTERS COMMON TO COUNTERVAILING AND ANTI-DUMPING ACTION

A brief word should be said about certain matters that are common to countervailing and anti-dumping action. In both countervailing and anti-dumping action, it is necessary to demonstrate that the subsidization or dumping is causing injury to the domestic industry of the importing country. The determination of injury will be examined in detail in the next chapter. Another common matter is procedure. The AD Agreement and the SCM Agreement lay down basically the same procedural rules for conducting anti-dumping and countervailing investigations. The only significant difference is that in countervailing investigations there is an additional requirement that consultations be held between representatives of the importing and the exporting country before the investigation is initiated. This follows from the fact that, unlike anti-dumping investigations, countervailing investigations concern action taken by sovereign states, for which there is also a remedy under the WTO dispute settlement mechanism. It is therefore as a matter of diplomatic courtesy that consultations are held before initiation of a countervailing investigation.

The procedures laid down by the AD Agreement and the SCM Agreement leave a certain amount of discretion to the WTO member countries. It is not the purpose of this work to examine procedures in any great detail. Mention should perhaps be made, however, of the fact that the Agreements say that it is desirable that investigations should take no longer than one year, but in no circumstances should the investigation last more than 18 months. The EU has adopted a stricter test and requires anti-dumping investigations to be completed within 15 months and countervailing investigations within 13 months. Moreover, under EU rules, if the investigation is not completed within the prescribed period, the investigation lapses and no duties can be imposed.

3.9   DISPUTE SETTLEMENT PROCEEDINGS AGAINST SUBSIDIES

As we remarked at the beginning of this chapter, our principal interest is in anti-dumping and countervailing action, not in dispute settlement proceedings against subsidies. There is, however, an important link between countervailing action and dispute settlement proceedings. It is that, if a remedy has been obtained by one WTO member country in dispute settlement proceedings against a subsidizing member country, that remedy would normally put an end to any injury caused by subsidization practices, and so it would not be appropriate to bring countervailing proceedings against the same subsidizing member country.[17] We will therefore summarize briefly, in concluding this chapter, the provisions for dispute settlement under the Dispute Settlement Understanding as applied by the SCM Agreement.

The basic principle of the SCM Agreement is that WTO member countries should not grant or maintain export or domestic input subsidies. Such subsidies are characterized by the SCM Agreement as 'prohibited subsidies'.[18] This means that a member country may bring WTO dispute settlement proceedings against the country granting the subsidy, without having to prove any adverse effects. The procedure for such proceedings can be summarized briefly as follows. Where a member country has reason to believe that a prohibited subsidy is being granted or maintained by another member country, it may request consultations with such other member.[19] The purpose of such consultations is to clarify the facts and seek to arrive at a mutually agreed solution.[20] The deadline for completion of such consultations is 30 days, on the expiry of which any party to the consultations may refer the matter to the WTO Dispute Settlement Body, for the matter to be solved through the dispute settlement procedure, namely by the setting up of a Panel, followed possibly by an appeal to the Appellate Body.

All other subsidies are 'actionable' and can be challenged in a procedure similar to that already described for prohibited subsidies,[21] provided (a) the subsidy is *specific*;[22] (b) the subsidy causes *adverse effects* to the interests of other member countries;[23] and (c) the request for consultations includes a statement of the available evidence with regard to the existence of the subsidy (and the fact that it is specific), and the adverse effects caused to the interests of other member countries.[24]

Adverse effects here means one of three things:

(a) injury to the domestic industry of another member of the kind that would warrant the opening of a countervailing investigation pursuant to Part V

---

[17] This follows from the injury requirement for the imposition of countervailing measures.
[18] SCM Agreement, Article 3.2.
[19] SCM Agreement, Article 4.1.
[20] SCM Agreement, Article 4.3.
[21] See SCM Agreement, Article 7. Some of the deadlines are different.
[22] SCM Agreement, Article 2.
[23] SCM Agreement, Article 5.
[24] SCM Agreement, Article 7.2.

of the SCM Agreement. This means (i) material injury to the relevant industry; (ii) threat of material industry to the relevant industry; or (iii) material retardation of the establishment of such an industry, and is assessed by applying the detailed provisions of Articles 15 and 16 of the SCM Agreement, as further discussed in Chapter 4 below;[25]

(b) nullification or impairment of benefits accruing directly or indirectly to other members under GATT 1994, in particular the benefits or concessions bound under Article II of GATT 1994; or

(c) serious prejudice to the interests of another member. Serious prejudice has a complex definition set out in Article XVI of GATT 1994 and Article 6, paragraphs 2 to 9 of the SCM Agreement. The definition of 'serious prejudice' is surprisingly, and, we would say, disproportionately, complex. For the purpose of the present work, it will suffice to understand that there is a defined state of affairs which constitutes 'serious prejudice'.

It should be noted by way of postscript that Part IV of the SCM Agreement provided that certain subsidies were non-actionable (and therefore also not countervailable) until the end of the year 1999. These provisions, which are now of only historical interest, allowed subsidies for certain research activities, for disadvantaged regions and to promote the adaptation of existing facilities to new environmental requirements imposed by law.

Special provisions were negotiated in the Uruguay Round to deal with agricultural subsidies: owing to the sensitivity of agriculture for all trading nations, a separate agreement was signed, the Agreement on Agriculture, in order to allow subsidization of agriculture to continue, although within a framework wherein it would be reduced by 31 December 2003.

---

[25] GATT 1994, Article VI.

4. Injury

4.1 IS INJURY THE INEVITABLE EFFECT OF COMPETITION?

International trade is based on the principle of comparative advantage.[1] In a free market, those industries with a comparative advantage will eventually replace those with a comparative disadvantage. Comparative advantage is not, however, a static concept. It changes over time, so that an industry which once had a comparative advantage may lose this as a comparable industry develops, perhaps in another country or region, or as technology changes.

With freely flexible exchange rates, the relative exchange rates between countries are influenced by the operation of comparative advantage, and they change as they reflect developments in comparative advantage over time.

It can be shown that the operation of comparative advantage works to the benefit of all parties: both consumers in countries or regions which are home to industries with a comparative advantage, and consumers in countries or regions which import the relevant products. Through the operation of this principle, consumers throughout the world obtain the products they need (in the absence of monopoly) at the lowest possible prices, based on the lowest possible costs.

The operation of comparative advantage is hindered by the presence of obstacles to international trade – obstacles such as tariffs, quotas and subsidies. But, as these obstacles are removed, in whole or part, considerable changes can come about in the pattern of industry between countries and regions. Such changes have already widely occurred in the textile and clothing industries, for example, and more took place following the end of the Multi-Fibre Arrangement on 31 December 2004, when the quotas associated with it were abolished. In these circumstances, comparative advantage will be able to play a fuller part in international trade in textiles and clothing than could formerly be the case.

---

[1] See, for example, L. Alan Winters, *International Economics*, Part I, 4th edn, Routledge 1991.

What economists who extol the virtues of free trade based on comparative advantage tend to play down, however, is the effect of such a regime on industries and countries who develop comparative *dis*advantages over time. In the long run all should be well, as resources move out of disadvantaged sectors into those which are more competitive. But in the short run much distress can be caused as industries become disadvantaged, and are forced to contract in size or close down altogether. In particular, their workforce may suffer. Not only may they face immediate unemployment, but they may possess skills which can no longer be used in the industries that remain. They may therefore stay unemployed for long periods of time, unless they are able to equip themselves for other types of task. The beneficial long run may therefore be of little comfort to them.

The operation of these forces will cause injury to those industries which become disadvantaged, either as a result of the removal of obstacles to trade or because of changes in comparative advantage over time. The injury will, however, have been caused by the normal operation of competitive forces. Consumers everywhere should in the long run benefit as a result, if not the workforce of the industries that have been injured.

The question that needs now to be considered, however, is whether injury which is associated with the practice of dumping, or of subsidization, can similarly be attributed to the inevitable operation of competition. The immediate answer that comes to mind is that such injury cannot be attributed to the inevitable effects of competition. This is because the implication normally associated with the beneficial effects of the workings of competition is that such competition should be 'fair', and the WTO-accepted rules of international trade are that dumping and subsidization are not fair methods of competition. Dumped imports, for example, are not considered fair because they may cause serious injury to the domestic industry of an importing country, even when true comparative costs favour the domestic industry. This may then possibly be followed by an increase in the price of the previously dumped imports, thus disadvantaging consumers in the importing country, and subjecting them to higher prices for the product than ruled before the dumping took place. Such an outcome would clearly be undesirable.

Experience does not, however, support such an extreme view of the likely effects of dumping. In general, some part of the domestic industry will probably remain in existence after dumping has taken place. The possible effect of the dumping is therefore to cause the domestic industry to diminish in size, or to expand less rapidly than it might have done, while the domestic price level is likely to fall. The domestic industry will have suffered injury on account of the dumped imports, but domestic consumers will have benefited from lower prices, which may well persist.

An interesting question is – how persistent is dumping likely to be?

Experience suggests that imports at low dumped prices are likely to persist, even after anti-dumping duties have been imposed. In this case, one may ask how exporting countries manage to keep on dumping. This will depend partly on the level of domestic prices in the exporting countries. If such prices are kept at a high level because of obstacles to imports, then export prices might be priced only slightly above the level of variable costs. While export prices based on variable costs might not be objected to at times of depressed demand, there are clear objections to exports which are consistently at such prices. In such a situation, industries in the importing countries, which need to cover their full costs in the long run, will be consistently subjected to imports based on variable costs only. If this is the case, the injury caused to domestic industries cannot reasonably be attributed to 'the inevitable effects of competition'.

But it has to be remembered that the issue of whether dumping has occurred or not is often the subject of controversy. Exporting countries may assert that their exports are not being sold at dumped prices. Such arguments may be especially persuasive when exports come from non-market economies, since in their case normal value (as used in anti-dumping cases) is likely to be determined on the basis of the price or constructed value in a market economy third country. It is well known that this criterion may result in an unrealistically high normal value, and hence a determination of high dumping based on this.

In addition, if one examines anti-dumping actions taken by rich countries or regions such as the USA or the EU, it is usually the case that such actions are predominantly taken against relatively poor countries, with much lower wage levels than those in wealthy countries.[2] It can be questioned, therefore, how far low-priced exports from poorer countries are really being dumped. In any event, even if technically they can be shown on occasions to have been dumped, it seems likely that consistently low export prices from such countries are based on low full costs of production, rather than prices below this level.

In so far as this is the case, the injury caused by these apparently dumped exports is more likely to be on account of the inevitable effects of competition, than of the consistent operation of unfair trade practices.

To put the argument another way: it is widely considered that China is becoming a more and more formidable competitor in world markets. Is this because of a fear that China will be consistently dumping or subsidizing its exports? The answer is clearly 'no'. China is formidable because it has very low wage costs, an enormous workforce, high levels of skill in many industries, and large inward investment, bringing with it technological progress and

---

2   See Aubrey Silberston, 'Anti-dumping rules – time for change?', *Journal of World Trade*, **37**(6), December 2003.

increased productivity. These are the factors that give China its great competitive strength. They are the inevitable effects of competition, not a reliance on unfair methods of competition.

4.2   DUMPING SUBSIDIZATION AND INJURY

The WTO Agreements, and the associated regulations in the USA and the EU, for example, are not concerned with these broader questions. They are concerned with dumping or subsidies, as defined in these instruments, and with the injury that such dumping and subsidization can cause. We now turn to an examination of this issue.

A finding that dumping has occurred on the part of an exporter, or that its exports have been subsidized, is not sufficient to generate anti-dumping or countervailing action in an importing country. In addition, it must be demonstrated that the industry concerned in the importing country has suffered injury, or is likely to do so. Unlike the determination of dumping and subsidization, however, which are basically arithmetic operations, the assessment of injury is to a large extent a qualitative exercise. Despite the guidance given in the WTO agreements on how injury might be assessed, it has been inevitable in practice that exporters have often felt that importing countries have not given them a fair deal as regards injury. It is not surprising, in these circumstances, that the assessment of injury has given rise to both economic and legal difficulties.

4.3   DEFINITION OF INJURY

The label 'injury' is a shorthand for three possibilities, outlined in the WTO Agreements: (a) the dumped or subsidized imports are causing material injury to the relevant industry of the importing country; (b) the dumped or subsidized imports are threatening to cause material injury to that industry; (c) the dumped or subsidized imports are materially retarding the establishment of that industry.

The first of these is the criterion most commonly used. Cases where duties have been imposed on the basis of the second criterion, threat of injury, are very rare (one being the EU case of synthetic handbags from China).[3] The third criterion, material retardation of the establishment of an industry, has virtually never been used, and never by the EU.

---

[3]   OJ L208, 2.8.97, p. 31.

4.4 CAUSATION OF MATERIAL INJURY

Because of the qualitative nature of industry assessment, such bodies as the European Court of Justice recognize that the EU Authorities, for example, have a wide margin of discretion in their assessment of economic elements such as injury. For these reasons it is difficult to show that the EU Authorities are manifestly wrong in their assessment of injury (manifest error being the test applied by the Court in deciding whether to interfere with the EU Authorities' findings). The EU Authorities, however, as with other comparable jurisdictions, have difficulty on occasions in proving injury. It is worth observing that, in about one-third of the cases initiated, the EU Authorities terminate the proceedings without proposing the imposition of protective measures, and that in about half of these cases the reason for termination is the finding of the absence of injury.

The principle underlying the whole of the analysis of injury, as laid down in the WTO Agreements, is that the findings must be based on positive evidence; that is to say, it cannot be based on speculation. Conclusions must be based on verified fact. At the end of the day, the hard facts which an investigating body has at its disposal are the values and volumes reported in the import statistics (provided the customs heading corresponds to the product under investigation) and, more important, the pricing and cost data provided both by domestic producers and by the exporters in their questionnaires, data which will have been verified at an on-site verification. The second principle is that the findings must be objective. Exporters frequently feel that the EU Authorities are biased in favour of the European industry, but the EU, for its part, has complained that the standards applied to its own exports by the USA, as well as by many developing countries, are often poor.[4]

It is indeed often far from easy to persuade the EU Authorities of the existence of injury. The EU Authorities are generally fair and objective in their assessment of injury, and the fact that about one sixth of the cases are terminated on the basis of no apparent injury is an indication of this. The basic rule is that a determination of injury shall be based on positive evidence and shall involve an objective examination of (a) the volume of the dumped or subsidized imports; (b) the effect of the dumped or subsidized imports on prices in the relevant importing market; and (c) the consequent impact of those imports on the domestic industry.

The determination of dumping or subsidization is made by reference to data in a reference or 'investigation period', usually the 12 months immediately

---

[4]   See Aubrey Silberston, 'Anti-dumping rules – time for change?', *Journal of World Trade*, **37**(6), December 2003.

preceding the initiation of the investigation. The relevant question is whether dumping or subsidization in this period has caused material injury to the industry concerned. Such an assessment cannot be made without looking at the trend of certain factors in the years preceding the investigation period. The EU Authorities, for example, usually examine the trend over four years preceding the investigation period, plus the investigation period itself.

4.5   VOLUME OF DUMPED OR SUBSIDIZED IMPORTS

If imports from the country concerned have increased in absolute or relative terms in relation to production or consumption in the importing country or region, that is an indicator that injury is being caused.

This rule needs to be read alongside another rule, defining negligible injury. The rule in the Anti-dumping Agreement defines negligible injury as imports from one country amounting to less than 3 per cent of total imports from all countries (unless all countries under the 3 per cent limit together account for 7 per cent or more of total imports).

The WTO rule is not expressed in the same way as in the EU AD Regulation. The latter regulation says that, if imports from the country concerned account for less than a 1 per cent share of the EU market, the injury is negligible and the case must be closed. The rule about closure of the case when imports are less than 1 per cent of market share does not apply if the case is brought against several exporting countries, each with less than 1 per cent market share, but with all the countries collectively accounting for 3 per cent or more of Community market. Thus it can be seen that, depending on the ratio of total imports to the total market, the EU rule can be more or less advantageous to the exporter than the WTO rule. The WTO rule also has the advantage of not depending on an assessment of the total Community consumption. It is relatively easy to determine total imports of a product, provided it corresponds to a customs heading. On the other hand, it can be difficult to estimate market size, especially if some domestic producers do not cooperate in the investigation.

It should also be noted that, unlike the WTO Anti-dumping Agreement, the SCM Agreement does not contain the 3 per cent/7 per cent rule at all, although it does refer to 'negligible' injury. This is generally assumed to refer to the 3 per cent/7 per cent rule in the AD Agreement.

Another aspect of volume is the issue of cumulation. It sometime happens that dumped imports are being made from more than one country. In such circumstances it is permitted[5] to assess the volume of the dumped or subsi-

---

[5]   Council Regulation (EC) No 384/96, OJ L56, 6.3.96, Article 3.4.

dized imports by reference to the total volume imported from all the countries subject to investigation, provided that:

(a) the margin of dumping is more than the 2 per cent *de minimis* level for each country concerned (or, in the case of subsidization the margin of subsidy is less than 1 per cent for developed countries, or 2 per cent for developing countries); and that the volume of imports from each country is not negligible, and

(b) a cumulative assessment is appropriate in the light of the conditions of competition between imported products, and the conditions of competition between the imported products and the like domestic product.

The second of these conditions requires further explanation. It means, in effect, that if dumped imports are being made from country A and from country B, the products from both these countries should be substitutable one for the other, and therefore compete with each other. In addition, the products from both country A and country B are substitutable for, and are competing with, the like product produced by the domestic industry.

4.6 EFFECT OF DUMPED OR SUBSIDIZED IMPORTS ON PRICES

The rule is that it has to be assessed whether there has been significant price undercutting by the dumped or subsidized imports, or whether the effect of such imports is otherwise to depress prices to a significant degree or prevent price increases, which would otherwise have occurred, to a significant degree. The EU Authorities seldom use this third test, prevention of price increases, because it involves speculation as to what levels prices might have risen to if there had been no dumped or subsidized imports.

In all cases where dumping or subsidization has been found, a price under-cutting calculation is made. This is a complex operation. First it requires an examination of the channels of trade, in the case of sales by domestic producers, and the channel of sale, in the case of sales by exporters. This is in order to determine which is the most appropriate level at which to make the price comparison, and this requires an examination of the behaviour of the users of the product. If the users place orders either with domestic producers or direct with the exporters, it is probably appropriate to make the price comparison between the duty paid cost, insurance and freight (CIF) price of the imported product and the ex-works price of the product of the domestic producers. In cases where the exporter does not sell direct to users, but only to distributors, whereas domestic producers sell direct to users, it would be appropriate to compare the price charged by the distributors, ex-warehouse, with the price charged by the domestic producers ex-works.

The above comparison may be complicated in cases where the product comes in many different product types, for example, telefax machines. In such cases it is necessary to ensure that price comparisons are made for product types which are similar and which are seen by users as substitutable. In such cases the procedure used by the EU Authorities is to calculate a separate undercutting margin for each of the product types, and then express the result as a weighted average.

In order to determine whether there has been depression of prices to a significant degree, the investigating body can only rely on trends over the years preceding the investigation period. Thus a finding of price depression is less exact than a finding of price undercutting, which is the result of a detailed calculation.

4.7   IMPACT OF DUMPED OR SUBSIDIZED IMPORTS ON THE DOMESTIC INDUSTRY

In determining the impact of the dumped or subsidized imports on the domestic industry, the investigating body must evaluate all relevant economic factors and indices having a bearing on the state of the industry. An illustrative list is provided in the WTO Agreement (Article 3.4) and in the EU regulation (Article 3.5). It is the EU Authorities' practice to deal with each item on the list in the reasoning for their decisions:

a.   the fact that the industry may be still in the process of recovering from the effects of past dumping or subsidization;
b.   the magnitude of the actual margin of dumping or subsidization (although the EU Authorities interpret this as simply requiring it to verify that the margin is not *de minimis*);
c.   actual and potential decline in sales, profits, output, market share, productivity, return on investments, utilization of capacity;
d.   factors affecting EU prices;
e.   actual and potential negative effects on cash flow, inventories, employment, wages, growth, ability to raise capital or investments.

The investigating body is obliged to verify that any injury caused by factors other than dumped or subsidized imports is not attributed to the dumped or subsidized imports. In particular, it is obliged to examine the effect of the volume and prices of imports not sold at dumped prices (and not subsidized), contraction in demand, changes in the pattern of consumption, restrictive trade practices, competition between third country and domestic producers, developments in technology and the export performance and productivity of the domestic industry.

As regards restrictive trade practices, the European Court of Justice has not hesitated to annul anti-dumping duties where the EU Authorities have failed to take account of possible anti-competitive conduct on the part of the EU industry. Thus in the case of *Calcium metal from Russia and China* the Court annulled anti-dumping duties because the EU Authorities had failed to examine whether the fact that the sole EU producer refused to supply one of the user–importers might have contributed to causing injury.[6] More recently, in the case of *Stainless steel bright bars from India*, the EU Authorities failed to give due weight to the fact that one component of the price of steel bright bars on the EU market was artificially increased under a restrictive practice among the EU producers.[7]

4.8   LESSER DUTY RULE

Article 19.2 of the WTO Subsidies and Countervailing Measures Agreement and Article 9.1 of the WTO Anti-dumping Agreement provide that it is desirable that the duty imposed should be less than the total amount of the subsidy (or the margin of dumping) if such lesser duty would be adequate to remove the injury to the domestic industry. The EU has given effect to this recommendation by incorporating the so-called 'lesser duty' into its regulations, but the USA has not done this, and works simply by the calculated dumping or subsidy margin.

The EU Authorities calculate the lesser duty in the following way. They establish the level of trade at which price comparisons should be made in the EU, having regard to the nature of the product and the structure of the market. The idea is to compare prices of the imported product with prices of the EU producers at the level at which the first independent customer purchases.

First, the EU Authorities determine the injury elimination level. This is done by taking the weighted average costs of production of the EU industry and adding a reasonable profit margin. This gives a price level, ex-works, which on average would enable the EU industry to make a reasonable profit. Next, the EU Authorities take a listing of all the import prices from a given exporter, and adjust these to the level of trade corresponding to sales ex-works of the EU producers. This is usually duty-paid, ex-warehouse at the European

---

6   Case C-358/89, *Extramet Industrie S.A.* v. *Council*, [1992] ECR I-3813.
7   Case T-58/99, *Mukand Ltd and Others* v. *Council*, [2001] ECR II-2521.

port. The European Authorities then calculate the amount of duty which, on average, would increase the import prices to the injury elimination level. This duty is the amount which is necessary to remove injury. The duty actually imposed is always the lesser of (i) the duty which would be necessary to remove injury, and (ii) the margin of dumping or subsidization. A simple illustration of this can be given:

Dumping/subsidy margin	35%
CIF price	100
EU industry's average costs of production	115
Reasonable profit margin (on sales)	8%
Injury elimination level (100 / 92 per cent)	125
Lesser duty (125 – 100)/100	25%

It should be noted that the lesser duty rule is applied individually for each cooperating exporter. In the case of exporters in China, for example, who qualify for individual treatment, or for market economy treatment, an individual calculation of the duty necessary to eliminate injury is carried out. For example, in the anti-dumping proceedings against *Compact fluorescent lights from China*, all the exporters who qualified for individual dumping margins, but one, had dumping margins that were less than the amount of duty necessary to remove injury, so that the duties imposed had to reflect these lower dumping margins. The remaining exporter, Philips & Yaming Lighting Co Ltd, Shanghai, on the other hand, had a dumping margin of 61.8 per cent, but the duty necessary to eliminate injury was found to be 39.2 per cent, so the anti-dumping duty imposed on this exporter was 39.2 per cent.[8]

4.9   CAN INJURY BE MEASURED QUANTITATIVELY?

It is obvious in the light of the above discussion that, with so many factors that have to be taken into account, the determination of any material injury caused by dumped imports cannot be an exact procedure. Any investigation of this sort must rely mainly on economic evidence, and for that reason the determination of causality can no more be precisely determined than many other issues that rely on economic analysis. Perhaps the greatest difficulty is determining which changes in the industry of the importing country are due to any dumping that may have occurred, and which to factors other than dumping.

---

[8]   Council Regulation (EC) No 1470/2001, OJ 2001 L195, 19.7.2001, p .8.

Suppose, for example, that the product manufactured in the importing country is becoming outdated, and that imports of a newer type of product have been coming in. The domestic industry will very likely contract in size as a result, unless it changes rapidly to the new product. This will be true whether imports of the newer product have been deemed to be dumped or not. If imports have been dumped, the penetration of the domestic market may well be speedier than would otherwise be the case, but this will simply be a matter of the rate at which the domestic industry contracts. How much of the contraction can be put down to dumping? In such a case the amount of injury due to dumping alone might be almost impossible to determine.

Another example, which illustrates the problems of determining injury, might concern a domestic industry which is expanding, but where imports are increasing faster than domestic production, so that imports are taking a larger share of the domestic market. Has the domestic industry been injured, even though it has been shown that some imports have been dumped? In this case it is again a question of the rate at which a change is taking place. Even if it is accepted that injury on account of dumping has occurred, how possible is it to determine the quantity of the injury caused by the dumping?

These examples could be multiplied. The difficulty in establishing a causal link between dumping and injury has been illustrated on many occasions when the Community and other authorities have attempted to investigate whether such injury has taken place as a result of dumping. As has been pointed out, a significant proportion of anti-dumping investigations in the EU have had to be terminated without action because injury could not be established.

An interesting case where the determination of injury caused some problems was that relating to *Unbleached (grey) cotton fabrics*.[9] In this case the Commission concluded that the situation of the Community industry had indeed deteriorated between 1992 and 1995, in particular in respect of production, sales, employment and profitability. Domestic prices fell during the period, while manufacturing costs rose, in spite of efforts to rationalize operations. But a major part of the increase in costs was due to sharp rises in raw cotton prices, and this may have depressed profitability, even in the absence of the allegedly dumped imports. Moreover, in discussing Community Interest, the Commission considered that the imposition of duties would not have a material adverse effect on the downstream industries.

In the event, a sufficiently large number of Community countries considered that their downstream industries would have been adversely affected by the imposition of duties. They argued that, overall, more injury would occur if action were taken on dumping than if it was not. As a result, the EU Council

---

[9] Commission Regulation (EC) 2208/96, OJ L295, 20.11.96, p. 3.

of Ministers decided, on balance, that the imposition of anti-dumping duties should not go ahead.

Another EU example concerns the recent *EU cellulose filament yarn case*.[10] It was concluded that the position of the Community industry had deteriorated between 1997 and 2001. Part of the deterioration was said to be due to a contraction in demand for the relevant product, but part was held to be due to dumping. It was therefore concluded that dumping had caused material injury to the Community industry. This conclusion was strongly contested by the importers, who cited other factors as being important in the movements that had taken place, including the fact that one Community producer had closed its production facility at the beginning of 2002, and had subsequently imported yarn from its facilities in the USA. The objections of the importers appear to have been strengthened by the subsequent withdrawal of the complaint by the trade association that had originally submitted it to the EU Authorities.

In the light of these and many other cases, it is not surprising that assertions about injury, and the causation of injury, have frequently been the subject of controversy. Importers into the EU or the USA have complained about many of the relevant findings, while the EU and the USA have themselves complained about injury alleged to have been caused, in such countries as India, by exports of their own, allegedly at dumped prices.

There are two major problems in this area. The first is to establish whether imports have been dumped. This raises all the problems of normal value that have been discussed above, together with the problem of establishing export prices, the dumping margin and so on. The second is whether, dumping having been established, material injury has been caused on account of it to a domestic industry. The analysis of this is complicated if both upstream and downstream domestic industries could be affected by the alleged dumping. But even if a convincing argument can be made for injury due to dumping, it is obvious, in the light of the considerations discussed above, that any such injury cannot be measured in an accurate quantitative sense.

4.10   THE PRICE–VOLUME RELATIONSHIP AND THE SPREADING OF OVERHEADS

As has been explained, there are two margins that the EU authorities consider in deciding on the level of anti-dumping duties to impose. The first is the dumping margin, that is, the comparison between the weighted average

---

[10]   Commission Regulation (EC) 1662/2002, OJ L251/9, 19.9.2002, p. 9.

normal value in the exporting country, and the weighted average export price. In the *EU cellulose filament yarn case*, for example, this was found to be 30.8 per cent in the case of exports from Lithuania and 104.8 per cent in the case of exports from the USA. The second margin is the margin of undercutting, that is, the extent to which imports from the countries concerned undercut the Community industry's prices. In the *EU cellulose filament yarn case* this margin was found to be between 4 per cent and 8 per cent for exports from Lithuania and between 0 per cent and 2 per cent for exports from the USA. Normally, on account of the lesser duty rule, anti-dumping duties are based on the lower of these two margins. In the case cited, therefore, they would normally be based on the margin by which the average price of dumped imports was below the injury elimination level. (The injury elimination level is the minimum price level in the EU market which would allow the EU industry to make a reasonable profit.)

It was, however, argued in this case that prices in the Community were depressed by the dumped import prices, so that anti-dumping duties ought to be imposed at a level sufficiently high to restore the Community industry to its appropriate normal level of profitability. It was suggested that a profit margin of 12 per cent on turnover could be regarded as an appropriate level which the Community industry could obtain in the absence of injurious dumping. On this basis, the injury elimination margins were established at 20.1 per cent in the case of Lithuania, and 16.3 per cent in the case of Celanese of the USA, and the levels of anti-dumping duties were accordingly set at these margins.

Community consumption decreased by 24 per cent between 1997 and the investigation period (2000–2001). The sales volume of the Community industry decreased by about 35 per cent during this period, while the volume of imports increased by 63 per cent. The Community consequently lost 12 percentage points of its market share, whereas the imports concerned managed to increase their market share by 14 percentage points during the period: from a 12 per cent market share in 1997 to 26 per cent in 2000–2001.

The EU Authorities had calculated that the imposition of anti-dumping duties at the levels estimated would raise prices in the Community, and restore profits in the Community industry to a level of 12 per cent on turnover. Following the imposition of measures, it was expected that the volume of sales of the product concerned by the Community industry on the domestic market would stabilize. This would enable the Community industry to recover lost market shares and, by increasing capacity utilization, decrease unit production costs and increase productivity. Prices would probably increase moderately, and this, together with further decreases in unit costs, would 'allow the Community industry to improve its financial situation'.

The consideration, by the EU Authorities, of the effect of duties on capacity utilization, and hence on unit production costs, was a comparatively new departure, since such considerations had not normally entered into previous analyses. Yet this is a potentially important point. Anti-dumping duties not only increase the price of imports. They are also likely to discourage imports at the new higher prices, thus enabling the domestic industry to increase its output. How far the domestic increase in output occurs, as a result, will differ from case to case. In the cellulose filament yarn case, for example, it can be asked whether the market share of the domestic industry would increase to its previous level of 88 per cent, as compared with its level during the investigation period of 74 per cent. Consumption in this period amounted to 29 000 tonnes. Assuming that this level was maintained, an increase from 74 per cent to 88 per cent of this total would imply an increase from 21 460 tonnes to 25 520 tonnes in the output of the domestic industry, an increase of some 19 per cent.

Such an increase in output would clearly have a beneficial effect on unit costs of production. According to the EU Authorities, in 1999 the unit cost of the Community industry increased by 16 per cent, mainly because of the decrease in production, and after restructuring was still 10 per cent above the 1997 level. It is not clear whether the reference here is to the change within a single year or over a period. Other evidence suggests that an increase in unit costs of this magnitude might have occurred when Community output fell from 88 per cent of 38 000 tonnes (apparent consumption in 1997) to 74 per cent of 29 000 tonnes (apparent consumption in 2000–2001), that is, when Community output fell from 33 440 tonnes to 21 460 tonnes – a decrease of some 35 per cent.

If, as a result of the imposition of duties, an increase in output from 21 460 tonnes to 25 520 tonnes were to take place, there would be a decrease in unit costs as overheads were spread over the larger output. The increase of 19 per cent in output would take place over a steeper portion of the average cost curve than the change from 33 440 to 21 460 tonnes. It is however unlikely that unit costs would fall by as much as 16 per cent, or even by as much as 10 per cent, but a fall of perhaps 5 per cent in unit costs might be possible.

The EU Authorities argued that, after the imposition of duties, domestic prices would in all likelihood increase moderately. The Community industry had just reached low profitability levels in 2000–2001, although these 'still remained far below sustainable profit margins'. These new levels of price were expected to give a profit margin of 12 per cent. When, in addition, a fall in unit costs of, say, 5 per cent is also taken into account, a profit level well above 12 per cent would be the likely result.

There is further possibility: an industry protected by anti-dumping duties may be more confident than otherwise in carrying out expenditure on research and development, or in investing in modern equipment. In that case anti-dumping duties would make it more likely that the domestic industry would bring down its long-run level of costs, or improve its products technologically. It would, however, obviously be difficult to take such possibilities into account when calculating the level of anti-dumping duties.

Ignoring these longer-run possibilities, it still follows that, when the effect on unit costs of increasing output, and thus of spreading overheads over a larger volume, is taken into account, the level of duties imposed (based on price differences alone) is likely to give the domestic industry a larger boost in profitability than would be at first sight apparent. The possible effect on unit costs of the likely increase in domestic output, following the imposition of duties, needs therefore to be considered. The implication is that a lower level of duties than that based on price differences would be appropriate, once economies from a higher level of output were taken into account.

4.11 CAN THREAT OF INJURY BE ASSESSED REALISTICALLY?

Injury is defined in the EU AD Regulation as material injury to the Community industry, threat of material injury to the Community industry, or material retardation of the establishment of such an industry.

Article 3.7 of Article VI of the WTO Agreement spells out the criteria required for the threat of material injury to be established. These are repeated in Article 3.9 of the Community's Regulation.

The relevant articles state that a determination of a threat of material injury must be based on facts and not merely on allegation, conjecture or remote possibility. The circumstances must be clearly foreseen and imminent. In making a determination regarding a threat of material injury, consideration should be given to such factors as the following:

a. a significant rate of increase of dumped imports into the domestic market indicating the likelihood of substantially increased imports;
b. sufficient freely disposable capacity of the exporter, indicating the likelihood of substantially increased dumped exports to the importing member's market;
c. whether imports are entering at prices which would, to a significant degree, depress prices or prevent price increases which would otherwise have occurred;
d. inventories of the product being investigated.

The totality of these factors must lead to the conclusion that further dumped imports are imminent and that, unless protective action is taken, material injury will occur.

Article 3.8 of the WTO Agreement adds another condition: 'where injury is threatened by dumped imports, the application of the anti-dumping measures shall be considered and decided with special care'.

In practice, the EU rarely imposes duties on the basis of threat of injury. The question of threat of material injury has usually been investigated by the Community in conjunction with the question of actual material injury. Where it has been investigated, the threat of material injury, whether in conjunction with actual material injury or not, has not usually been substantiated. The question of threat of injury alone was considered, for example, in the case of *Refined antimony trioxide from the People's Republic of China.*[11] Here there was a significant increase in dumped imports, but no actual injury due to the high profits being registered by the Community industry. The EU Authorities took the view that, given the levels of profitability and the resilience of the industry, it was not clearly foreseeable that the current situation was likely to develop into imminent material injury.

There have been a few cases where the EU Authorities have found – for example, in *Methylamine from the German Democratic Republic and Romania* – both actual material injury and, at the same time, a threat of injury, but such cases have been rare.[12]

An interesting example of threat of injury can be found in the case of *Leather handbags from China.* In this case the EU Authorities found, at the provisional duty stage, that the high volume of imports from China, combined with price undercutting in the range of 28 per cent, had caused material injury to the Community industry.[13] However, at the definitive stage, the Community authorities limited themselves to saying that imports from China were threatening to cause injury. This was possibly the result of a political compromise with Member States, some of which were not in favour of the measures. By making a finding of threat of injury instead of actual material injury the Community authorities had to release the calculated provisional duties that had been imposed earlier on.[14] This is because, in application of the principle in Article 7.1 (ii) of the WTO Anti-Dumping Agreement, and Article 10(2) of the EU Regulation, the EU collects provisional duties only when they are necessary to prevent actual injury, not the threat of injury. Even so, a definitive anti-dumping duty was imposed in this case from the date of the final determination of the threat of injury.

It will be seen that the list of conditions that have to be satisfied before the threat of material injury can be established is a formidable one. Not only must

---

[11]   OJ L176, 9.7.94, p. 41, recital (34).
[12]   OJ L238, 13.8.82, pp. 35–6.
[13]   OJ L33, 4.2.97 p. 11
[14]   OJ L208, 2.8.97, p. 31.

the conditions set out be present, but it must be established that material injury is likely to be caused as a result of their operation. Considering the problems involved in assessing whether actual material injury has taken place, it is clearly even more difficult to establish that there is a threat of such injury. This is probably just as well, as this regulation could easily be used as a protectionist device.

4.12   CAN MATERIAL RETARDATION OF A NEW INDUSTRY BE ASSESSED REALISTICALLY?

The question of material retardation has never been a decisive factor in any of the cases decided in the Community. Unlike a threat of material injury, no special factors which would justify such a finding are contained in the WTO Agreement. Presumably similar factors would apply as to a threat of material injury.

For material retardation to be established it would presumably be necessary to show, for example, that dumped or subsidized imports would make it difficult for an investor in the domestic market wishing to establish a new industry to do so, because adequate profits could not reasonably be anticipated. Proof would presumably be needed that such an investor had plans at an advanced stage to establish the industry concerned. Such proof is, however, likely to be difficult to obtain, since a potential investor is unlikely to take advanced steps to establish a new industry if he is aware of the existence of low-priced, possibly dumped, imports. These might well make his venture unprofitable, even if an anti-dumping duty were imposed. In any event, a problem would be to determine the appropriate anti-dumping duty, in the absence of actual production in the importing country.

An interesting illustration of the effect of dumped imports on a barely established industry can be found in the *EU Japanese DRAMs case*.[15] Here the volume of dumped imports, the prices at which they were offered, and the condition of the Community industry, led the EU Authorities to determine that the effect of the dumped imports had caused injury to the Community industry. The facts of the case were considered to support a finding both of material injury and of injury in the form of material retardation.

It was considered in this case that huge financial losses resulting from the non-utilization of Community plant and manpower had to be considered as material, whether related to an established industry or to an existing industry which was in an infant or nascent state. In the latter instance the dumped

---

[15]   Regulation (EEC) 165/90, OJ L20, 25.1.90.

imports had 'clearly materially retarded the development of a Community industry, established or otherwise, by causing delays in the adoption of decisions that would have occurred in a fair market environment'. The EU Authorities therefore were of the opinion that the question of whether the Community industry was established at the time could, in these circumstances, be left open.

In this case an initial attempt had been made to establish the industry within the Community. Plant had been installed and considerable investment had taken place, but cheap imports had caused the installed plant to be largely unutilized. In the circumstances the EU Authorities seemed undecided whether to class the Community industry as established or merely 'nascent'.

In any event, the EU Authorities' remedy in this case was to persuade the leading Japanese exporters to enter into price undertakings. At a later stage voluntary restraints on Japanese exports were agreed, thus enabling the 'nascent' Community industry to establish itself. This in itself appears to be sufficient proof that, in the absence of these measures, material retardation of the establishment of the Community's industry had taken place.

A somewhat later but similar case concerned the import of *CD-Rs from India*.[16] The Community's consumption of CD-Rs increased from some 459 000 units in 1998 to some 2 460 000 in 2001, but Community production increased only from some 76 000 in 1998 to some 390 000 in 2001, and amounted to some 16 per cent of the total in the latter year. As from 2001, the increase in Community capacity was limited, and could be mainly explained by investments to replace machinery of the first generation.

In this case it was not dumping that was found by the EU Authorities, but an illegal subsidy, and a countervailing duty was therefore imposed. It was concluded that the Community industry had suffered material injury, because it had been prevented from benefiting from cost reductions, and because the investment programmes for CD-Rs had been significantly reduced, owing to the declining trend of sales prices.

There is not much doubt that, in the absence of low priced imports from India (and also, principally, from Taiwan), the production of the Community industry would have increased much more strongly, and that it would therefore have taken a larger share of the Community market for CD-Rs than has actually been the case. There was undoubtedly therefore material retardation of the establishment of the Community industry, resulting from the low-priced imports, although this cause of injury was not cited by the EU Authorities.

It is, however, an interesting question whether material retardation of an infant industry, if it occurs, is likely to be mainly on account of dumping or

---

16   Regulation (EC) 960/2003, OJ L138, 5.6.2003.

subsidization. What is at issue is the conditions under which an industry can be firmly established. Does it seem likely that such a development can be prevented or hindered largely on account of imports being dumped (or subsidized), which in any event might well be a temporary problem? What seems more likely is that, if the threat to the development of a domestic industry comes from cheap imports, whether alleged to be dumped or not, it seems probable that comparative advantage for the product concerned lies with the exporting industry. This is almost certainly the case as regards Indian CD-Rs. It is also difficult not to conclude that the production of CD-Rs in Taiwan has a strong comparative advantage over production in the Community.

This is not to deny that dumping may hinder the development of an existing industry in an importing country, or slow down the establishment of a new industry. What seems less plausible is that an 'infant' or 'nascent' industry can be prevented from developing altogether into a firmly established industry, simply on account of dumping or subsidization. When a domestic industry fails to establish itself, this seems very likely to be mainly because an industry elsewhere possesses a comparative advantage in producing the good in question. In such circumstances, the industry in the importing country can only become established behind a shield of heavy protection, as occurred in the case of Dynamic Random Access Memory (DRAMs) in the EU.

5. Anti-dumping action – problems arising

The AD Agreement raises a number of problems. These relate firstly to the problems of interpreting several articles contained in the Agreement, and secondly to possible deficiencies in the Agreement itself, which ideally should be corrected. The present chapter deals with problems of interpretation, with reference principally to the EU AD Regulation, and to a lesser extent, to the US AD Regulation.

5.1 DOMESTIC PRICE AND SALES AT A LOSS[1]

As we have explained in Chapter 2, the domestic price in the country of export must be used as a measure of normal value, provided the relevant product is made in the ordinary course of trade, in sufficient quantities to be representative, and in a normal market situation. A domestic price is not regarded as being in the ordinary course of trade if it is charged to a related or associated party, for example a price charged by one company to another company when they are owned by the same holding company. Equally, a domestic price is not regarded as being in the ordinary course of trade if there is a compensatory arrangement between the parties. For example, suppose that an exporter A of PET (polyethylene teraphthalate) chips supplies PET chips to a local company B, but the local company B provides the first supplier A with monoethylene glycol. Because they are making cross-supplies the parties agree a pricing structure which they would not otherwise use in normal market conditions.

Domestic sales cannot be used as a measure of normal value unless they are in representative quantities. They are not considered to be in representative quantities unless their volume is at least 5 per cent or more of the volume of relevant exports to a given country or region. Equally, domestic sales cannot generally be used as a measure of normal value if they are loss making. The rules here are very technical. The AD Agreement formulates them in terms of

---

[1]   The rules discussed in this section can be found in Articles 2.1 to 2.3 of the AD Agreement.

when the investigating authorities *may* disregard loss-making sales, and when they may not.

As we have explained in Chapter 2, sales below unit costs may be disregarded in calculating normal value only if two conditions are satisfied: (a) such sales are in substantial quantities and over an extended period of time; and (b) such sales do not provide for recovery of costs within a reasonable period of time. The extended period of time has normally to be one year, but in no case should be less than six months.

As far as concerns condition (a), sales below unit costs should be considered to be in substantial quantities, within such a period, when it is established that (i) the weighted average selling price is below the weighted average unit cost, or (ii) that the volume of sales below unit cost is not less than 20 per cent of sales being used to determine normal value. As far as concerns condition (b), if prices which are below costs at the time of sale are above weighted average costs for the period of the investigation, such prices must be considered to provide for recovery of costs within a reasonable period of time.

These various tests for establishing sales in substantial quantities, below costs of production, which may be treated as not being in the ordinary course of trade, give rise to a number of problems. The condition (b) above envisages that costs of production (costs of manufacture plus sales, general and administrative expenses) may be determined transaction by transaction, or on a short-term basis. This may be appropriate where there are significant seasonal variations or when high inflation countries are involved. Such an approach may disclose prices which are below unit costs of production at the time of sale. But before such sales can be disregarded in computing normal value, they must be compared with the weighted average costs of production for the entire investigation period. If it is found that the prices exceed weighted average costs, then they are treated as providing for recovery all costs within a reasonable period of time, and cannot thus be disregarded. So the only candidate sales for being disregarded are those at prices which are less than average costs of production. But before they can be excluded, it has to be determined that they are in substantial quantities (condition (a)), for which there are two alternative tests.

Under the first alternative test, sales below unit cost are deemed to be made in substantial quantities if the weighted average selling price of all domestic sales of the product under consideration is less than the weighted average unit cost of production. If this is the case, then all the sales at prices less than weighted average cost have to be excluded. The normal value is thus the weighted average of all the sales which are at prices above weighted average costs.

The second alternative test is that, if the volume (quantity) of sales at unit prices below unit costs of production is not less than 20 per cent of the volume of domestic sales of the product, sales at below unit cost are deemed to be made in substantial quantities and may be disregarded. If this is the case, then all the sales at prices less than weighted average costs have to be excluded and normal value is determined as the weighted average of the remaining sales.

It follows from these two tests that, if the domestic sales at less than weighted average costs amount to less than 20 per cent of all domestic sales, *and* the weighted average price of all domestic sales is greater than the weighted average costs, then normal value is determined as the weighted average of *all* domestic sales.

The 20 per cent criterion can give rise to paradoxical situations. If, say, 10 per cent of domestic sales are loss-making, then these sales can be ignored, and 100 per cent of sales will be included in the calculation of normal value. But if, say, 25 per cent of sales are loss-making, the position appears to be that only the other 75 per cent of sales (all of which are by definition profitable) will be included in the normal value computation. In the 10 per cent situation, the weighted average selling price is depressed by the loss-making sales. In the 25 per cent situation, the loss-making sales are ignored, thus resulting in normal value being based on profitable sales only. Indeed, one could imagine two exporters, each of which had unit costs of 10, and had total domestic sales of 100 units for a total value of 1080, giving each of them a profit of 80. However, suppose the first exporter sold 90 units at 11 and 10 units at 9: his normal value would be 10.80, the average for all domestic sales. Suppose that the second exporter sold 75 units at 11.40 and 25 units at 9: his normal value would be 11.40, the average for the sales above unit costs of production. Thus, for the same total turnover, and the same overall profit, two different exporters could have different normal values.

In an extreme case where, say, 89 per cent of sales are loss-making (the EU Authorities normally regard 90 per cent as a cut-off value), normal value will be based on the profitable 11 per cent of sales only. This clearly makes little sense, and gives a computation of normal value which is far removed from the average level of domestic prices, thus increasing the likelihood that export prices will be below this somewhat bizarre 'normal value'. Taking the same unit cost of production of 10 as in our earlier example, one could imagine an exporter who sold 89 units at $9.00 and 11 units at $13.50. His total revenue would be $950, giving him an overall loss of $50, but his normal value would be $13.50, higher even than that of the two profitable exporters in the previous example.

Another problem arises out of the fact that condition (a) can lead to an abrupt and discontinuous change in normal value for no justifiable reason. If unit costs of production are $10, and 100 per cent of sales are at $11, the normal value will be $11. If, now, the price of 10 per cent of the sales is reduced to $9, the normal value becomes $10.80. If the price of 15 per cent of the sales is reduced to $9.00, the normal value becomes $10.70. If the price of 19 per cent of the sales is reduced to $9.00, the normal value becomes $10.62, but if the price of 20 per cent of the sales is reduced to $9.00, the normal value moves back to $11.00.

More fundamentally, it may be asked why, in those cases, taking all sales, when average prices are above average costs, loss-making sales should be excluded at all. This device serves to put up normal value, thus increasing the likelihood that dumping will be found. But if, on the average of all sales, a profit is being earned, why should not the normal value be accepted on this basis, which reflects the true profitability over the period of the domestic situation?

In any event, it is obvious that, for these various criteria to be satisfied, a number of complex calculations have to be carried out. In particular, weighted average selling prices over the extended period have to be calculated as well as weighted average unit costs. The proportion of domestic sales sold at below weighted average costs over the extended period has also to be calculated.

The calculation of weighted average selling price raises questions of variations in selling prices over time, while that of weighted costs of production gives rise to accounting problems. So does the comparison between the relevant weighted prices and costs. There are also problems in comparing export prices with the normal value or, in appropriate cases, with the relevant costs of production of the exports. In such comparisons the problem of 'zeroing', among others, arises. These and other related questions are addressed in Chapter 6 of this study.

5.2   PROBLEMS OF LIKE PRODUCT[2]

A major problem in the measurement of normal value concerns the question of whether there are sales of a 'like product' on the domestic market of the exporting country and, if so, whether the domestic sales exceed the 5 per cent limit. A like product is defined in the AD Agreement (Article 2.6) as 'A product which is identical, i.e. alike in all respects, to the product under consideration, or in the absence of such a product, another product which, although not alike in all respects, has characteristics closely resembling those of the product under consideration.'

The question of like product arises in the case of injury as well as in the calculation of normal value; an important consideration is how far a dumped

---

[2]   The rules discussed in this section can be found in Articles 2.4 and 2.6 of the AD Agreement.

product affects prices in the import market for like products. For the moment, however, it is best to concentrate on the problem of whether domestic sales and allegedly dumped exports are or are not 'like products'.

The question as to whether or not there are sales of a 'like product' on the domestic market of the exporting country is apparently a simple matter of fact. So is the question of whether such sales constitute 5 per cent or more of the sales volume of the product under consideration exported to the importing WTO member country. Products made for the export market may, however, differ from those made for the domestic market of the exporter. At the simplest level there may be differences in the electrical voltages that pertain between domestic and export markets. Or there may be differences in TV or DVD standards.

The AD Agreement does not say how one is to make the adjustment for physical differences, and so this is left to the individual WTO member countries. Article 2(10(a)) of the EU AD Regulation requires that, where there are differences in the physical characteristics of the product concerned – for example if there are several different varieties or models of the same product – adjustments may be made which correspond to a reasonable estimate of the market value of the difference. But such estimates may be difficult to arrive at. This is likely to present difficulties when different varieties are made for home and export. But there is likely to be particular difficulty when the product manufactured for export is not manufactured at all for domestic consumption. There may be perfectly rational reasons for such a situation to exist, but the consequence will be that a comparison between domestic and export prices for like products simply cannot be made.

A different problem arises when it is suspected by an importing country, allegedly suffering from dumping, that even though a like product to that being exported is also being sold domestically, the domestic price is not regarded as being in the normal course of trade. This may be because it is alleged that sales of the like product in the domestic market of the exporting market have been below unit (fixed and variable) production costs plus administrative selling and general costs (SG&A) over an extended period and in substantial quantities.

In this case, or when there are insufficient or no domestic sales of the like product in the ordinary course of trade, normal value is calculated on the basis of ex-factory cost of production in the country of origin of the exported commodity (plus a reasonable amount for administrative selling and general costs and for profit). In practice, when the European Commission, for example, examines an allegation of dumping, it invariably investigates costs of production in the exporting country of like products if they exist, and of the exported commodity, where no like domestic sales exist. This attitude is taken because, without such an investigation, the Commission cannot necessarily accept that normal value in the exporting country, calculated on the domestic selling price of the like product, is sufficient to cover full unit costs of production plus administrative selling and general costs, plus profits.

What it comes to in practice, therefore, is that, even when a like product is held to exist, the domestic price of such a product is not simply accepted as determining normal value. This is all the more likely to be the case when no like domestic product exists, or when the domestic variety is different from the exported variety. In all cases, therefore, the measurement of normal value entails an examination of costs of production, although the relevant costs of production may differ according to the circumstances.

5.3   THE PROBLEM OF NO LIKE PRODUCT[3]

The question of what should be done where there is no like product being sold on the domestic market raises a problem of principle. According to EU practice, in these circumstances normal value is be calculated on the basis of ex-factory manufacturing cost in the country of origin of the exported commodity, plus a reasonable amount for SG&A and profits.

This provision is obviously an attempt to construct a (domestic) normal value for the exported commodity, even though such a normal value does not exist. This is in line with the fundamental principle of EU practice: what has to be investigated is the relationship between the domestic and the export price or, failing that, between domestic costs and the export price.

There may, however, be market circumstances where this constructed normal value may not be appropriate. Any firm selling a product in export markets must have regard to its competitiveness in such markets. It may have developed a special line for export which it has to sell at only a modest profit margin, because of the competition from exporters in other countries. Or it may be trying to break into a market, and therefore charging a low price initially. Another possibility is that trade may be depressed, and the exporter is only able to sell abroad, at least for a time, at a price just above variable costs. In the long run the exporter would, however, hope to cover his full unit costs, by offsetting temporary low prices against higher prices in more prosperous times.

None of these strategies would appear to be reprehensible to an economist. But all of them would be ruled out under the present rules, when there is no like product, which demand that prices should be based on a simulated normal

---

[3]   The rules discussed in this section can be found in Article 2.2 of the AD Agreement.

value. It would make more sense in these circumstances if the export price, averaged over time, were to be investigated, and its relationship to the costs of producing that export were to be determined, taking due account of the long-term strategy of the exporting firm. Unfortunately, the present rules are not sufficiently soundly based in economic logic to allow such a solution to be adopted.

It is of course true that, even if there were a like product domestically, it may seem attractive to an exporter to pursue strategies such as those outlined above. But under the present rules such strategies would certainly be regarded as involving dumping, at least over certain periods of time. Perhaps in the long run even the rules for exports of like products should be changed, but in the present situation there is an argument for the authorities to take an especially flexible approach in the case of unlike products.

5.4   CONSTRUCTION OF NORMAL VALUE, SG&A AND PROFIT[4]

As has been explained, the calculation of normal value, while nominally based on the prices paid for the like product in the ordinary course of trade in the exporting country, in practice involves an examination of the costs of producing the like product – in other words, the 'constructed value'. Where there is no like product being sold in sufficient quantities on the domestic market, the constructed value is likely to be based on the costs of producing the exports of the allegedly dumped product.

In order to arrive at a constructed value, direct and indirect costs of production have to be taken into account, plus SG&A (selling, general and administrative expenses). One problem in ascertaining the constituents of direct and indirect costs is that accounting systems differ from country to country, in spite of international efforts to harmonize accounting procedures. This affects in particular the distinction between direct and indirect costs. The usual practice, however, is to start by accepting the accounting records of the exporter.

But costs in accounting records may be questioned for a number of reasons. For example, inputs into direct costs may be purchased from a related party at prices less than their costs of production. In such cases, the authorities of the importing country or region will wish to adjust the price to reflect the relevant costs of production plus reasonable SG&A and profits. As another example, the appropriate social security and other charges may not have been added to

---

[4]   The rules discussed in this section can be found in Article 2.2 of the AD Agreement.

direct labour costs, but treated as a general overhead. In such cases it would be necessary to re-allocate such charges to the accounting costs of the direct labour employed.

Indirect costs present greater problems. There is the major problem of the allocation of overheads between different products. This is discussed below. More generally, the practice of exporters in allocating capital costs over time needs to be examined. This involves a study of depreciation rates and periods, allowances for capital expenditure and other development costs. In some cases capital costs are treated as part of current expenditure. More commonly they are spread over the notional life of the investment, the amount for depreciation in the accounts varying according to the number of years adopted. There may be queries over this and other calculations. In addition, there is the question of the accounting treatment of interest payments on borrowed capital, including the plausibility of the rates of interest assumed.

These and other accounting problems lead to the situation that the accounting records of exporters are unlikely to be taken at their face value by the authorities of importing countries. This results in there being ample scope for argument and disagreement over the calculation of costs of production between exporting and importing nations.

In addition to the problems discussed so far, there is the question of arriving at a reasonable amount for SG&A (selling, general and administrative expenses) and profits. According to the AD Agreement, the amounts for this 'shall be based on actual data pertaining to production and sales, in the ordinary course of trade, of the like product, by the exporter or producer under investigation.' When such amounts cannot be determined on this basis the amounts may be determined on the basis of the following:

(a) the actual amounts applicable to production and sales, in the ordinary course of trade, of the same general category of products for the exporter or producer in question in the domestic market of the country of origin;
(b) the weighted average of the actual amounts determined for other exporters or producers subject to investigation, in respect of production and sales of the like product in the domestic market of the country of origin;
(c) any other reasonable method, provided that the amount for profit so established shall not exceed the profit normally realized by other producers or exporters on sales of products of the same general category in the domestic market of the country of origin.

It should be noted that, when constructed value has to be based, in the absence of a domestic like product, on the unit costs of producing the relevant exported product, the SG&A and profits to be included in the calculation must be that appropriate to the domestic sales (not the export sales) of a product in one of the above categories. This provision clearly raises serious problems of estimation.

In any event, it is obvious that the set of criteria for calculating SG&A and profits, presumably in descending order of preference, can give rise to differing interpretations by different authorities. The problems of allocation may also arise in these cases.

A particular question in assessing SG&A and profits may arise in the case of the appropriate rate of profit to be included in the calculation. The regulation provides that profits, together with the other relevant cost elements, should be based on actual data or, where these cannot be determined, on the criterion given in the third method mentioned above – the profit normally realized by other exporters or producers on domestic sales of products of the same general category.

In practice, domestic rates of profit may vary over time, being high at times of strong demand and low at times of depressed demand. Or keen competition in the domestic market may keep profits at a continuously low level. There is therefore a danger that the rate of profit actually included in SG&A calculations by the importing authority may tend in practice to be set at an unrealistically high level: for example, at a rate high enough to make a relevant industry profitable in the long term. Such a value for profits would increase the chances that normal value would be set at so high a level that exports will inevitably appear to be at dumped prices.

5.5   HOW SHOULD COSTS BE ALLOCATED?

In the case of costs of production, certain costs, such as costs of labour and materials, may usually be specific to a given product, and are therefore attributed to that product as direct costs of production. On the other hand, manufacturing overheads, interest charges, selling costs (excluding the direct costs of sales), SG&A and profits, are indirect costs of production. When more than one product is being produced, indirect costs have to be allocated to individual products. This gives rise to a number of problems.

Before overheads can be allocated, the exact division between direct and indirect costs has to be ascertained. Different divisions between direct and indirect costs, in a given allocation situation, will give rise to differences in the value of overheads to be added to the direct costs of the product under consideration, and will hence affect the calculation of normal value. The relevant division, therefore, has to be made with some care. Inevitably, in calculations of this description there may be room for argument, even when accountants have been called in to help make a decision.

Article 2.2.1.1 of the AD Agreement requires that the allocation of costs should be in accordance with the methods that have been historically utilized. Cost records should also be in accordance with the generally accepted accounting principles of the country concerned. In the absence of a more appropriate method, preference may be given to the allocation of (overhead) costs on the basis of turnover. Another frequently used method of allocation, presumably acceptable if generally accepted historically in a country, would be the allocation of overheads based on the direct costs of producing the different products which are subject to common overheads.

The correct allocation of overheads, when the manufacture of several products is involved, has been subject to much discussion among economists. There is general agreement that the calculation of direct costs should be made as accurately as possible. Any overheads directly attributable to the manufacture of a particular product should be established, and included in the calculation. But where truly common overheads are concerned the conclusion generally reached is that any allocation to individual products is likely to be a fruitless exercise. Enterprises should price their products at a level above direct costs, and aim to make a sufficient margin on all their products taken together to cover their overheads and desired level of profit.

Any other approach may well lead to wrong decisions. For example, the loading of a proportion of overheads on a particular product, according to some chosen principle, such as relative turnover, may make it appear that that product is unprofitable, and should no longer be produced and sold. But if the question is asked, 'what would happen to the profitability of the firm if the revenue received from sales of the product were to cease?', the answer may well be that the firm's profitability would suffer. There may be a number of reasons for this, including links between the sales of this product and sales of related products. A decision to cease producing the product, based on a particular allocation of overheads, will therefore have been the wrong decision.

While the economists' approach to dealing with the problem of overheads may be the correct one, this does not solve the problem facing authorities concerned with cases of alleged dumping. In such cases normal value has to be calculated and, as has been explained, the calculation of normal value nearly always involves a calculation of costs of production plus SG&A and profits. For this purpose full costs need to be established, that is, both direct and indirect costs. An allocation of overheads must therefore be made, despite the arbitrary nature of many such allocations.

The chief contenders for such an allocation are direct costs of production or turnover. As between these two, turnover is perhaps the better alternative. This is because turnover reflects prices, and the prices of products are likely to include a margin above direct costs. Those products yielding higher margins will be making a greater contribution to overheads than those yielding lower margins. They are therefore presumably more able to bear a higher proportion of overheads, if these need to be allocated. An allocation of overheads based on direct costs, on the other hand, would give no guidance as to the particular products which are best able to carry a large share of overheads.

The underlying arbitrariness of allocating common overheads however, always needs to be borne in mind. When a question of allocation arises, therefore, it is a matter for consideration which method of allocation should be chosen in an individual case. Since in principle no method of allocating common overheads is correct, it is necessary to find that method which appears to be the least objectionable in all the circumstances.

5.6   PROBLEMS OF START-UP SITUATIONS[5]

Article 2.2.1.1 says that costs shall be adjusted when they are affected by start-up situations. A footnote to this provision says that the adjustment made for start-up operations shall reflect the costs at the end of the start-up period or, if that period extends beyond the period of investigation, the most recent costs which can reasonably be taken into account by the authorities during the investigation. Expanding on this, Article 2(5) of the EU AD Regulation provides as follows:

> Where the costs for part of the period for cost recovery are affected by the use of new production facilities requiring substantial additional investment and by low capacity utilization rates, which are the result of start-up operations which take place within or during part of the investigation period, the average costs for the start-up phase shall be those applicable, under the abovementioned allocation rules, at the end of such a phase, and shall be included at that level, for the period concerned, in the weighted average costs referred to in the second sub-paragraph of paragraph 4.

It follows from the wording of the regulation that the rule about start-up operations cannot be invoked for all types of new investment, such as that incurred as a result of maintenance or the installation of replacement parts. The investment must represent a material increase in capital spending, intended to bring on a stream of new production facilities, and must be accompanied by low capacity utilization rates.

What the AD Agreement and the EU AD Regulation appear to contemplate is that an investigation period, in a start-up situation, may be divided into two shorter periods, the first relating to the period of the start-up, and the second

---

5   The rules discussed in this section are found in Article 2.2.1.1 of the AD Agreement.

to a period of normal operation following this, when capacity utilization is at its more normal level. If a start-up phase extends beyond the investigation period, information relating to costs just after the end of the start-up phase should be 'taken into account'.

In so far as start-up costs involve substantial additional investment, it is appropriate for such investment to be taken into account in the calculation of costs. This will normally be done by choosing an appropriate period for depreciation of the new facilities. Low capacity utilization will raise costs per unit. Direct costs may not be greatly affected by low utilization rates, but overheads will be spread over a lower volume of production than will eventually be made possible, thus increasing indirect costs per unit.

In practice, the regulation regarding start-up is applied by the Community authorities to refer to the level of costs at the end of the start-up phase. At this point, capacity utilization is assumed to be at its new normal level, so that overheads will be spread over the 'normal' volume of output. In order for this calculation to be made, however, the end of the start-up period needs to be ascertained.

The regulation provides that the length of the start-up phase 'shall be determined in relation to the circumstances of the producer or exporter concerned, but shall not exceed an appropriate initial portion of the period for cost recovery'. The length of such an initial period will differ from case to case, but it is understood that the EU Authorities normally consider that the period for cost recovery should be 12 months, and the appropriate initial portion should be of the order of three months but never exceeding six months.

In these circumstances, the weighted average for the period under investigation (normally a year) will be based on average costs per unit after the three to six months period. The high level of average start-up costs per unit, spread over initial low capacity utilization, will not therefore apparently apply to the calculation of weighted average costs. Even so, it may be doubtful whether the normal level of capacity utilization will have been reached as soon as three to six months. In that case, a comparatively high level of weighted average costs per unit is likely to apply for the whole period under investigation. This will bring up the level of the normal value, and make it more likely than otherwise that exports (whose prices may have to conform to the world level) will be found to have been dumped.

5.7 IMPORTS FROM NON-MARKET ECONOMY COUNTRIES

The AD Agreement does not say anything about market economy countries. A note to Article VI of GATT 1947 provides as follows:

It is recognized that, in the case of imports from a country which has a complete or substantially complete monopoly of its trade and where all domestic prices are fixed by the State, special difficulties may exist in determining price comparability for the purposes of paragraph 1, and in such cases importing contracting parties may find it necessary to take into account the possibility that a strict comparison with domestic prices in such a country may not always be appropriate.

It is pursuant to this provision that the EU has adopted a complex system for dealing with the determination of dumping in relation to imports from non-market economy countries. This system is set out in Article 2(7) of the EU AD Regulation, which has been amended on several occasions as thinking on this subject evolved.

5.7.1 Analogue Country

It will be recalled that, in the case of imports from non-market economy countries, prices and costs are considered to be unreliable as a basis for determining normal value. It is therefore provided that normal value shall be determined on the basis of the price or constructed value in a market economy third country, or the price from such a third country to other countries, including the importing domestic market, or, where those are not possible, on any other reasonable basis. The EU Authorities may even use the price actually payable in the EU for the like product, duly adjusted to include a reasonable profit margin. It is also required that an appropriate market economy third country be selected in a not unreasonable manner. Even so, this 'analogue country' provision has given rise to a number of problems.

The countries which the EU, for example, considered to be non-market economies in 2006 included Albania, Armenia, Azerbaijan, Belarus, Georgia, North Korea, Kyrgyzstan, Moldova, Mongolia, Tajikistan, Turkmenistan and Uzbekistan.

In selecting the analogue market economy country the European Commission is obliged to take account of the criteria laid down by the European Court of Justice in the *Chinese paint brushes case*. In that case the Court of Justice ruled that the anti-dumping duties were illegal because the European Commission had failed to select the analogue country on a reasonable basis. The criteria laid down by the Court were as follows:

a. representativity of the market in the analogue country, such as the size of the market and whether the volume of transactions used in the analogue country to determine normal value amounted to at least 5 per cent of the quantity exported from the country under investigation;

b. openness of the market, laid down by the Court as follows: for example, whether producers in the analogue country are subject to effective competition among themselves or from imports;

c.   access to basic raw materials: for example, whether there were any significant differences between access to raw materials in the analogue country and in the country subject to investigation.

The problem with use of an analogue country to determine normal value is that sometimes the EU Authorities choose a country which is highly developed, whereas the exporting country is still in the course of development. For example, if one determines the normal value of polyethylene terephthalate (PET) chips in the USA as an analogue for normal value of PET chips produced in China, it is not difficult to see that the costs of production in a high cost country such as the USA may well be out of proportion with the costs that one expects to find in a developing country such as China. This problem translates into the fact that dumping margins may tend to be particularly high when recourse is made to normal value in an analogue country.

One can, however, understand the dilemma of the EU Authorities when faced with the analogue country problem. When seeking an analogue country in the case of exports from China, for example, there may be no low-cost country with production and exports of the like product. In the case of *Barium carbonate from China*, for example, three Chinese exporters suggested South Korea, Russia and India as suitable analogue countries. On investigation, the EU Authorities found that none of these countries had appropriate production and export circumstances.

To be fair to the EU Authorities, it should be added that they did seek cooperation from India, Japan and Brazil, but that no producer in these countries was willing to cooperate. Possibly producers there may have feared that they themselves might one day be subject to anti-dumping actions, and therefore did not want to expose themselves unnecessarily.

The EU Authorities therefore had to fall back on the USA as their preferred analogue country, in spite of the fact that the USA was a far more advanced country than China. The USA was, however, more efficient as a producer, and to that extent it had a comparatively lower normal value than might otherwise have been the case. It is not surprising, in these circumstances, that two Chinese exporters, granted market economy status (see below) were found to have dumping margins of 11.2 per cent and 24.4 per cent respectively, while all other exporters were found to have the higher dumping margin (based on normal value in the USA) of 34 per cent.

Reliance on analogue countries can clearly have serious flaws, but it is not easy to see how the position can be improved. Analogue countries with a cost basis similar to that of the exporting country can reasonably be used to construct normal value, but the use of non-comparable analogue countries, such as the USA, raises obvious problems. The situation can be alleviated as a result of permitted adjustments, to allow for differences between the export price and normal value, including differences between the analogue country and the country under investigation. However, the range of adjustments permitted by the Courts has been a narrow one. Account may be taken of natural comparative advantages enjoyed by producers in non-market economy countries, but this has been interpreted to omit potentially important factors. For example, differences in access to raw materials may be taken into account, but not what is likely to be a major consideration, differences in labour costs.

Perhaps the most satisfactory solution would be to attempt, when a serious problem of comparability arises, to discover what reasonably reliable production and other costs can be found for the exporting firms concerned in their own country. This process could be greatly helped by reference to any firms found to be exporting the like product, in the same country, which had been granted market economy treatment.

5.7.2 Individual Treatment

Another problem with the approach to imports from a non-market economy country is that it is considered that, in such a country, it may not be possible to grant individual exporters individual treatment. For example, if exporter E has an export price of 110 while exporter F has an export price of 100, and normal value in the analogue country is found to be 120, the dumping margin of exporter E will be 10, whereas the dumping margin of exporter F will be 20. The EU does not normally impose an anti-dumping duty of 10 on exports made by E and a duty of 20 on exports made by F. Instead it calculates the average dumping margin, say 15 in this case, and imposes a duty of 15 per cent on all imports from the country concerned, whatever the identity of the exporter. The reason for this is that the EU assumes that, in a non-market economy country, the state can control the export activities of all economic operators. Thus, if a duty of 10 were imposed on exports made by E and a duty of 20 were imposed on exports made by F, the state could intervene, and arrange that all of F's production was sold to E for export in its own name, thus benefiting from the lower duty of 10.

In the particular cases of Russia and China, as their economies became more liberal, the EU recognized that there might be circumstances in which individual treatment would be justified. Thus the practice started in about 1996 of granting individual treatment to exporters. This means that any anti-dumping duties levied may differ among exporting firms in a given exporting country, depending on their individual circumstances. The first Chinese cases in which this was done concerned investments in mainland China that were made and controlled by Hong Kong companies. The Hong Kong investors were considered to be sufficiently independent of the State to allow individual treatment to be granted without risk of circumvention. One of the early cases in which this was done was ring binder mechanisms and handbags. Since those early cases the rules have been formalized and inserted in Article 2(7) of the EU AD Regulation. In order to obtain individual treatment it is necessary for the exporter to show the following:

a. Foreign investors are free to repatriate the capital invested in the exporting company;
b. Export prices and quantities, and conditions and terms of sale, are freely determined;
c. The majority of the shares of the company belong to private persons. If State officials appear on the Board of Directors or hold key management positions, it has to be shown that they are in a minority or that the company is nonetheless sufficiently independent from State interference;
d. Exchange rate conversions are carried out at the market rate; and
e. State interference is not such as to permit circumvention of measures if individual exporters are given different rates of duty.

Individual treatment does not, however, mean that the domestic prices and costs of the firms concerned can be taken to represent normal value. Recourse still has to be made to an analogue country in order to obtain the appropriate normal value, which can then be compared with the individual firm's export value.

5.7.3   Market Economy Treatment

In 1998 and 2000, the EU AD Regulation was amended in order to allow market economy treatment to be granted to Russian and Chinese exporters (as well as to those from the Ukraine, Vietnam and Kazakhstan, plus any non-market-economy country which is a member of the WTO) under certain conditions. Under a 2002 amendment, exporters from Russia were automatically treated as being subject to market economy conditions.

Exporters from China and elsewhere are able to qualify for market economy treatment in those situations in which they can demonstrate that they are operating in market economy conditions. In order to do this they have to show the following:

a. decisions of firms regarding prices, costs and inputs, including for instance raw materials, cost of technology and labour, output, sales and investment, are made in response to market signals reflecting supply and demand, and without significant State interference in this regard, and costs of major inputs substantially reflect market values;

b. firms have one clear set of basic accounting records which are independently audited in line with international accounting standards and are applied for all purposes;
c. the production costs and financial situation of firms are not subject to significant distortions carried over from the former non-market economy system, in particular in relation to depreciation of assets, other write-offs, barter trade and payment via compensation of debts;
d. the firms concerned are subject to bankruptcy and property laws which guarantee legal certainty and stability for the operation of firms; and
e. exchange rate conversions are carried out at the market rate.

Companies who are able to show that they operate in market economy conditions are treated in all respects as exporters in market economy countries. In other words, an individual normal value is determined for the company, based on its own prices and costs, and an individual dumping margin is determined, based on a comparison of its own export prices with its own individual normal value.

The introduction of these rules has demonstrated that, where individual Chinese companies, for example, have been able to show that they operate in market economy conditions, they are quite often able to show very low or zero dumping margins. Meanwhile those companies who are unable to show that they operate in market economy conditions, but are able to qualify for individual treatment under the 2002 rules, generally have higher dumping margins than those who are considered to operate in market economy conditions. This is because the normal value in the analogue country applies, and this is generally higher than the normal value for those individual Chinese companies who are considered to operate in market economy conditions.

In the light of these considerations, China has worked hard to try to persuade the EU to recognize that China is indeed a market economy country, in the same way as the EU has now recognized Russia as being a market economy country. Many in China would indeed consider that their economy has less State interference than in Russia. It is important to realize, however, that it is no solution for the EU to recognize China formally as a market economy country if the underlying reality is different. For example, one of the criteria on which many Chinese exporters have fallen down in trying to obtain market economy status has been the failure to demonstrate that the exporter has one clear set of basic accounting records, which are independently audited in line with international accounting standards, and are applied for all purposes.

If, in a market economy case, when the European Commission is verifying the exporter's questionnaire, it finds that the accounting records of the company are unreliable, the Commission will reject the exporter's accounting records and make its findings on the basis of the facts available. As a general rule, recourse to the facts available tends to result in a larger dumping margin than that which the exporter considers to be the appropriate margin, based on its own data.

Thus it can be seen that, even if China, for example, were formally recognized as a market economy country, but many of its exporters failed to keep proper accounting records, this recognition would not help them. In such cases their normal value would be determined on the basis of the facts available, and this gives the European Commission even greater flexibility than if it is tied to the rule that requires it to determine normal value in an analogue country. For example, one of the first things that the Commission checks in an anti-dumping investigation is whether total production plus opening stock is equal to total sales plus closing stock. If there is a discrepancy, this casts doubt not just over the stock records but also over the production and the sales records. This is the sort of problem that several Chinese companies have faced when they sought to obtain market economy treatment.

Another consequence of recognizing China or other countries as market economy countries would be to open the countries up to countervailing investigations. The countervailing instrument is not generally used by the EU against imports from China, for example, on the grounds that, in a non-market economy country with considerable State interference, practically everything is likely to be subsidized in some manner or other. Thus if China, for example, were formally recognized as a market economy country, while there was still a large degree of State interference, the country would become a sitting target for countervailing action.

It is clear from this discussion that the treatment of non-market economy countries in anti-dumping cases raises a number of difficult problems. Obviously the choice of an unsuitable analogue market economy needs to be avoided as far as possible, since this almost certainly results in a finding of dumping on the part of the non-market economy. Apart from this, however, there are many remaining problems that cannot readily be solved, since they arise from the structure and practice of the non-market economies themselves.

5.8 PROSPECTIVE OR RETROSPECTIVE?[6]

Once the definitive dumping margins have been determined, the question arises as to what is the most appropriate means of offsetting the dumping. In answering this question it has to be remembered that the purpose of anti-dumping

---

[6]   The rules discussed in this section are contained in Article 9.3 and 9.4 of the AD Agreement.

measures is not to punish the exporter, but merely to counteract the injurious effects caused by his dumping practices. For this reason, any anti-dumping duty may not be greater than the margin of dumping, and it is desirable that it should be less if such lesser duty would suffice to remove injury. A similar rule applies to price undertakings.

If one were to take this rule literally, a notional customs officer clearing the goods should verify first whether the normal value had changed since the definitive determination, and if necessary make an adjustment. He should then take the actual export price declared for customs purposes, work back to an ex-factory level, and then compare the result with the normal value in order to determine the margin of dumping for the particular import under consideration. In this way an anti-dumping duty could be collected by the customs officer that was exactly equal to the margin of dumping (and obviously, if the export price were greater than or equal to the normal value, no duty would be payable).

This ideal solution is not workable in practice, for the simple reason that the authorities do not generally have the resources available to recalculate the dumping margin for each import shipment. Thus some form of approximation has to be found. The AD Agreement authorizes two methods, the prospective method and the retrospective method of collecting anti-dumping duties. Under the retrospective method, the method used in the USA, an amount is paid on account of duties at the time of import. (This amount is not a provisional duty – it is a payment on account of definitive duties, the exact amount of which has still to be assessed.) Under the prospective method, the method used in the EU, it is assumed that the weighted average rate of dumping found to exist in the investigation period continues to apply in the future, so a definitive anti-dumping duty is collected at the rate corresponding to the average rate of dumping found during the investigation period. Under this system, the WTO Agreement requires that an importer be entitled to apply for a refund of duty if it can show that the amount of dumping actually applicable to the relevant imports was less than the amount of duty collected. The EU has implemented this rule in the EU AD Regulation. In addition, it is possible for any interested party to ask for a review of a prospective duty so that a new prospective duty is determined based on a subsequent investigation period.

This form of review differs from the review in the USA in that the US review takes place every year to determine retrospectively the amount of duty that should be paid, whereas a (non-automatic) review in the EU determines a new rate of duty to be paid in the future.

It is not difficult to see that both the prospective and the retrospective methods have their advantages and disadvantages. The advantage of the retrospective method is that it offers an incentive to exporters to increase their prices, thereby avoiding duty. The disadvantage of the method is that the importer can never be wholly certain what the amount of duty is going to be. On the other hand, the advantage of the prospective method is that the amount of duty is known in advance by both exporter and importer. The disadvantage of the method is that refund procedures are relatively slow and complex, and this lessens the incentive for the exporter to increase prices in order to reduce the amount of duty paid. Indeed, the effect of a prospective duty is generally to encourage the exporter to reduce his prices still further, so that the duty paid price is acceptable to the importer. The result of this is to increase the margin of dumping which leads, in the case of a review, to an increase in the rate of the actual duty.

In rare cases the EU authorities temper the effects of the prospective duty by providing for a variable duty, namely a duty equal to the amount by which the CIF price is below a certain threshold (where the threshold corresponds to an undumped or non-injurious price). However, this approach is disliked because it publicizes the undumped price level for the exporter (or the non-injurious price level for the Community industry). In addition, it tends to encourage all market operators to align their prices on the threshold, thus removing competition.

6. Zeroing and the full degree of dumping

6.1 THREE METHODS OF CALCULATION

In the real world the ideal method of collecting anti-dumping duties cannot be achieved. One has therefore to live with either the prospective or the retrospective method, and their respective advantages and disadvantages. The ideal, namely the case where the customs officer reassesses normal value and export price for each import, is nevertheless a useful theoretical tool for dealing with difficulties that arise in the imposition and collection of anti-dumping duties.

One such difficulty is the question of undumped shipments and what is known as 'zeroing'. Under the prospective system, and before the Uruguay Round, the EU authorities used to calculate the weighted average dumping margin by treating all undumped shipments as having a dumping margin of zero; that is, on determining the weighted average they did not give the undumped shipments their arithmetic negative value. When one thinks about this, it has a certain logic. The purpose of determining a weighted average dumping margin as a percentage of the weighted average CIF price is to calculate the weighted average duty that would have been collected if each individual import made during the investigation period had been subject to a duty equal to the amount of dumping. It is then assumed that duty will continue to be due, in the future, at this same average rate per value CIF imported. In this model, the customs officer is not going to make a rebate of duty if an individual shipment has a negative dumping margin. He is simply not going to charge any anti-dumping duty. It is therefore logical that the dumping margin should be treated as zero, and not as a negative figure, when determining the weighted average dumping margin, corresponding to the flat rate of duty to be imposed in the future, that is to say, prospectively. Thus one could conclude that, from an economic point of view, it is correct to use zeroing in calculating the weighted average dumping margin.

This approach was challenged before the European Court of Justice in the *Mini-ball bearings case* in 1989. The Court approved of the Commission's practice, although not on the analytical basis that has just been explained. The Court's reasoning was as follows:

The transaction by transaction method is the only method capable of dealing with certain manoeuvres in which dumping is disguised by charging different prices, some above the normal value and some below it. The application of the weighted average method in such a situation would not meet the purpose of the anti-dumping proceeding, since that method would in essence mask sales at dumping prices by those which are known as 'negative' dumping prices, and would thus in no way eliminate the injury suffered by the Community industry concerned.[1]

The Court's approach was understandable. The Court was naturally concerned about the possibility of misuse of 'negative' dumping prices in order to circumvent the purpose of anti-dumping measures, which is to prevent injury being caused to the domestic industry by unfair dumping practices. The Court's approach could be criticized, however, for failing to distinguish between those cases where negative dumping is used by the exporter consciously as a means of avoiding the full extent of anti-dumping action, and those cases where negative dumping is the result of seasonal or market changes that are beyond the control of the exporter.

Thus, before the Uruguay Round, one can argue that both the law and economic common sense were in favour of the proposition that it was correct to use zeroing when calculating a dumping margin. The Uruguay Round changed all that, however.

Article 2.4.2 of the AD Agreement, provides as follows:

Subject to the provisions governing fair comparison in paragraph 4, the existence of margins of dumping during the investigation phase shall normally be established on the basis of a comparison of a weighted average normal value with a weighted average of prices of all comparable export transactions or by a comparison of normal value and export prices on a transaction-to-transaction basis. A normal value established on a weighted average basis may be compared to prices of individual export transactions if the authorities find a pattern of export prices which differ significantly among different purchasers, regions or time periods, and if an explanation is provided as to why such differences cannot be taken into account appropriately by the use of a weighted average-to-weighted average or transaction-to-transaction comparison.

Article 2.4.2 is rich in concepts which require critical analysis in order to come to a coherent theory for the determination of weighted average dumping margins. For ease of reference in the following discussion, the three methods mentioned in Article 2.4.2 will be referred to in the following discussion as follows:

---

[1] Case 240/84, *NTN Toyo Bearing Co., Ltd.* v. *Council*, [1987] ECR 1809, at para 23.

1. 'First Symmetrical Method': comparison of a weighted average normal value with a weighted average of all comparable export transactions;
2. 'Second Symmetrical Method': comparison of normal value and export prices on a transaction-to-transaction basis;
3. 'Asymmetrical Method': comparison of normal value established on a weighted average basis with prices of individual export transactions.

6.2   GENERAL OBSERVATIONS ABOUT ALL THREE METHODS

The first thing to be observed is that it can be demonstrated mathematically that the First Symmetrical Method will always produce a weighted average dumping margin that is equal to, or less than, the weighted average dumping margin under the Asymmetrical Method (which by implication introduces zeroing). The two methods will produce the same result when every individual shipment is dumped, but the First Symmetrical Method will produce a lesser weighted average dumping margin as soon as one or more of the transactions are not dumped (because negative dumping is given its full negative value in the First Symmetrical Method).

If it had been intended by the drafters of the AD Agreement to prohibit zeroing they would not have provided the Asymmetrical Method as an alternative to the First Symmetrical Method because, if zeroing is not used, the Asymmetrical Method produces the same result as the First Symmetrical method in all cases. Thus it must be deduced that the drafters of the AD Agreement intended implicitly to allow the practice of zeroing.

The difficulty one has with the First Symmetrical method is that it goes against the common sense argument developed above, which says that zeroing should be used in all cases. Because the First Symmetrical Method involves a comparison of the weighted average export price with the weighted average normal value, it takes into account the negative margins of undumped transactions. This is not in accordance with the ideal paradigm of the notional customs officer who assesses each individual shipment, and does not pay money to the importer if a transaction has a negative dumping margin. Thus one has to conclude that Article 2.4.2 does not make economic sense, however much it may have satisfied the diplomatic lobbies at the time.

Another difficulty with Article 2.4.2 is that it introduces the notion of the Second Symmetrical Method. This method is unknown in the EU and the US, but is used in some countries, for example New Zealand. It is not clear under this method, since it is scarcely ever used, whether zeroing is implicit in its operation or not.

At first sight also, the Second Symmetrical Method seems to be totally unworkable in cases where a product is imported in a large number of ship-ments, because it seems to require one to determine a separate normal value for each of the shipments and compare this with the export price actually prac-tised for that shipment. The Second Symmetrical Method would seem, at first sight, to be more suited to anti-dumping investigations concerning large items of capital equipment, for which there may have been only two or three export transactions during the investigation period. This is an unsatisfactory solution, however, in the light of the judgment of the ECJ in the case *Petrotub v. Council.*[2] In that case the ECJ ruled, in effect, that the EU institutions had to examine the possibility of using the First Symmetrical Method and the Second Symmetrical Method before proceeding to use the Asymmetrical Method. It is only after the EU institutions have satisfied themselves that neither the First Symmetrical Method nor the Second Symmetrical Method would reflect the full degree of dumping being practised, that they could move to the Asymmetrical Method. In the light of this, the EU institutions have developed a *pro forma* way of dismissing the Second Symmetrical Method, by saying that the number of export transactions renders it impractical to make a comparison of each export price with the normal value at the time of export. This, however, is a reason *passe partout* and so renders the Second Symmetrical Method otiose. The drafters of the AD Agreement must presum-ably have intended something more than this. It will now be demonstrated how a sensible meaning can be given to the Second Symmetrical Method.

6.3 HOW COULD THE SECOND SYMMETRICAL METHOD WORK?

Upon a cursory reading of the description of the Second Symmetrical Method it appears that the investigating authority has to look for a domestic transac-tion occurring at about the same time as the export transaction under consid-eration, check that the domestic price is profitable and representative, and then use it as the normal value for the export transaction. The logistical problems involved in undertaking this, one would suggest, could give rise to an arbitrary approach – and this is also the view of the European Commission.[3]

However, this should not be a reason for rejecting the Second Symmetrical Method out of hand. Although the European Commission refers to the imprac-ticalities of examining thousands of domestic transactions,[4] one would suggest

---

2   Case C-76/00P, *Petrotub SA and Republica SA v. Council*, [2003] ECR I-79.
3   See, for example, Recordable compact disks originating in Taiwan, Council Regulation (EC) No 1050/2002, OJ L160, 18.6.2002, at recital (29).
4   Ibid.

that the correct approach, under the Second Symmetrical Method, is to determine the normal value for successive sub-divisions of the investigation period. The European Commission does this, even when using the First Symmetrical Method or the Asymmetrical Method, when substantial inflation of the local currency of the exporter makes it difficult to determine an average cost of production or an average price for the whole investigation period.[5] It is suggested that such an approach is equally valid under the Second Symmetrical Method, because one cannot decide questions such as whether an individual domestic sale is profitable (and so can be used as a measure of normal value) without taking into account all costs over a given period, however short, in which the domestic sale takes place. In addition, it is an inherent principle of anti-dumping practice that all comparable transactions, both domestic and export, that occur in the normal course of trade during the investigation period, have to be taken into account.

Thus, when using the Second Symmetrical Method, the reference to the normal value at the time of the export transaction should be interpreted, it can be argued, not as a reference to an individual domestic sale, but as a reference to the weighted average normal value, over a sub-division of the investigation period (which could be quite short) in which the export transaction falls. The interesting characteristic of the Second Symmetrical Method is that it takes account of variations in normal value throughout the investigation period, unlike the First Symmetrical Method and the Asymmetrical Method, which simply take a weighted average normal value for the whole investigation period.

6.4   IS IT LEGITIMATE TO ALLOW ZEROING WITH THE SECOND SYMMETRICAL METHOD?

If sub-divisions of the investigation period are to be employed, on what principle should these be determined? It is suggested that the sub-divisions should relate to periods of time in which the normal value remains approximately constant. The investigation period would then be divided into a number of sub-periods, the number depending on how often the normal value was subject to appreciable change.

Having proposed a meaningful use for the Second Symmetrical Method, this inevitably gives rise to the question: is it permitted, under the Second Symmetrical Method, to use zeroing within a period for which the normal

---

[5]   For example, provisional anti-dumping duties on seamless pipes and tubes from, inter alia, Romania, Regulation (EC) No 981/97, OJ L141, 31.5.97, p. 36.

value is constant? And, irrespective of the answer to this question, is it permitted to allow zeroing between dumping margins determined for different periods, that is, for different normal values? The texts do not provide any guidance on this, and the virtual absence of practice increases the problem further. As far as concerns the first question, it would seem, by analogy with the First Symmetrical Method, that zeroing should not be allowed among export transactions made within a period during which the normal value remains constant. This is because the First Symmetrical Method simply takes a weighted average of normal value and a weighted average of comparable export transactions, whether or not individual dumping margins are positive or negative. By analogy, it would seem that the Second Symmetrical Method should follow the same procedure, albeit for each period of time that is separately distinguished.[6]

As far as concerns the second question, it could be argued that an exporter should be expected to change his export price if the normal value changes, and if the exporter does not do this, he is following a policy which may possibly involve a deliberate attempt to dump. If for some periods such a policy involves negative dumping, it would seem to follow that the exporter should not be able to take credit for such negative dumping margins. The appropriate practice to be followed therefore should be to take an average, over the investigation period, of the dumping margins in those sub-periods when positive dumping has taken place. Sub-periods of negative dumping should be ignored.[7]

6.5   WHEN CAN RECOURSE BE MADE TO THE ASYMMETRICAL METHOD?

Having dealt with the First and Second Symmetrical Methods, the crucial question is what are the conditions that need to be satisfied before the investigating authority can have recourse to the Asymmetrical Method? The investigating authority has first to consider both the First Symmetrical Method and the Second Symmetrical Method before he can move to the Asymmetrical Method.[8] He can only use the last method if he has come to the conclusion that

---

[6]   This is the approach adopted by the WTO Appellate Body in *United States – Measures relating to zeroing and sunset reviews (Complainant Japan)*, WT/DS322/AB/R of 9 January 2007, section 5.1.1.

[7]   See case cited in previous footnote where the Appellate Body says that zeroing is not permissible at any time under the Second Symmetrical Method,. It therefore does not agree with us on this point.

[8]   Case C-76/00P, *Petrotub SA and Republica SA* v. *Council*, Opinion of Advocate General Jacobs of 25 April 2002, paragraphs 64ff. The Court of Justice followed the Advocate General on this point (see judgment of 9 January 2003, paragraph 62).

he cannot adequately deal with the varying pattern of export prices using the First Symmetrical or the Second Symmetrical Methods, or, to use the language of the EU, that neither of these methods would reflect the full degree of dumping being practised.[9]

There is strength in the view of the EU Authorities that the Second Symmetrical Method would produce arbitrary results if the investigating authority were allowed to select individual domestic transactions at random and compare them with individual export transactions.[10] This is primarily because it would in practice normally be impossible to determine the normal value for every single export transaction. It has been demonstrated above, however, that the Second Symmetrical Method can and should be used in a manner that does not produce such arbitrary results, a manner that takes account of the relative weighting of normal value over the investigation period (and which can be further refined by using zeroing in cases where the exporter does not adjust his export prices in phase with changes in his normal value). When used in this manner, the Second Symmetrical Method will give a better reflection than the First Symmetrical Method of the degree of dumping being practised, in cases where the normal value is changing during the investigation period. This measure of dumping may be greater or less than under the First Symmetrical Method, depending on the relative loading of domestic and export sales quantities in different periods.

6.5.1   Asymmetrical Method v. First Symmetrical Method

If, having tried the First Symmetrical Method and the Second Symmetrical Method, the investigating authority considers that neither of these methods enables it to take appropriate account of variations in export prices, it may use the Asymmetrical Method. It must, however, give an explanation as to why it has to use this method. As between the Asymmetrical Method and the First Symmetrical Method, it cannot be sufficient for the investigating authority to say that the former gives a larger arithmetical result than the latter method.[11] If this were a valid reason, Article 2.4.2 of the AD Agreement would never have mentioned the First Symmetrical Method because, as has been shown,

---

[9]   Article 2(11), Council Regulation (EC) No 384/96 (OJ L56, 6.3.96).
[10]   See, for example, Recordable compact disks originating in Taiwan, Council Regulation (EC) No 1050/2002, OJ L160, 18.6.2002, at recital (29).
[11]   Case C-76/00P, *Petrotub SA and Republica SA* v. *Council*, Opinion of Advocate General Jacobs of 25 April 2002, paragraphs 74 to 81. It seems that, out of considerations of judicial economy, the Court of Justice chose not to rule on this particular point, since it was able to annul the anti-dumping duties on the basis of the sole fact that the Commission had failed to consider the Second Symmetrical Method at all.

the result under the Asymmetrical Method is always greater or equal to the result under the First Symmetrical Method. There has to be an additional element. If one returns to the reasoning of the European Court of Justice in the *Mini-ball bearings case* cited above, it can be seen that the objective of the Asymmetrical Method is to counter practices whereby the exporter hides dumping by charging different prices. It is submitted that it is inherent in this principle that the exporter is consciously adopting a policy of discriminating in his pricing between different areas, periods or clients, knowing that he can maintain higher prices in some areas than in others. The result of such a policy of discrimination is that the exporter would be able, under averaging, to hide dumping in certain areas with negative dumping in other areas.

One would argue, therefore, that it is appropriate to have recourse to the Asymmetrical Method in those cases where such intention on the part of the exporter can be proved, or at least presumed, from all the surrounding circumstances. What does one mean by this? One means that the exporter is not able to demonstrate an objective explanation for the variations in export prices that is consistent with his not having any intention to 'target' his dumping in certain areas. If, however, the exporter can show that the variations in export prices are the result of seasonal or market variations that he and all other market operators have been obliged to follow, then it cannot be said that he has adopted a conscious policy of 'targeting' his dumping.[12] Such an approach would be similar to that followed in the competition law area when one examines whether a dominant supplier has adopted a discriminatory pricing policy that amounts to an abuse of his dominant position.[13]

6.5.2 Asymmetrical Method v. Second Symmetrical Method

As between the Asymmetrical Method and the Second Symmetrical Method, there must be a very good reason for comparing individual export prices with a weighted average normal value for the whole investigation period rather than with a normal value individualized for a relatively short period in which the export has taken place. It is argued that the basic approach should be the same as when comparing the Asymmetrical Method and the First Symmetrical Method, namely whether there is an of intentional targeting of dumping. But the targeting can be of two kinds. For example, the exporter may have thought to himself, 'I can dump in the month of March because I can take some credit for the negative dumping margins that results from the fact that I had a very low normal value last December.' However, as we have argued above, this sort

---

[12] A more difficult case is that where the exporter charges lower prices to certain customers because they are unable to meet the price generally charged.
[13] For example, in the European Community, under Article 82 EC.

of conduct can be taken care of adequately under the Second Symmetrical Method, using zeroing.[14] Thus, in order to be able to reject the Second Symmetrical Method in favour of the Asymmetrical Method, it is argued that the targeting practised by the exporter must be directed at something that cannot adequately be taken care of by the use of differing normal values for different periods. For example, if an exporter was targeting his dumping at a particular region, or particular customer, irrespective of time, this would seem to be a good reason for rejecting the Second Symmetrical Method and using the Asymmetrical Method.

6.6   THE DECISION TREE

To summarize, it follows from the previous arguments that the decision tree should be as follows:

1. As between the First Symmetrical Method or the Second Symmetrical Method, which does one choose?
    Answer: choose the First Symmetrical Method if normal value does not vary throughout the investigation period. If normal value does vary, and the quantities sold on the domestic market also vary, choose the Second Symmetrical Method.
2. If, in step (1), one has chosen the First Symmetrical Method, in what conditions may one reject this method and use the Asymmetrical Method?
    Answer: if there is evidence of an intention to target particular periods, regions or customers, the Asymmetrical Method may be used.
3. If, in step (1) the Second Symmetrical Method has been chosen, can one use zeroing?
    Answer: there are good arguments that zeroing should be allowed if there is evidence that the exporter has intentionally failed to adjust his export price in phase with changes in the normal value.[15]
4. If, in step (1), one has chosen the Second Symmetrical Method, in what conditions may one use the Asymmetrical Method instead of the Second Symmetrical Method?
    Answer: if there is evidence of an intention to target particular regions or customers or periods, use the Asymmetrical Method. Note that, if there is evidence of an intention to target particular periods, it must first be exam-

---

[14]   This argument fails if one accepts the approach in the Appellate Body's ruling of 9 January 2007, cited above.
[15]   This argument also fails if one accepts the approach in the Appellate Body's ruling of 9 January 2007, cited above.

ined whether the periods correspond to changes in normal value. If they do, then such targeting could perhaps be taken into account in (3) above, in which case it would not be a justification for recourse to the Asymmetrical Method.

6.7 NEGATIVE DUMPING, ZEROING AND THE INVESTIGATION OF INJURY

6.7.1 Negative Dumping and the Causal Link

Does the existence of negative dumping affect the establishment of whether a domestic industry has been injured or not by dumped imports? Suppose that, during the investigation period, there have been some imports which have been dumped and some which have been subject to negative dumping. One can assume that imports which have been dumped will normally come in at prices below the domestic price level in the importing country and will therefore cause injury. But what about imports subject to negative dumping? Some of these imports may also have come in at prices below the domestic price level, but there may be circumstances where others have come in at prices above this level.

Article 3.5 of the AD Agreement says, in effect, that injury caused by imports not sold at dumping prices should not be attributed to the dumped imports. Taking this literally, it would seem that, in its injury assessment, the investigating authority should eliminate from consideration the volumes and prices of all the transactions that have negative dumping margins. This would require a very detailed analysis of the data relating to exports from the country concerned, and this is not carried out in the EU. Moreover, it is not carried out in the US because there a separate body makes the determination of injury, and so does not get involved in the dumping calculations. But we would argue that, in a perfect world, it is precisely this sort of analysis that should be carried out, particularly if there are substantial quantities of transactions with negative dumping margins. Causation of injury, in other words, should be based only on an assessment of import transactions which are dumped.

6.7.2 Zeroing and the Determination of Underselling

'Underselling' is not a term used in the AD Agreement. It is a term used in the EU to describe the amount by which the dumped imports are at prices below the level necessary to eliminate injury. This level is calculated by taking the weighted average costs of production of the complainant industry, and adding a reasonable margin for profit. The calculation is very similar to the calculation of the dumping margin, except that, instead of comparing export prices with a normal value (usually at ex-works level), export prices (usually at CIF duty paid level) are compared with the injury elimination level (usually at the ex-works level, EU producer). If the margin of underselling is less than the margin of dumping, the EU imposes a duty equal to the margin of underselling, pursuant to the 'lesser duty rule' which the EU has opted to apply. The calculation of the underselling can be carried out transaction by transaction and so raises questions of zeroing. However, the AD Agreement provides no guidance on how the transactions with negative underselling should be treated.

An argument can be advanced to say that zeroing should *not* be used in an underselling calculation. If an export transaction is above the injury elimination level, any domestic producer competing on price against this transaction would be able to quote a price higher than the injury elimination level, but less than the imported product, and get the business. Thus this particular export transaction will have enabled the domestic industry to make more than a reasonable profit. For this reason we would argue that, in determining the overall level of underselling, negative underselling should not be zeroed, but should be taken into account at its full negative value.

6.8   THE END OF ZEROING?

The *Indian bed-linen case*,[16] considered by the WTO, dealt a severe blow to the practice of zeroing. India had argued (under Article 2.4.2 of the AD Agreement) that the EU had acted inconsistently with Article 2.4.2 of the AD Agreement by counting negative dumping amounts as zero for certain types of bed linen, when calculating the overall weighted average dumping margin for the like product, bed linen.

India asserted that the EU had established the dumping margin by applying the First Symmetrical Method, that is, by comparing the weighted average normal value with a weighted average of prices of all comparable export transactions. But it had not in practice calculated a true average, because it had given negative dumping a zero value.

In India's view, the practice of zeroing was not consistent with the requirement that this comparison should take into account 'the weighted average of prices of all comparable export transactions'. There was no justification for excluding certain amounts in establishing an average. This EU method, India

---

16   'European Communities – anti-dumping duties on imports of cotton-type bed linen from India', Report of Panel,WT/DS141/R, 30 October 2000, and Report of the Appellate Body, WT/DS141/AB/R, 1 March 2001.

argued, would always lead to a higher dumping margin than was envisaged by the AD Agreement.

The EU maintained that its practice in calculating the dumping margin was consistent with the requirements of Article 2.4.2, since its methodology focused on those product types where dumping had been found. However, the types of products that are found to have margins less than zero (and which are not therefore being dumped) are nevertheless kept in the calculation (albeit at notional zero margins) on a weighted average basis, and thereby reduce the overall weighted average dumping margin determined for that product.

Egypt and Japan agreed with the Indian view, but the USA argued that Article 2.4.2 does not prohibit the practice of zeroing. In its view, for products with no dumping margins, the amount of dumping duties which the importing country is permitted to collect is properly considered to be zero.

The finding of the Panel was that Article 2.4.2 'obligated an investigating authority to make its determination in a way which fully accounts for the export prices on *all* comparable transactions'. The EU methodology took less than full account of exports at negative margins and therefore did not accomplish this goal. The Panel therefore concluded that the EC acted inconsistently with Article 2.4.2 in establishing dumping margins on the basis of a methodology which included treating negative price differences as zero.

The Appellate Body, after consideration at some length, upheld (at paragraph 66) 'the finding of the Panel in paragraph 6.119 of the Panel report that the practice of 'zeroing' when establishing 'the existence of margins of dumping', as applied by the European Communities in the anti-dumping investigation at issue in this dispute, is inconsistent with Article 2.4.2 of the Anti-Dumping Agreement'.

It should be noted however, when considering the *Indian bed-linen case*, that this is basically about the use of the First Symmetrical Method, not the use of the Asymmetrical Method. The Panel ruling says in effect that if, when using the First Symmetrical Method, the investigating authority finds that certain product types are dumped and other product types are not dumped, that is, have negative dumping margins, it cannot apply zeroing to the negative dumping margins. This is because that would amount, in practice, to a partial application of the Asymmetrical Method, without having first established that the conditions for recourse to this method were satisfied.

The Asymmetrical Method requires that three types of targeted dumping can be addressed: that is, it can be employed if there is a 'pattern of export prices which differs significantly among different purchasers, regions or time periods' and 'such difference cannot be taken into account appropriately by the use of' the First or Second Symmetrical Methods, or, in the language of the EU AD Regulation, if the First or Second Symmetrical Methods 'would not reflect the full degree of dumping being practised'. In the *Indian bed-linen case*, the EU tried to argue that certain types of product might also be targeted, but the Appellate Body argued that the Anti-Dumping Agreement makes no provision for this type of product targeting.

In the more recent *EC-Brazil malleable cast iron tube or pipe fittings dispute*,[17] the WTO panel again argued that the EU had acted inconsistently with its obligations by applying zeroing in its dumping determination. The EU had again calculated the dumping margin by using the First Symmetrical Method, that is, by comparing the weighted average normal value with the weighted average export price. Here also it had employed zeroing in cases of negative dumping, although it argued that this practice had a relatively limited impact on the result (a dumping margin of 34.82 per cent as opposed to 32.09 per cent).

The Panel found (paragraph 7.216) that the EU did not fully take into account the actual values pertaining to certain export transactions in establishing the margin of dumping, and it therefore found that the EU had violated Article 2.4.2 of the AD Agreement by failing to consider the weighted average of 'all comparable export transactions'. It found support for this finding in the EC *Indian bed-linen dispute*, where the Appellate Body had upheld the Panel's finding that the practice of zeroing did not fully take into account the prices of all comparable transactions, as required by Article 2.4.2.

The question that arises from these cases is whether the practice of zeroing has in effect now been outlawed by these WTO rulings. They were, however, both based on what the WTO considered to be an inappropriate application of the First Symmetrical Method. It is therefore possible that the WTO might rule differently in a case where the use of the Second Symmetrical Method, or more probably the Asymmetrical Method, might be considered to be justified.

On the other hand, the EU appears at first sight to have taken the view that all cases of zeroing should henceforth be outlawed. This seems to follow from their announcement on 17 February 2004[18] that the EU was requesting the establishment of a WTO panel to examine the WTO compatibility of the United States' use of zeroing when performing its dumping calculations. 'This is no longer permitted by WTO rules,' argued the EU, citing the decision in the EC *Indian bed-linen dispute*. Although the *Indian bed-linen case* was concerned with the EU practice, 'it unambiguously condemned the zeroing methodology as such when used in well-defined circumstances. The current US practice in anti-dumping investigations is identical to that condemned in Bed-Linen. The EU furthermore considers that the use of zeroing by the US

---

[17]   'European Communities – anti-dumping duties on malleable cast iron tube or pipe fittings from Brazil', Report of Panel, WT/DS219/R, 7 March 2003.
[18]   'Trade Issues, Respecting the Rules. Anti-Dumping', Press release by DG Trade, European Commission, 17 February 2004.

administration when conducting annual reviews to determine the final dumping liability is equally incompatible with the Anti-Dumping Agreement'.

The US zeroing practice, the EU argued, was having a significant adverse economic impact on EU exporters in a number of sectors. It went on to claim that 'in most cases, without zeroing, the dumping margin on the EU exports concerned would have been *de minimis* or even negative'.

It is not, however, entirely clear that this attack on US zeroing practice means that the EU has set its face against the use of zeroing in all possible circumstances. It should be noted that, in its press release of 17 February 2004, the EU, referring to the *Indian bed-linen case*, says that in this case the WTO condemned the zeroing methodology 'in well defined circumstances'. This appears to imply that in other circumstances – for example, when the use of the Asymmetrical Method was justified – the practice of zeroing might be considered by the EU to be acceptable. On the other hand, as has been said, the EU began its press release by stating categorically that zeroing 'is no longer permitted by WTO rules'.

The EU's situation is therefore ambiguous, while the USA has stated firmly that its position is that the use of zeroing is permissible, and that it will continue to apply this methodology. Apparently therefore, the jury may still be out on this issue. However, a further signal that the practice of zeroing may be losing support lies in the WTO ruling in the case on the methodology of calculating dumping margins, brought by the EU and others, against the USA.[19] The panel in that case concluded that 'the United States acted inconsistently with Article 2.4.2 of the Anti-dumping Agreement when . . . it did not include in the numerator used to calculate weighted average dumping margins any amounts by which average export prices in individual averaging groups exceeded the average normal value for such groups'. In other words, zeroing was unacceptable when the First Symmetrical Method was employed, and the EU's contention was therefore upheld.

The panel also found that the USA's zeroing methodology was inconsistent with Article 2.4.2, as it relates to *original investigations*. In other words, the panel was arguing that, in such investigations, zeroing is never justified, whatever methodology was employed to arrive at the measure of dumping.

On the other hand, the panel found that zeroing was not inconsistent with Article 2.4.2 when the Asymmetrical Method, comparing average monthly normal value with individual export prices, was employed in administrative reviews. The logic of these findings could reasonably have been based on the fact that administrative reviews take place retrospectively. To disallow zeroing in such reviews might encourage exporters deliberately to dump certain exports during the relevant period, knowing that negative dumping could override the

---

[19]   WT/DS294/R. Panel report circulated 31 October 2005.

cases of dumping. In this way they could claim that dumping had not on balance occurred, and that therefore the importers could claim back the dumping duties to which they had been subject.

However, this was not the panel's reasoning. This appears to have been based on a narrow interpretation of the term 'during the investigative phase' in Article 2.4.2 of the Anti-Dumping Agreement. In a powerful dissenting opinion, one member of the panel argued that it was inconsistent to outlaw zeroing in the case of the original investigation, but not in the case of administrative reviews. In this opinion, therefore, zeroing was held not to be permissible in all the instances investigated by the panel (although targeted dumping was considered to be an exception).

This case was considered by the Appellate Body, in its report of 31 March 2006.[20] The Appellate Body found that the zeroing methodology, as it relates to original investigations in which the weighted-average-to-weighted average comparison method was used to calculate margins of dumping, can be challenged. The Appellate Body therefore upheld the panel's conclusion that in this case the zeroing methodology was inconsistent with Article 2.4.2 of the Anti-Dumping Agreement. As regards administrative reviews, the Appellate Body overturned the panel's view that the zeroing methodology was not inconsistent with the relevant Articles of the Anti-Dumping Agreement and of the GATT 1994.[21] Zeroing, therefore, was not allowed in this case either.

In short, therefore, zeroing has not been generally outlawed, but when the First Symmetrical Method is employed, one may not break out product groups separately and use zeroing for particular product groups. As regards administrative reviews, zeroing is also not permissible when the First Symmetrical Method is employed (that is, in the absence of targeted dumping).[22]

Thus we can summarize the situation as follows:

• First Symmetrical Method: zeroing is not permitted in any circumstances whatsoever.
• Second Symmetrical Method: there is no ruling on whether and when zeroing can be used under this method. We have argued earlier in this chapter

---

[20]   WT/DS294/AB/R, 31 March 2006.
[21]   A communication from the United States – 'United States – Laws, Regulations and Methodology for Calculating Dumping Margins ('Zeroing')', dated 12 June 2006 – WT/DS294/18 – took exception to these conclusions of the Appellate Body, and asserted that, with the exception of average-to-average comparisons in investigations (where they now acknowledge that zeroing is unacceptable), the GATT 1994 and the Anti-Dumping Agreement do not preclude zeroing.
[22]   Since writing, the decision of the Appellate Body of 9 January 2007, WT/DS322/AB/R cited above says that zeroing cannot be used when the Second Symmetrical Method is used, whether in originating investigations or reviews.

that zeroing might be justified if an exporter did not adjust his prices to take account of periodic variations in his normal value.[23]

• Asymmetrical Method: provided the conditions for recourse to this method are satisfied, that is, where there is targeted dumping, zeroing is permitted under this method.[24] In a US-style administrative review the conditions for targeting are more likely to be present than in original investigations, but whether they are in fact present is a matter of fact to be investigated in each individual case.

ANNEX 1   COMPARISON OF FIRST SYMMETRICAL AND ASYMMETRICAL METHODS

A common element of the First Symmetrical Method and the Asymmetrical Method is the determination of the weighted average normal value. More will be said about this later. For the time being one will assume that one knows how to do this, and the symbol N will be used to designate the weighted average dumping margin expressed in value per unit quantity. (Throughout this study, references to normal value will be to normal value net of all deductions permitted by Article 2.4 of the WTO Anti-Dumping Agreement, and for ease of discussion it will be assumed that all domestic prices are profitable and comparable to export prices.) Let e_i now be used to signify the export price per unit of the 'i'th export transaction. (Again, throughout this study, references to export prices are references to export prices net of all adjustments permitted by Article 2.4 of the WTO Anti-Dumping Agreement.) Let us also indicate the quantity of the 'i'th export transaction by q_i and let us assume that all the export transactions are dumped. One can now (under the Asymmetrical Method) express the dumping margin per unit of the 'i'th transaction as $(N - e_i)$ where $N > e_i$ for all values of i. The total dumping margin for the 'i'th transaction is then $(N - e_i)q_i$ and the total dumping margin for all transactions is $\Sigma(N - e_i)q_i$, where Σ means the sum for all values that the index i takes. In order to obtain the weighted average, one needs to divide by the total quantity, which is Σq_i, thus arriving at the following result:

$$D_3 = \Sigma(N - e_i)q_i / \Sigma q_i,$$

(where D_3 is the dumping margin using the Asymmetrical Method).

---

[23]   See note 22.

[24]   This is the view taken by the European Court of First Instance in Case T-274/02, *Ritek Corp and Prodisc Technology Inc* v. *Council*, Judgment of 24 October 2006 (not yet reported).

One can rearrange this as follows:

$$D_3 = \Sigma N q_i / \Sigma q_i - \Sigma e_i q_i / \Sigma q_i$$
$$= N - \Sigma e_i q_i / \Sigma q_i.$$

However, $\Sigma e_i q_i / \Sigma q_i$ is none other than the weighted average export price, which will be symbolized by E, and so one has:

$$D_3 = N - E.$$

But one can also see with very little difficulty that the dumping margin D_1 obtained by using the First Symmetrical Method is simply:

$$D_1 = N - E.$$

And so one has the result that $D_1 = D_3$ when all the individual export transactions are dumped. Let us now suppose that some of the export transactions have negative dumping margins. Let us symbolize the undumped export transactions as having prices e_j and quantities q_j for some j in the series of export transactions defined by the collection $\{i\}$. In order to reduce the negative dumping margins to zero, one needs to add back the amounts $(e_j - N)q_j$ in order to annul the effect of all the negative $(N - e_j)q_j$ included in the formula $\Sigma(N - e_i)q_i$. Thus one can write:

$$D_3 = \{\Sigma(N - e_i)q_i + \Sigma(e_j - N)q_j\} / \Sigma q_i$$
$$= \{N - E + \Sigma(e_j - N)q_j\} / \Sigma q_i$$
$$= D_1 + \Sigma(e_j - N)q_j / \Sigma q_i.$$

Now $\Sigma(e_j - N)q_j\} / \Sigma q_i$ is positive, since by definition all e_j are greater than N, and so one has:

$$D_3 > D_1 \text{ (in all cases where there are some undumped transactions).}$$

ANNEX 2   A THEORY FOR USE OF THE SECOND SYMMETRICAL METHOD

Using the same notation as above, one can write the dumping margin, as determined under the Second Symmetrical Method, in the following terms:

$$D_2 = \Sigma(n_k - e_i)q_i / \Sigma q_i$$

or, rearranging this:

$$D_2 = \Sigma n_k / \Sigma q_i - \Sigma e_i q_i / \Sigma q_i$$
$$= \Sigma n_k q_i / \Sigma q_i - E.$$

It is important here not to fall into the trap of thinking that $\Sigma n_k q_i / \Sigma q_i$ is the weighted average normal value, N. It is not. It is a weighting of the individual normal values on export quantities, not on domestic quantities. If one symbol-izes by v_k the domestic quantity corresponding to the normal value n_k, one has $N = \Sigma n_k v_k / \Sigma v_k$ which is not the same as $\Sigma n_k q_i / \Sigma q_i$. It can be seen that D_2 will be greater or less than D_1, depending on the relative distribution of quantities sold on the domestic market and sold for export. This is best illustrated by two examples.

In both examples, the export price is systematically one unit less than the domestic price and the quantity exported per month is constant. In the first example, the domestic sales increase both in quantity and price.

If one compares the pricing month by month, one can see at a glance that the dumping margin is 1 per unit exported. This is the result under the Second Symmetrical Method. However, the First Symmetrical Method gives a larger dumping margin. The reason for this is that, by taking a weighted average normal value, the First Symmetrical Method gives greater weight to the larger

Table 6A.1   Domestic sales: increase in quantity and price

Month	Export Quantity	Export Unit price	Export Total value	Domestic Quantity	Domestic Unit price	Domestic Total value	D_1 Dumping margin	D_2 Dumping margin
1	100	10	1 000	100	11	1 100	N/A	100
2	100	11	1 100	120	12	1 440	N/A	100
3	100	12	1 200	140	13	1 820	N/A	100
4	100	13	1 300	160	14	2 240	N/A	100
5	100	14	1 400	180	15	2 700	N/A	100
6	100	15	1 500	200	16	3 200	N/A	100
7	100	16	1 600	220	17	3 740	N/A	100
8	100	17	1 700	240	18	4 320	N/A	100
9	100	18	1 800	260	19	4 940	N/A	100
10	100	19	1 900	280	20	5 600	N/A	100
11	100	20	2 000	300	21	6 300	N/A	100
12	100	21	2 100	320	22	7 040	N/A	100
Total	1 200		18 600	2 520		44 440		1 200
Average		15.50			17.63		2.13	1.00

quantities of domestic product sold at higher prices towards the end of the investigation period. In fact it is easy to see that, if the domestic price and the export price were the same month by month, there would be no dumping under the Second Symmetrical Method but there would be some dumping under the First Symmetrical Method.

Let us now look at the case where the domestic sales increase in volume but decrease in price (Table 6A.2).

In this case there is no dumping (in fact negative dumping) under the First Symmetrical Method. Nevertheless, an examination month by month shows that there is clearly dumping of one per unit, the result given by the Second Symmetrical Method.

Based on these two examples it is suggested that the Second Symmetrical Method is the more appropriate one to use where the exporter has been exporting constant quantities but has been increasing (or decreasing) the quantities sold on the domestic market. The reason is that the Second Symmetrical Method eliminates the effects of the lop-sided distribution of domestic sales quantities. One can generalize this and say that the Second Symmetrical Method will be more appropriate than the First Symmetrical Method in any case where the ratio of domestic sales quantities to export sales quantities varies significantly during the investigation period.

Table 6A.2   Domestic sales: increase in volume, decrease in price

Month	Export Quantity	Export Unit price	Export Total value	Domestic Quantity	Domestic Unit price	Domestic Total value	D_1 Dumping margin	D_2 Dumping margin
1	100	21	2 100	100	22	2 200	N/A	100
2	100	20	2 000	120	21	2 520	N/A	100
3	100	19	1 900	140	20	2 800	N/A	100
4	100	18	1 800	160	19	3 040	N/A	100
5	100	17	1 700	180	18	3 240	N/A	100
6	100	16	1 600	200	17	3 400	N/A	100
7	100	15	1 500	220	16	3 520	N/A	100
8	100	14	1 400	240	15	3 600	N/A	100
9	100	13	1 300	260	14	3 640	N/A	100
10	100	12	1 200	280	13	3 640	N/A	100
11	100	11	1 100	300	12	3 600	N/A	100
12	100	10	1 000	320	11	3 520	N/A	100
Total	1 200		18 600	2 520		38 720		1 200
Average		15.50			15.37		0	1

ANNEX 3   ZEROING UNDER THE SECOND SYMMETRICAL METHOD

Consider the following example (where $D_2(Z)$ indicates the dumping margin under the Second Symmetrical Method using zeroing). In this example the export price remains constant at 15 during an investigation period of 12 months. During the same period the domestic prices increase from 10 to 21. It is argued that the exporter should not be able to take credit for the negative dumping when the normal value was at 10. He ought to have increased his export prices by the time the normal value had increased to 15. The argument on this point is similar to that concerning the conditions under which recourse may be made to the Asymmetrical Method.

Table 6A.3   Illustration of zeroing under the Second Symmetrical Method

	Export	Export	Export	Domestic	Domestic	Domestic	D_1	D_2	$D_2(Z)$
Month	Quantity	Unit price	Total value	Quantity	Unit price	Total value	Margin	Margin	Margin
1	100	15	1 500	100	10	1 000	N/A	−500	0
2	100	15	1 500	120	11	1 320	N/A	−400	0
3	100	15	1 500	140	12	1 680	N/A	−300	0
4	100	15	1 500	160	13	2 080	N/A	−200	0
5	100	15	1 500	180	14	2 520	N/A	−100	0
6	100	15	1 500	200	15	3 000	N/A	0	0
7	100	15	1 500	220	16	3 520	N/A	100	100
8	100	15	1 500	240	17	4 080	N/A	200	200
9	100	15	1 500	260	18	4 680	N/A	300	300
10	100	15	1 500	280	19	5 320	N/A	400	400
11	100	15	1 500	300	20	6 000	N/A	500	500
12	100	15	1 500	320	21	6 720	N/A	600	600
Total	1 200		18 000	2 520		41 920		600	2 100
Average		15.00			16.63		1.63	0.50	1.75

ANNEX 4   ILLUSTRATION OF COMPARISON OF THE THREE METHODS

In this example, all three methods show a dumping margin. The varying ratio of the domestic quantities to the export quantities would be a reason for using the Second Symmetrical Method rather than the First Symmetrical Method.

Table 6A.4 *Comparative illustration of dumping margins under all three methods*

Month	Export Quantity	Export Unit price	Export Total value	Domestic Quantity	Domestic Unit price	Domestic Total value	D_1	D_2	$D_2(Z)$	D_3
1	100	26	2 600	100	23	2 300	N/A	−300	0	363
2	100	29	2 900	120	24	2 880	N/A	−500	0	63
3	100	26	2 600	140	25	3 500	N/A	−100	0	363
4	100	26	2 600	160	26	4 160	N/A	0	0	363
5	100	26	2 600	180	27	4 860	N/A	100	100	363
6	100	29	2 900	200	28	5 600	N/A	−100	0	63
7	100	26	2 600	220	29	6 380	N/A	300	300	363
8	100	30	3 000	240	30	7 200	N/A	0	0	0
9	100	26	2 600	260	31	8 060	N/A	500	500	363
10	100	30	3 000	280	32	8 960	N/A	200	200	0
11	100	26	2 600	300	33	9 900	N/A	700	700	363
12	100	30	3 000	320	34	10 800	N/A	400	400	0
Total	1 200		33 000	2 520		74 680		1 200	2 200	2 667
Average		27 50			29.63		2.13	1.00	1.83	2.22

Note: the values in the final column are derived by comparing the individual export value with the average domestic unit price of 29.63.

Moreover, zeroing would be appropriate under the Second Symmetrical Method because the exporter did not increase his undumped export price by the time the domestic price had increased to the same level as the export price. However, if it could be shown that the variations in export price were the result of an intention to target the dumping at certain areas or customers, rather than just a failure to adjust to changes in normal value, it would be appropriate to use the Asymmetrical Method which, in the present example, gives the highest dumping margin of all three methods.

7. Subsidies and countervailing action – problems arising

In Chapter 3 we outlined the rules for the determination of the existence of subsidies and their amount. We will now examine how the application of these rules can raise some difficult questions. In the first three sections we will be looking at three problems arising out of the allocation of subsidies. The first problem arises out of the allocation of subsidies over several years, and adjustments for the time-value of money. The second problem is related to the first. It concerns the question whether interest should be charged when a subsidy is received and expensed in the investigation period, that is to say, when the subsidy is not allocated over two or more years. The third problem is about whether subsidies should be allocated per unit or per value. In the fourth section we examine the relationship between countervailing action and anti-dumping action, a subject which leads inevitably to the question, 'Why are undumped subsidized exports countervailable at all?', a question we explore in our fifth section. This involves a discussion of the difference between export subsidies and domestic subsidies, and whether some subsidies are of a 'hybrid' nature, having characteristics of both export subsidies and domestic subsidies. We end this chapter with the examination of a subject that is still disputed between the EU and the US, namely the extent to which subsidies granted to a state-owned enterprise continue to be countervailable after the privatization of that enterprise.

7.1 ALLOCATION OF COUNTERVAILING DUTIES OVER TIME: SUBSIDIES LINKED TO THE ACQUISITION OF FIXED ASSETS

The SCM Agreement says nothing about how to allocate subsidies over time, taking into account the time-value of money. This is hardly surprising because there is a general consensus among accountants and financiers as to the basic techniques for working out the equivalence between a present-day capital sum and a future income stream of constant annuities. This is none other than making adjustments for the time-value of money. Where a subsidy is received in connection with the acquisition of a capital asset, such as plant and machinery, the effect of the subsidy is to reduce the costs of acquisition of the asset. Since the costs of acquisition of a capital asset are not expensed in the year, but are written down over the depreciation period of the asset, it seems normal that the subsidy should be allocated over the depreciation period of the asset. This is basically the approach of the EU and US Authorities, although there are differences in the fine details. The methodology used by the EU Authorities raises some interesting points of principle, which we shall examine here.

Article 8(7) of the EU AS Regulation says that a subsidy linked to the acquisition of fixed assets shall be calculated by spreading the subsidy across a period which reflects the normal depreciation period of such assets in the industry concerned. The EU Authorities have published guidelines on how the interest factor should be taken into account in such cases. The example given by the EU Authorities concerns a lump sum grant of, say, $100 000[1] for the acquisition of an asset with a normal depreciation period of five years. On a straight-line basis, the annual depreciation is $20 000. Thus the subsidy is allocated over a five-year depreciation period giving an annual subsidy of $20 000. At the beginning of the depreciation period, the total unamortized subsidy is $100 000, and this amount decreases by $20 000 every year. One also needs to take account of interest, however. The annual benefit to the exporter is not just the $20 000, but also the interest or the time-value factor arising out of the fact that the exporter receives $100 000 at the beginning of the five years, rather than an annual sum of $20 000 every year. Assuming an annual rate of interest of 10 per cent, the EU Authorities reason that the interest charge in the first year is 10 per cent of $100 000, namely $10 000, and that the interest charge in the fifth year is 10 per cent of $20 000, namely $2000. The EU Authorities then conclude that the annual interest charge should be the average of the two, namely $6000. Thus the total amount of the annual subsidy plus interest is $26 000.

This method has the advantage of simplicity, but it is a far cry from the notions of compound interest that one learns in secondary school. The correct way of calculating the annual amount of the subsidy plus interest is to determine the constant sum which, if paid annually to the exporter over five years, together with compound interest on those sums, would give the same value at the end of the five years as a fixed grant of $100 000 paid at the beginning of the five years together with compound interest over the same period. If we assume that the annual amount in question is A, and the annual interest rate is

---

[1]   The example published by the Commission uses different figures, but we have changed them so that the numbers are comparable with other examples we shall be looking at.

10 per cent, the value of the five annual payments together with compound interest at the end of the five years (assuming that the payments are deemed to be made at the beginning of each year) will be:

$$(A \times 1.10^5) + (A \times 1.10^4) + (A \times 1.10^3) + (A \times 1.10^2) + (A \times 1.10).$$

The sum of this geometric progression is: $A \times (1.10^6 - 1.10) / (1.10 - 1) = A \times 11 \times (1.10^5 - 1) = A \times 6.716$.

The other figure we need is the value of $100 000 at the end of five years, which will be $100 000 \times 1.10^5 = $161 051$.

In the hypothesis, these two computations must give the same value. Thus $A \times $ 6.716 = $ 161 051$, or $A = $ 23 980$. This is considerably less than the figure of $26 000 obtained using the EU Authorities' method.

Let us now look at the generalized case. Let us assume that (a) the capital grant is C; (b) the depreciation period is n years; (c) the annual interest rate is r; and (d) the annual value of the subsidy is A. Then the generalized case requires that

$$C(1 + r)^n = A(1 + r)[(1 + r)^n - 1] / r$$

whence:

$$A = Cr(1 + r)^{n-1} / [(1 + r)^n - 1].$$

On the other hand, the Commission's methodology gives $A' = (C/n)[1 + r(n+1)/2]$. These two formulae are very different. The only way one can measure their relative effects is to compare a few examples, as is done in Table 7.1. In all these examples the total subsidy calculated under the Commission's method is greater than the total subsidy calculated on the basis of the method we advocate. On the other hand, if one makes the same comparison for interest rates of 15 to 20 per cent over depreciation periods of 15 to 20 years, the Commission's method is more favourable to the exporter than our method. But the typical case does not involve such long periods and such high rates of interest. So, for all practical purposes, one can conclude that the Commission's method is less favourable than the method we advocate. We would argue that our method is the correct method, because it applies generally used techniques for determining the constant annuity over a period of years generated by a capital sum contributed at the beginning of the period.

Proponents of the EU Authorities' method will no doubt argue that this method has the advantage of simplicity and that the difference between the two methods is too small to be worth arguing about. For example, suppose that, in a capital intensive industry, the capital to turnover ratio is 1 and that the exporter benefits from a capital grant of 30 per cent of his investment. Let us suppose also that the investment is written off over five years, and that the prevailing annual interest rate is 7.5 per cent. The annual export subsidy will be 22.99 per cent of the capital grant under the correct method and 24.50 per cent of the capital grant under the Commission's method. Since the capital grant amounts to 30 per cent of the total investment (and also 30 per cent of the annual turnover) this translates into a subsidy of 6.90 per cent of sales under the correct method, and 7.35 per cent of sales under the EU Authorities' method. The difference of 0.45 per cent of sales, some might say, is not significant. We would not agree. While 0.45 per cent of sales may not seem like a large number on its own, it has to be borne in mind that anti-subsidy investigations are usually looking at exporters who receive many different subsidies at the same time. If, for each subsidy, there is an error of 0.45 per cent to the disadvantage of the exporter, this can soon add up to a material sum. Then there is the question of principle. An investigating authority should, in all cases, strive to use the method which is correct. Only if there were serious calculation difficulties might one consider taking some short cuts. But we would suggest that the calculation involved in our method is straightforward and could easily be incorporated in standard practice.

Table 7.1   Relative effects of the two formulae

Per cent			Correct method A	Commission method A´	Difference	Per cent
C	r	n				
100	10.00	10	14.80	15.50	0.70	4.7
100	7.50	10	13.55	14.13	0.57	4.2
100	5.00	10	12.33	12.75	0.42	3.4
100	2.50	10	11.15	11.38	0.23	2.1
100	10.00	5	23.98	26.00	2.02	8.4
100	7.50	5	22.99	24.50	1.51	6.6
100	5.00	5	22.00	23.00	1.00	4.5
100	2.50	5	21.00	21.50	0.50	2.4
100	10.00	3	36.56	40.00	3.44	9.4
100	7.50	3	35.77	38.33	2.56	7.2
100	5.00	3	34.97	36.67	1.69	4.8
100	2.50	3	34.16	35.00	0.84	2.5

7.2   INTEREST CHARGES ON SUBSIDIES RECEIVED FOR CURRENT TRANSACTIONS MADE DURING THE INVESTIGATION PERIOD

We will now consider the question examined in the previous section and ask ourselves, 'What happens if the subsidy should be expensed 100 per cent in the year of its receipt?' One way of answering this question would be simply to put $n = 1$ in the formula. The EU Authorities' formula:

$$A' = (C/n)[1 + r(n + 1)/2]$$

would become $A' = C[1 + r]$. In other words, the amount of the subsidy should be increased by an interest charge for one year. If we do the same in our formula,

$$A = Cr(1 + r)^{n-1} / [(1 + r)^n - 1],$$

we obtain $A = C$. In other words, the amount of the subsidy is simply the face value of the subsidy without any addition of an interest charge.

The EU Authorities' practice is, in fact, to charge interest on all subsidies received in the investigation period and wholly expensed in that period, that is to say, not allocated over several years. The Commission does this not only in the case of receipt of a capital sum, but also in the case of recurring subsidies, for example any subsidy which accrues every time an export is made throughout the investigation period. The EU Authorities' argument is as follows. The subsidy could have been received at the beginning of the investigation period, but, equally, it could have been received at the end of the investigation period. If the subsidy is received at the end of the investigation period there is no need to make an interest charge for the time-value of money. On the other hand, if the subsidy is received at the beginning of the investigation period, an interest charge should be made for the year during which the exporter has had the subsidy. Since subsidy payments could occur at any time in the year, the EU Authorities argue that it is appropriate to take an average, namely interest over six months. On this basis the EU Authorities have established a long-standing practice of increasing the amount of all subsidies on current transactions by an interest charge calculated on the amount of the subsidy for a period of six months using prevailing borrowing rates in the exporting country.[2]

---

2   See, for example, PET film from India, OJ L219, 19.8.1999, p. 14 at recitals (23) and (44).

This ingenious approach relies on a basically sound principle that money received at the beginning of a year has greater value than money received at the end of the year. However, in applying this principle, the EU Authorities have not thought through all the ramifications. The following considerations will demonstrate that the EU Authorities are wrong in their approach.

Imagine that a lump sum of $120 is paid to an exporter on the first day of the investigation period, and this sum is expensed in the year, that is to say, it is not amortized over more than one year. Suppose that, during the year, the exporter exports 10 units per month, giving a total of 120 for the year. In accordance with normal practice the subsidy would be allocated over total exports, giving a rate of subsidization of $1 per unit. If countervailing duties are imposed at the rate of $1 per unit imported, and imports continue at the rate of 10 units per month, the importing country will collect $120 in countervailing duties every year. In addition to collecting the duties, it will have the benefit of interest on those duties. The $10 collected in the first month will earn interest for 12 months, the $10 collected in the second month will earn interest for 11 months, and so on. On average, the countervailing duties will earn interest for six months. But it should be remembered that the EU Authorities will already have increased the subsidy by a six-monthly interest charge. In this way it is not difficult to see that the methodology of the EU Authorities results in double counting, and is wrong.

The approach of the EU Authorities amounts, in effect, to taking into account the time-value of money day by day, month by month. Thus $10 received in January is worth more than $10 received six months later in July. Equally $10 paid in January is a heavier burden than $10 paid six months later in July. The error of the EU Authorities arises from the fact that they make a time-value adjustment to the amount of the subsidy, but they do not make a time-value adjustment for other financial data. If an investigating authority wishes to make such adjustments, it is argued that they should apply the methodology consistently. They must not only convert the value of subsidies received for the time-value of money, but they must also convert all financial revenues and costs on the same basis. By so doing the rate of subsidization will be unaffected by the addition of interest, as Table 7.2 illustrates. In this example we have actualized the monthly export turnover to a value as at the end of the year, using an interest rate of 5 per cent per annum. For the purposes of the example, we have supposed that the export subsidy received every month is equal to 10 per cent of the value exported.

In the second and third columns of the table we have taken the total annual subsidy without an interest charge and divided it by the total annual turnover. As a result it is determined that the average rate of subsidization is 10 per cent of turnover. In the fourth and fifth columns we have actualized the subsidy and the turnover to its value as at the end of the period (31 December) by charg-

Table 7.2   Subsidization, interest and actualized export sales

	Exports CIF (US$)	Export subsidy (US$)	Exports actualized to 31 December	Export subsidy actualized to 31 December
January	1 000.00	100.00	1 047.92	104.79
February	1 000.00	100.00	1 043.75	104.38
March	1 000.00	100.00	1 039.58	103.96
April	1 000.00	100.00	1 035.42	103.54
May	1 000.00	100.00	1 031.25	103.13
June	1 000.00	100.00	1 027.08	102.71
July	1 000.00	100.00	1 022.92	102.29
August	1 000.00	100.00	1 018.75	101.88
September	1 000.00	100.00	1 014.58	101.46
October	1 000.00	100.00	1 010.42	101.04
November	1 000.00	100.00	1 006.25	100.63
December	1 000.00	100.00	1 002.08	100.21
Total	12 000.00	1 200.00	12 300.00	1 230.00
Subsidy rate		10.00%		10.00%

ing interest at the rate of 5 per cent per annum. In this case the total actualized subsidy divided by the total actualized turnover, namely the rate of subsidization, is still 10 per cent.

We will now look at the generalized case. In abstract terms we can say that if, for a series of exports of values (CIF) $e_1, e_2, e_3, e_4, \ldots, e_n$, countervailable benefits are received of $b_1, b_2, b_3, b_4, \ldots b_n$, and the factors necessary to adjust each of these for the time-value of money are $a_1, a_2, a_3, a_4, \ldots, a_n$, then the rate of subsidization is:

$$\Sigma \, (b_i \times a_i) \, / \, \Sigma \, (e_i \times a_i)$$

where Σ signifies the sum for all values of i from 1 to n.

Let us suppose that for each 'i', the ratio b_i/e_i is constant, namely that the rate of subsidy is a fixed proportion of the value exported for every shipment. In such a case it can be demonstrated arithmetically that the above formula simply reduces to $\Sigma \, (b_i) \, / \, \Sigma \, (e_i)$, namely the total benefit divided by the total export value, without any adjustment for the time-value of money. If the ratios b_i/e_i are not all the same, but the exports are spread more or less equally throughout the year, and the adjustment for the time-value of money is small, it can still be demonstrated that $\Sigma\ (b_i \times a_i)\ /\ \Sigma\ (e_i \times a_i)$ is close to $\Sigma\ (b_i)\ /\ \Sigma\ (e_i)$. In fact this is a matter of common sense. In countries with low inflation we do not take into account the time-value of money within the same year. We happily make statements such as 'I pay social security contributions of 12.5 per cent of my salary' or 'My annual mortgage commitments are just about equal to one third of my salary' without taking account of the time-value of money. The conclusion we draw from the foregoing is that the Commission is wrong to charge interest on subsidies that are expensed in the year in which they are received, that is, subsidies which are not depreciated over more than one year.

7.3   THE RELATIONSHIP BETWEEN DUMPED AND SUBSIDIZED EXPORTS REVISITED

Article VI(5) of GATT 1994, which we have already discussed in Chapter 3, provides as follows: 'No product of the territory of any contracting party imported into the territory of any other contracting party shall be subject to both anti-dumping and countervailing duties to compensate for the same situation of dumping or export subsidization.'

As we explained in Chapter 3, the investigating authority needs to set off, against the gross dumping margin, that part which is countervailed as an export subsidy, and then impose an anti-dumping duty in respect of the remainder of the dumping margin. On the other hand, any domestic subsidies, that is, subsidies which are not contingent on export performance, can be countervailed without having to set them off against the amount of the dumping margin. This seems to be general practice of many investigating authorities. For example, in a case involving PET film from India, the EU Authorities found that the dumping margin, namely the difference between the export price and the normal value, was X per cent of the CIF value. They found that the margin of export subsidization was Y per cent of the CIF value. In addition, they found the existence of a domestic subsidy equal to Z per cent of the CIF value. So the EU Authorities imposed a countervailing duty of Y per cent + Z per cent and an anti-dumping duty of X per cent – Y per cent, giving a duty (anti-dumping plus countervailing) of X per cent + Z per cent.

In most cases, the above approach will produce the correct results. We would suggest, however, that the principle underlying Article VI(5) is simply to avoid what one might characterize as 'double counting'. One can imagine situations in which double counting can arise but which are not dealt with if one applies blindly the principle that export subsidization is deducted from the dumping margin, but domestic subsidization is not. We will give two examples, one based on domestic subsidization and one based on export subsidization.

7.3.1   Example based on Domestic Subsidization

Imagine that the unit costs of production of the product concerned are 92, but this is due to a domestic subsidy of 8 which has the effect of reducing the gross cost of 100 to 92. Suppose that the unit domestic price is 98 and the unit export price is 88. At first sight it appears that there is a dumping margin of 98 – 88 = 10 and a domestic subsidy of 8. Applying Article VI(5), the investigating authorities would impose a countervailing duty of 8 and an anti-dumping duty of 10. There is no question of deducting the subsidy from the dumping margin because the subsidy is a domestic subsidy. However, in the context of the anti-dumping investigation, the investigating authorities could possibly take the view that the real cost of production was not 92, but 100, namely the costs of production without the deduction of the subsidy. On this approach the domestic price would no longer be more than unit costs, and so the normal value would have to be determined on some other basis, that is, by using the export price to a third country, or costs of production plus a reasonable profit margin.

There are good arguments to say that the normal value should simply be adjusted by adding the subsidy to the domestic price, giving a normal value of 106. In this way the dumping margin would become 106 – 88 = 18. Applying Article VI(5) blindly, one would calculate the countervailing duty as 8 and the anti-dumping duty as 18, without making any deduction for the amount of the subsidy, which, after all, is a domestic subsidy. However, the amount of the dumping margin has been increased from the initial assessment of 10 to a larger figure of 18 by adjusting the costs of production for the amount of the domestic subsidy. We would argue that this is a situation which should be covered by the principle of Article VI(5). In other words, the countervailing duty should be deducted from the dumping margin to the extent that the subsidy countervailed has contributed to the amount of the dumping margin. So the countervailing duty should be 8 and the anti-dumping duty 18 – 8 = 10, giving a total duty of 18. This is exactly the same result as that obtained above, where normal value was taken as being equal to the subsidized domestic price.

There are, of course, other ways in which the normal value could be determined, using third country export prices, or costs of production plus a reasonable profit margin. Suppose that the normal value thus determined was 110. The dumping margin would become 110 – 88 = 22. Applying Article VI(5) blindly, one would impose a countervailing duty of 8 and an anti-dumping duty of 22, giving a total duty of 30. We would argue, however, that the correct approach would be to impose a countervailing duty of 8, and an anti-dumping duty of 22 – 8 = 14, giving a total duty of 22.

7.3.2   Example based on Export Subsidization

We can take the previous example and vary the facts slightly so that the subsidy of 8 granted for production is in fact contingent on export performance. The subsidy of 8 would therefore constitute an export subsidy and fall clearly within the scope of Article VI(5). If the exporter did not have any domestic sales at all, his normal value for dumping purposes would have to be determined by reference to third country export prices or costs of production. If the investigating authority decided to construct normal value using costs of production plus a reasonable profit margin, it would find that the costs of production of the exporter were 100 but that these had been reduced to 92 by the export subsidy. One approach would be to correct the costs of production by excluding the subsidy. If the investigating authority chose to do this, it would take the costs of production to be 100 and add a reasonable margin for profit. To stay within the same parameters as the previous example, we will assume that a reasonable margin for profit would be 10, so that the constructed value would be 110. This would give a dumping margin of 110 − 88 = 22. So the investigating authority would impose a countervailing duty of 8 and an anti-dumping duty of 22 − 8 = 14, giving a total duty of 22.

If the investigating authority had not made any adjustment to the costs of production, but had relied on the subsidized costs, it would have determined the normal value to be 92 + 10 = 102. This would give a dumping margin of 102 − 88 = 14. The dumping margin has already been reduced by the fact of using the subsidized costs of production to determine normal value, and so there is no reason to deduct the margin of subsidization from the dumping margin. It would be erroneous on the part of the investigating authority to deduct the amount of the export subsidy from the dumping margin under this latter approach. Thus the anti-dumping duty should be 14, the countervailing duty 8, giving a total duty of 22.

These two examples illustrate that Article VI(5) does not require the blind application of a rule: export subsidies are deducted from the dumping margin but domestic subsidies are not. It is a question of examining carefully whether the methodology used to determine the margins of dumping and subsidization involve double counting or not.

7.4   WHY ARE UNDUMPED SUBSIDIZED EXPORTS COUNTERVAILABLE?

It is possible to have a situation where there is export subsidization, but no, or a *de minimis*, dumping margin, as illustrated by the EU case of *CDRs from India*. There is no reason why the exporter should necessarily reduce his export prices just because he has an export subsidy. He could maintain equality of his export and domestic pricing, and pocket the export subsidy as an extra windfall. One may legitimately ask the question: 'Why can an importing country impose a countervailing duty if there is no dumping?' Put in a different way, if the subsidy does not cause the exporter to engage in price discrimination, where is the unfair trading practice? Let us imagine a case where the export price is 100 and the (profitable) domestic price is 95. There is no dumping. If, in addition, there is an export subsidy of 5, a countervailing duty of 5 can be imposed. But let us consider what would happen if the exporting country were to withdraw the export subsidy. In theory, the exporter would be obliged to increase his export price by 5 in order to compensate for the loss of subsidy, with the result that his export price would become 105 as against an already profitable domestic price of 100. But since his export price of 100 is not dumped, the exporter could simply maintain his price at this level and undergo the loss of additional income provided by the export subsidy. This would be a quite viable strategy from an economic point of view. Countervailing practice seems to be based on the theory that subsidization causes an exporter to reduce his prices. This may be true in the majority of cases, but it is not a necessary consequence of subsidization.

So where is the unfair trading practice? The answer would seem to be that an export subsidy encourages a producer to export more than he would be inclined to do in the absence of the subsidy. Thus, even if it is profitable for a producer to export without any subsidy, the granting of an export subsidy encourages him to concentrate his efforts on exporting rather than on domestic sales. The exporting country might have a motivation for this, notably to improve the balance of payments and to earn foreign currency, but such a practice is condemned by the SCM Agreement.

An interesting consequence of this is the following. Since export subsidization can be countervailed even in the absence of dumping, and since anti-dumping duties may not be imposed to deal with that part of the dumping margin which has been countervailed, a producer who obtains an export subsidy has an incentive to practise dumping at the same time. By practising dumping he can be more competitive in the export market, but without exposing himself to any greater duty. For example, if he sells on the domestic market for $100 per unit (which is above costs of production) and sells for export at the same price of $100, but receives an export subsidy of $5, he can be countervailed with a duty of $5. If, now, he reduces his export price to $95, he will have a dumping margin of $5, but this will already be covered by the countervailing duty of $5, so no additional dumping duty can be imposed.

7.5   A HYBRID EXPORT SUBSIDY?

A well known form of subsidy is to grant a benefit, for example an exemption from import duties on capital goods, provided the producer exports a certain percentage, say 70 per cent, of his production. If the exporter does not export 70 per cent of his production, he will be obliged to pay the import duties from which he was exempted. This looks like an export subsidy because it encourages the producer to export at least 70 per cent of his production. Provided the exporter exports at least 70 per cent of his production, however, he will benefit from a given reduction in his investment costs whether he exports 70 per cent, 80 per cent, 90 per cent or all of his production. This given reduction in his investment costs will reduce his annual depreciation cost, and this in turn will reduce his costs of production overall, whether the production is exported or not.

So is it fair to allocate the total amount of subsidization only to exports, and not to allocate it over domestic and export sales? The EU Authorities take the view that the total amount should be allocated only to export, but from a strict cost point of view this does not seem to be fair. The reduced amount of depreciation reduces the cost of production overall, and so one would expect it to have an effect on the exporter's pricing both in the domestic market and in export markets. Moreover, EU Authorities' approach has the undesirable consequence of encouraging the exporter to export all of his production, even if he only needs to export 70 per cent in order to qualify for the subsidy. The amount of the subsidy is a fixed quantity of depreciation, and so the larger the export volume, the lower the rate of subsidization. Thus, by exporting more than 70 per cent of his total production, the exporter can reduce the rate of subsidization. This does not concur with common sense. The subsidy has the effect of reducing unit costs of production and so should be allocated over all production. In effect, the proportion of the subsidy allocated to the production that was exported should be characterized as an export subsidy, and that part allocated to the production sold on the domestic market should be treated as a domestic subsidy.

7.6   SUBSIDY ALLOCATION: PER UNIT OR PER VALUE?

The SCM Agreement says that the subsidy shall be allocated per unit. In other words the assumption of the SCM Agreement is that export subsidies are contingent on export performance, and export performance is measured by the number of units exported, not by their value. This could be questioned from an economic point of view. If the policy behind the export subsidization was to earn foreign currency, then it would be more logical to measure export performance in value terms rather than units. Moreover, the structure of many subsidies is value-based rather than unit-based. For example, an exemption from corporate income tax on export revenues is clearly based on the value of turnover, rather than the number of units exported. That being said, the text of the SCM Agreement says that the allocation should be made per unit. This rule is not always followed, however, by investigating authorities. Departure from the SCM Agreement text can produce different results if the prices of exports to the country imposing the countervailing duties are not the same as the prices of exports to other countries, as the following example will illustrate.

Suppose that, during the investigation period, an exporter has total export sales of the product concerned to all countries of US$10 million. Suppose also that his exports to the country concerned are in fact made up as in Table 7.3. It can be seen that, by allocating the export subsidy over quantities rather than over turnover, the subsidy margin, expressed as a percentage of turnover, diminishes as the unit price increases. There is some logic in this. As we have argued in the previous section, export subsidization tends to contribute to dumping by encouraging the exporter to lower his export price. Thus the higher the per unit subsidization, the lower one would expect the export price to be. The demonstration in the Table 7.3 is just that this is the result if one allocates the subsidy on a per unit basis rather than in proportion to value. This supports our argument that the correct method of allocation is on a per unit basis, although we recognize that this may not always be practicable, for example, when the product consists of a wide variety of types and sizes. There

Table 7.3   Comparison of allocation per unit, and per value

Exports	Total/ average	Country concerned	Other countries
Total value (US$)	10 000 000	7 500 000	2 500 000
Unit export price (US$)	76.19	75.00	80.00
Total quantity (units)	131 250	100 000	31 250
Total export subsidy allocated on turnover	500 000	375 000	125 000
Percentage duty based on per turnover allocation	5	5	5
Total export subsidy allocated on units	500 000	380 952.40	119 047.60
Percentage duty based on per unit allocation	5	5.08	4.76

may also be cases where allocation on a per value basis is more appropriate. It is nevertheless important to remember that the rule in the SCM Agreement is allocation on a per unit basis, so this should be the starting point in any discussion of how the subsidy should be allocated.

Last of all, it should be observed that, as in our example in section 7.1 above, the percentage difference between the two methods is small. But as we have already remarked, several small percentages calculated on an annual export turnover of millions of dollars can soon add up to a material sum.

7.7   CONTINUATION OF SUBSIDIES AFTER PRIVATIZATION

Since 1999 there has been continuing litigation between the USA and the EU before the WTO Dispute Settlement Body as to whether the USA's methodology for determining the continuation of subsidization when a state enterprise is privatized is consistent with the SCM Agreement. The dispute is very complex and the rules of the Dispute Settlement Body turn, to a certain extent, on procedural issues. It will be helpful first to approach the matter *de novo* by applying general principles to a few simple scenarios.

If a state-owned enterprise A, a producer of widgets, has received a capital grant from the government, and has used this grant to invest in assets, the benefit to the enterprise will continue throughout the period of depreciation of the assets. If the enterprise A sells the assets for fair market value to another widget producer, B, B acquires the assets, but does not acquire any benefit from the capital grant given to A. B pays fair market value for the assets, while A still has the benefit of the capital grant, since it has used the grant to purchase the asset, and then sold the asset for fair market value. B cannot therefore be subject to countervailing action in respect of the subsidy granted to A. If A retains some production facilities and so remains in the business of producing and exporting widgets, it could continue to be subject to countervailing action in respect of the financial benefit conferred on it at the time it acquired the assets. This conclusion would appear to be supported by the panel findings in *United States – Imposition of Countervailing Duties on Certain Hot-Rolled Lead and Bismuth Carbon Steel Products Originating in the United Kingdom,* findings which were upheld by the Appellate Body.[3]

If now we consider a variant on the above, where, instead of B acquiring the assets for fair market value, B acquires all the shares in A. A thus becomes a wholly-owned subsidiary of B; in fact A and B form a single economic entity

---

[3]   WT/DS138/AB/R of 10 May 2000.

because both A and B are widget producers. This economic entity comprising B, and its wholly owned subsidiary A, continues to benefit from the subsidy granted originally to A. The position of the US in such cases is to consider that a countervailing duty can continue to be imposed on imports of widgets produced by A. The US position was held not to be compatible with the SCM Agreement by a panel in *United States – Countervailing Measures concerning certain products from the European Communities*. The Appellate Body gave a more nuanced ruling, however, saying that it could not be assumed automatically from the privatization process that no benefit continued to accrue to the privatized producer.[4]

What price should B pay for the shares in order to avoid the continuation of a subsidy in A? Reasoning from first principles, it seems that B should pay the state the market value of the shares. If it could be shown that the market value of the shares took into account the remaining value of the capital subsidy that A had received, it could be argued that B had paid back the remaining value of the subsidy. In other words, it would have to be demonstrated that the price paid was equivalent to the sum of (i) the market value of the company estimated on the basis that it had no remaining benefit from the subsidy, plus (ii) the remaining unamortized value of the subsidy. In this way B would put an end to subsidization and should therefore be able to apply for a review of the countervailing duties. Alternatively, B could pay less than a market price for the shares in A. Here there would be additional subsidy consisting in the advantage conferred on B by the state selling at less than market value. So the economic entity consisting of the two companies A and B could be subject to countervailing action in respect not only of the capital grant made to A, but also of the sale at an undervalue to B.

Coming now to a possible second variant on the above, let us suppose that, instead of B purchasing the shares in A, these shares are offered for sale on public markets and are taken up by a wide variety of investors who have nothing to do with widget producing. In this scenario it seems to us it is not possible to say that the shareholders and A all form a single economic entity. The price these shareholders pay for the shares has no effect on A's business and so can have no effect on the subsidy analysis. A continues to benefit from the subsidy granted by the state and can be subject to countervailing action irrespective of the change in shareholders, and irrespective of whether these shareholders paid more or less than fair market value for the shares.

---

[4]   WT/DS212/AB/R, of 9 December 2002.

8. Public policy considerations

The fundamental objection to such practices as dumping or subsidizing exports is not simply that they adversely affect producers in importing countries, but that in doing so in an unfair manner they adversely affect the broad public interest. This means that they adversely affect not only producers and workers in the enterprises directly affected, but also enterprises and workers who are indirectly affected, such as those in user industries, and in addition they adversely affect consumers. Consumers clearly benefit from low import prices, but it can be argued that this is often a short-term gain only, and that in the longer run they benefit more as consumers – let alone as possibly affected workers – from 'fair' international trade rules.

This is not of course a universally held view. Some economists would argue, for example, that low prices on account of dumping benefit consumers in importing countries in the long as well as the short run. Stories of how domestic industries will be driven out of existence and, following that, import prices will be raised to monopolistic levels, are much exaggerated. Competition in export markets will keep import prices low. But this ignores the advantages that consumers may gain from having product manufactured in close proximity in the domestic market. It also neglects the possibility that domestic production may be a safeguard against the possibility of vital imports being cut off for political reasons. There is also the point that low-priced exports may be being subsidized by high prices in protected home markets in exporting countries, thus adversely affecting consumers in those countries.

The purpose of this chapter is to explore further these issues, which might properly be called public policy considerations. In doing this it is necessary to bear in mind Article 19.2 of the SCM Agreement and Article 9.1 of the AD Agreement. These provide that it is desirable that 'the imposition [of duties] be permissive'. Most countries have a stage at which political intervention is possible to decide that it is not appropriate, on general policy considerations, to take anti-dumping or countervailing action in a particular case. In the EU, the consideration of general policy considerations is formalized into a necessary part of the investigation. The EU has given effect to this recommendation by incorporating the 'Community interest' test in the EU AD Regulation and the EU AS Regulation. More widely, this 'desirability' provision provides a good deal of latitude in terms of the practice of the EU.

8.1 COMMUNITY INTEREST

The EU AD Regulation and the EU AS Regulation provide that anti-dumping and countervailing duties may not be applied where the authorities, on the basis of all the information submitted, can clearly conclude that it is not in the 'Community interest' to apply such measures. It should be noted that the word 'Community' here refers specifically to the European Community, namely the economic 'pillar' of the EU.

For several years past, the EU Authorities have systematically carried out a separate examination into the Community interest, taking into account the interests not only of the importers and the EU industry, but also of users and consumers, together with considerations of public interest such as the need to preserve competition, the employment situation, certainty for investors and considerations of external trade policy.

It is, however, rare for the EU Authorities to conclude that it is not in the Community interest to impose measures, once dumping or subsidization causing injury has been found. In the case of *Gum Rosin from China*,[1] however, the EU Authorities did give preference to the interests of user groups over those of the EU industry. Gum rosin is a primary product used by a number of industries, including tyre manufacturers, the paint industry, adhesive producers and the production of varnish. The case was closed without the imposition of duties on the following grounds:

1. The EU industry consisted of medium-sized firms located in a single Member State which made use of limited available natural resources;
2. Even if anti-dumping measures were imposed, EU users would continue to be largely dependent on imports since the EU industry's capacity for production could only supply a fraction of EU demand for the product;
3. The goods produced by the EU users were of high added-value and these industries supported a substantial workforce;
4. The imposition of duties would result, for EU user industries, in a substantial increase in their respective costs of production because of the need for a steady and abundant supply of the product.

More recently, the EU authorities decided, in *Synthetic handbags from China*,[2] that it was not in the EU interest to impose anti-dumping measures because:

---

[1]   OJ L41, 12.2.94, p. 50.
[2]   OL L208, 2.8.97, p. 31.

1. It was unlikely that the imposition of duties would increase the volume of synthetic handbags sold by the EU industry, since this would merely increase imports from other countries;
2. The imposition of duties would have a negative impact on employment in the industry, with around 4100 employees;
3. The imposition of duties would create a shortage of supply, thus reducing consumer choice.

These cases where the Community interest has been decisive are comparatively rare, however. In most instances the Community interest appears in practice to be treated as virtually synonymous with the interest of the EU's own domestic producing industries. It can be argued therefore, on the basis of this experience, that the explicit provisions on the Community interest in the EU regulations lead to no greater benefits to the EU as a whole than the absence of such provisions in, for example, the US legislation. This is probably unfair to the EU Authorities, however, since they now increasingly devote attention to the wider aspects of proposed anti-dumping and countervailing actions.

8.2   BENEFITS TO PROCESSING INDUSTRIES

Anti-dumping duties and countervailing duties are applied to a wide variety of imported products. Many of these are raw materials. In 2002, for example, definitive anti-dumping duties were imposed by the EU on imports of urea, glyphosate, ferro molybdenum, zinc oxides, ammonium nitrate and powdered activated carbon.[3] Duties are also applied to more finished products, such as, in 2002, magnetic discs, recordable compact discs, bicycle parts, tube and pipe fittings, polyester textured filament yarn, ring binder mechanisms and colour television receivers. This latter group can, in its turn, be divided into intermediate products, such as bicycle parts, polyester yarn and ring binder mechanisms, and finished products, such as recordable compact discs and colour television receivers.

It is clear, from this, and from both previous and later evidence, that a high proportion of the duties imposed are placed on raw materials and intermediate products. These products are then further processed by domestic industries. The imposition of duties on these products thus tends to disadvantage processing industries, by increasing the price of their inputs.

A somewhat surprising feature of many of the EU cases concerning

---

[3]   European Community, Eur-Lex, 11.60.40.20, Anti-dumping measures.

processing industries is that the domestic manufacturers concerned, when asked by the EU Authorities for their comments on the proposed imposition of duties, fail to register a protest against these. Accordingly, the EU Authorities can then, when considering the scope of injury and the Community interest in the relevant cases, dismiss objections to the proposed duties on the grounds that no serious objections by users have been put forward to them.

In the *Cellulose filament yarn case*,[4] for example, it was stated that the main user of the product concerned was the textile industry, producing linings, women's apparel and furnishings. Questionnaires were sent to 40 domestic users, but only seven of these returned a completed questionnaire. In addition, several users sent letters, outlining their concerns at the possible imposition of duties. The EU Authorities' comment was that cellulose acetate represents on average around 27 per cent of the users' cost of production of products incorporating the input concerned. The impact of the duty would therefore have an impact on their costs of production. But, as the Community industry had free cellulose acetate capacity, and there was a possibility of sourcing from countries not subject to anti-dumping duty, price increases, if any, were expected to be moderate.

It could be argued, conversely, that as the countries on which duties were imposed had increased their market share of Community consumption from 12 per cent in 1997 to 26 per cent in 2000–2001, there would have needed to be quite a big switch to other producers or importers for the duties to be avoided. It seems likely therefore that, in practice, the imposition of duties (20 per cent on imports from Lithuania and 16.3 per cent on imports from the USA) would have had a significant adverse effect on users' costs of production.

It is interesting that, possibly for this reason (although no explanation was publicly given) the trade association which had brought the original complaint later withdrew it, so that no duties were eventually imposed. Although the EU Authorities had discounted users' complaints, the trade association was perhaps in the end more sensitive to them. It may also have been sensitive to complaints from such a large player as Celanese, the US company affected by the proposed duties.

Another interesting case concerning user industries was that of *Unbleached (grey) cotton fabrics*.[5] The dumped imports represented some 42 per cent of the Community market, in spite of the existence of import quotas. Representations had been made in this case by importers and users of the dumped products, to the effect that the imposition of measures would have adverse effects, sometimes serious, on downstream industries. These industries would be

---

4   Commission Regulation (EC) 1662/2002, 19.9.2002, OJ L251, p. 9.
5   Commission Regulation (EC) 2208/96, OJ L 295, 20.11.96, p. 3.

subject to rising raw material costs and would also face a different (and more serious) kind of pressure from imports from the countries subject to duties, since the measures might result in exporters moving their production down the production ladder. The imposition of duties, it was argued, would therefore bring about an increase in imports of finished textiles in the longer term.

The European Commission noted in this case that only a very small number of Community importers and users had made themselves known and had provided information within the time limits set. It was, however, clear from those submissions that had been received from downstream industries that grey cotton fabrics undergo a number of transformations, making an assessment of the possible effects of the potential duties particularly difficult. Grey cloth was first bleached, then printed or dyed, and thereafter cut or sewn. Each additional stage in the production chain added significant value and increased product differentiation.

The Commission concluded from this that, 'given the proportion of input costs represented by unbleached cotton fabrics and the variety of uses, a clear conclusion on the effect of the proposed duties on the downstream industries cannot be reached'. Even so, given the variety of sources of supply and the competitive nature of the Community market, the situation of the processing industries 'will not be substantially affected'. As regards the possible import of finished fabrics, the Commission did not consider that these presented a serious threat. It also stressed the beneficial effect of duties on certain upstream industries, in particular yarn production.

The *Unbleached (grey) cotton fabrics case* had been considered twice before the quoted (1996) enquiry. It was obviously controversial, since some Member States, such as France, were producers of grey cotton cloth and were therefore unhappy about allegedly dumped imports, while other Member States, such as the UK, had only a small grey cotton cloth industry remaining, and were happy with low import prices. The UK and other Member States in a similar position were not therefore in favour of the proposed imposition of duties, since these would adversely affect their processing industries. In the event, the UK and its allies outvoted France and its allies in the EU Council, and the duties were never imposed.

In the light of this and other cases, it is not easy to explain why objections from processing industries tend to be so weak at the investigation stage. It may be that the dumped input sometimes represents such a small part of costs of production that, even when duties are added, the resulting cost is not significant. It could also be that domestic prices have been forced down by low-priced imports, and that, even when duties are likely to be imposed, domestic prices are expected to remain low and competitive. There may also be problems for small firms in completing a detailed questionnaire, while other firms may have reasons for not wishing to put their heads above the parapet. Another possibility is that trade associations' members consist of both producers of the primary input and processors of it, and that internally in the trade association the producers win.

A further possibility is that processors are aware that they may be able to obtain the relevant product from a source different from that which is likely to be subject to duties. For example, the manufacture of ring binder mechanisms was transferred by a British firm to Malaysia, for cost reasons. Duties were then imposed by the EU on imports from Malaysia and also from China.[6] The Malaysian operation was transferred to India, and the Chinese operation to Indonesia. Dumping and countervailing subsidy cases were then brought against Indonesia. Then ring binder mechanisms started to come from Vietnam, India and Thailand. As a result of this merry-go-round, EU importers were able to avoid duties, at least for some time.

In any event, since the relevant authorities are generally faced with complaints from producers of the product concerned, they have to take these complaints especially seriously. It has to be said, however, that the EU Authorities, in their public interest considerations, often give the impression of playing down the interests of processors. Perhaps it may be suspected that the officials concerned are a little too keen to support the relevant domestic industries? Processors are not always without their supporters, however, as the *Unbleached (grey) cotton fabrics case* illustrates. The Member States who were against the duties would not have taken the attitude they did without strong lobbying on the sponsoring government departments, from the processors concerned. The somewhat surprising general feature, however, is the comparatively late stage at which lobbying from processors appears to take place. Perhaps they only wake up to the threat when it is staring them in the face.

However, the situation may be changing, at least as far as importers of finished products are concerned. In 2006, formidable difficulties were faced by the EU Authorities in attempting to impose anti-dumping duties on imports of footwear from China and Vietnam. Here the northern EU countries, largely importers of footwear, opposed duties, while countries which manufacture footwear, such as Italy, Portugal, Spain and Greece, favoured them.

8.3   BENEFITS TO CONSUMERS

As has been said, it would appear at first sight to be in the interests of consumers in importing countries that no duties should be placed on imports

---

6   OJ L22, 24.1.1.97, p. 1.

that have allegedly been dumped, or have been subject to export subsidies. In the absence of duties, cheap imports would be free to enter, hindered only by tariffs and any quotas that may survive. As far as consumers are concerned, therefore, the lower the barriers set by tariffs and quotas, the better it will be for them (at least in the short term) since cheap imports will be free to come in with little hindrance. Cheap imports of raw materials should result in lower prices for finished goods at the retail stage, while cheap imports of finished products should be of direct benefit to consumers.

The passing on of cheap imports to consumers is not of course an automatic process. If there is some degree of monopolization among importers, processors or retailers, the benefits of cheap imports might accrue to them, in the form of higher profits, rather than to consumers. Much depends, therefore, as far as consumers are concerned, on the strength of competitive forces in the importing and using industries. This strength tends to vary across industries, although in highly industrialized countries, such as the USA or Britain, there is plenty of competition in industries such as food or textiles, so that low import prices for products such as these tend to be reflected in low final prices to the consumer.

A number of studies have been made of the benefit to consumers of dismantling import barriers set by quotas in particular. Effectively such studies would also apply, *mutatis mutandis*, to the removal or reduction of high import tariffs, and to the non-imposition of anti-dumping or countervailing duties. The quota studies concerned have referred especially to the EU and USA textile and clothing industries, protected by the MFA (Multi-Fibre Arrangement) from 1975 until the end of 2004. The clothing industry in particular is extremely competitive in advanced countries, so that the ending of the MFA would be expected to lead to lower wholesale and retail prices for clothing. One estimate, derived from quota premia in Hong Kong, suggested that the ending of the MFA would cause retail clothing prices in the UK to fall by 5 per cent.[7] Other estimates have suggested even bigger reductions in retail clothing prices in all regions and countries protected by the MFA.

Certainly, immediately after the MFA came to an end, there was a rush of cheap clothing imports into the EU in the early months of 2005, especially from China. So great was the volume that the European Commission entered into negotiations with China to cut down the volume of Chinese clothing imports, although it did this in such a manner as to cause much disruption in the affected importing industries.

---

    [7]   Z.A.Silberston, with M.Ledic, 'The Future of the Multi-Fibre Arrangement', HMSO 1989.

The reduction of import barriers is, however, likely to have adverse effects on those employed in import-competing industries. As consumers they would benefit from low prices, but as producers they would lose. It could be that their industries would contract greatly, or even cease to exist, when imports became more competitive. Many hundreds of thousands of textile and clothing jobs have indeed been lost in Europe and the USA as a result of competition from cheap imports. A recent result of this competition was the attempt to safeguard the US clothing industry by the imposition, in November 2003, of punitive tariffs on certain Chinese clothing imports. In addition, following the end of the Multi-Fibre Arrangement from 1 January 2005, there were moves in the USA, as well as in the EU, to invoke safeguard provisions on textile and clothing imports from China.

It should not be forgotten that those employed in declining industries are often among the most poorly paid industrial workers. If they succeed in gaining employment in more prosperous industries, once they leave their original industries, they might well have higher earnings than previously. An example of this potentially beneficial effect was the transfer of employment from the Lancashire textile industry to the newer electrical industry, that took place in the 1960s and later, after a cartel in the textile industry had been declared illegal by the UK Restrictive Practices Court at the end of the 1950s.

It might be the case, however, that the specialized skills, the age or the location of displaced workers would make it difficult or impossible for them to obtain alternative employment. In that case the benefits they derive as consumers of imported products might be more than offset by their losses as employees. Their distress might be such as to require government assistance, and they might never be employed again. In the long run, however, assuming the maintenance of a high level of employment in the economy as a whole, the gross national product and workers as a whole should benefit from cheap imports, as should consumers generally.

As has been said, it is sometimes suggested that low-priced imports might be used in a predatory manner. The domestic industry might be destroyed or severely damaged by such imports and, following this, the prices of imports might be raised monopolistically, to the benefit of the formerly low-priced exporting countries. Experience does not, however, support such a hypothesis. Low-priced imports are likely to continue to be low-priced, after the freeing of trade, especially if the industry concerned is the subject of strong international competition. The experience of the international clothing industry is a clear example of such behaviour.

In addition to the interests of consumers in importing countries it is important to consider consumers in countries exporting low-priced products. Duties against their exports will adversely affect workers in these countries, who are often very poor. The reverse of such policies as the MFA, therefore, is that they work against the interest of workers and consumers in countries with very low standards of living.

Sometimes, however, poor countries can do themselves harm. If the countries concerned have high tariffs and other barriers against imports, prices on their home market may be set at a high level, partly in order to enable exports to be made at subsidized prices. In that case, consumers in the countries exporting cheaply will be adversely affected by these domestic tariff and pricing policies. They will also be disadvantaged by lack of access to imported products, which might be of higher quality than domestic products, more technologically advanced or relatively cheap. Such a scenario is not fanciful. Until recent years, for example, imports into India were hindered by high import barriers, thus disadvantaging Indian consumers.

If, on the other hand, low-cost countries do not have a policy of high protection, they stand to benefit from the working of international comparative advantage. Their exports are likely to be at low prices, because their costs of production are low, while their imports will come in from the rest of the world at comparatively low prices. Those industries which are internationally competitive will flourish, while those that are not will wither away or fail to grow. Over time, such a situation will lead to rising standards of living in low-cost countries – a rise in standards that will be inhibited if rich countries block the entry of low-priced products from these developing countries.

Comparative advantage does tend to change over time, however. Countries which maintain low import barriers will benefit greatly from the international division of labour. But they must be prepared for adjustments to their industrial structure, as international comparative advantage changes. In the short run such adjustments will not be comfortable, and may be cushioned by governmental or other policy. But in the long run it is essential that such adjustments take place if countries are to maintain their prosperity and to grow in wealth over time, to the great benefit of their consumers.

9. Anti-dumping action – alternative approaches

9.1 MARKET CIRCUMSTANCES AND DUMPING

It has been demonstrated that there are many problems associated with the present rules regarding anti-dumping action. To a considerable extent these are inevitably associated with the way the regulations have been drafted, and with the detailed investigations that have to be made when dumping has been alleged.

A feature of the anti-dumping regime is the frequency with which anti-dumping action has been taken (at least until comparatively recently) by the leading participants in international trade. In the past the EU and the USA have led the way with anti-dumping actions. Now, however, such countries as India and China have become very active in bringing actions against allegedly dumped imports.[1] By the mid-1990s, indeed, new users accounted for over half of anti-dumping filings.[2]

Another striking feature of anti-dumping action is the number of cases brought by the developed countries and regions against relatively low-cost countries. For example, between 1999 and 2002, the EU Authorities adopted some 200 anti-dumping regulations and decisions. Of these some 35 per cent were against low wage countries such as China and India, while some 60 per cent were against relatively low wage countries, mainly in Asia and Eastern Europe. Only 5.5 per cent were against high cost countries such as Japan and the USA.[3]

Even as late as the second half of 2005, exports from China in particular remained by far the most frequent subject of new measures, when considering all countries taking anti-dumping action against China.[4]

---

[1]   For some of the statistics involved, and for a more extended discussion of what follows in this section, see Aubrey Silberston, 'Anti-dumping rules – time for change?', *Journal of World Trade*, December 2003.

[2]   See Taro Hallworth and Matloob Piracha, 'Macroeconomic fluctuations and anti-dumping filings: evidence from a new generation of protectionist countries', *Journal of World Trade,* June 2006.

[3]   Aubrey Silberston, op. cit., section on 'Anti-dumping action by the EC'.

[4]   WTO Secretariat, Press/441, 8 May 2006, 'Anti-Dumping'.

Recent research has revealed, however, that factors other than the threat of dumping by exporting countries may stimulate anti-dumping action by importing countries. It has been argued in particular that macroeconomic factors may play a part in sparking anti-dumping action. A study of four 'new' user countries, Argentina, Brazil, India and South Africa, has suggested that these countries are more likely to initiate anti-dumping action when their exchange rates strengthen or when the rate of growth of their GDP (Gross Domestic Product) declines.[5] There is a certain logic here. When the exchange rate of an importing country strengthens, imports become cheaper on the domestic market of the importer. When GDP growth declines, the domestic industries of the importer are likely to do less well than formerly, so that low-priced imports become a greater threat. Action against imports is therefore stimulated by these macroeconomic changes, irrespective of any change in the degree of dumping by exporting countries.

As Hallworth and Piracha put it,[6] 'Countries named in AD filings appear to be unfairly taking the blame for macroeconomic fluctuations, particularly in the filing country, on which they have no influence.' Factors such as these clearly need to be borne in mind when anti-dumping investigations are carried out. In particular, the analysis of the causes of injury needs especial attention in the light of these findings.

To return now to the main issues to be analysed in this chapter, which concerns possible alternative approaches to anti-dumping regulations, it is important to enquire first how likely it is that low wage, and relatively low wage, countries are in fact likely to resort to dumping.

9.2   LOW WAGE COUNTRIES

Low-wage countries are likely to have relatively low costs of production, provided that they are able to combine their low wages with relatively efficient methods of production. They may also have considerable economies of large-scale production. In such countries the domestic price level may be relatively low (but still possibly above total costs of production), and if exports are priced at the domestic level this may be at, or even below, world market prices. In this case, no dumping will be necessary in order to compete in world markets.

However, many low wage countries have high import tariffs. These may have been adopted as a revenue raising measure, or alternatively to protect a

---

[5]   Hallworth and Piracha, op. cit.
[6]   Ibid., p. 420.

domestic industry, or for both reasons. In any event, in these circumstances the domestic price level in the protectionist country would very likely settle at above the world market price, and exports would have to be dumped, in order to be competitive. In addition, the quality of the products concerned, manufactured as they have been behind high tariff barriers, may not be sufficiently high to be competitive, if charged at developed country prices.

Even relatively efficient firms in low-wage countries might, however, wish to export at prices below the domestic price level, at least for a time, perhaps in order to maximize their earnings of foreign exchange. In that case also, dumping will have taken place. Variable costs will provide a lower limit to export prices, unless one is dealing with a state-run country. Such a country might be prepared simply to maximize foreign exchange earnings, regardless of the level of its costs of production (which, in any event, may not be calculated according to market economy criteria).

In general, however, it seems implausible that low-wage countries, producing products of acceptable quality on a large scale, will need to export at dumped prices. Their levels of productivity may not be high, but their low wages, their skills and – in many instances – their high levels of output, will all help to ensure that they have low costs of production, and therefore low export prices.

China is probably the leading country to which such conditions are likely to apply, even though, as a non-market economy, subject in the past to the analogue country syndrome, it has often technically been found to have been dumping. Now however, in individual cases, when market economy conditions have been applied to Chinese exports, it has been shown that dumping is less likely to be established in these cases. When, eventually, China joins Russia in being treated as a market economy country, dumping will no doubt be even less likely to be found than under present circumstances.

9.3 COUNTRIES WITH NO IMPORT BARRIERS

It is sometimes argued that dumping can occur even in the case of countries with no import barriers, such as Hong Kong. This argument does not seem to be convincing. If such a country wished to export a 'like' commodity at a lower price than its domestic price level, arbitrageurs would readily be found who would buy up the cheap exports and re-import them, to sell at the higher domestic price. The consequence would then be to bring down the level of the domestic price.

How far the domestic price could be brought down would depend on the relative volumes of the previous domestic and export sales. If the export quantities were relatively large, the resulting domestic price would be brought down to the export price, or to somewhere near to it, so that home and export prices would be equalized. Dumping would not then arise (assuming that the domestic price was still above total costs of production). If, on the other hand, the export quantities were relatively small, the domestic price would remain above the previous export price after re-importation, and dumping would continue in the case of the remaining exports, but probably not on any significant scale.

More fundamentally, it is worth asking whether a market such as that of Hong Kong, which has no import tariffs, would find it attractive to sell at an export price below its domestic price level. Given the competitive nature of such a tariff-free market, there will be strong internal forces keeping domestic prices down to levels which give only a moderate level of profit to the marginal firm. In such circumstances, exporting at a lower price than the domestic price is unlikely to prove an attractive proposition.

It is of course true that costs might rise to such a level in a market of this sort as to render prices high by world standards. In that case there will be a strong incentive to abandon domestic production and to import the commodities concerned. Domestically based firms might choose to manufacture in a low-cost country, or in a separate customs area – mainland China, for example, in the case of Hong Kong (China). They could then import low-cost manufactures for their own use, and possibly also re-re-export them to the rest of the world. In such a situation, it is unlikely that such territories as mainland China would find it necessary to dump its exports to Hong Kong, and Hong Kong, in its turn, would not need to dump in order to re-export at competitive prices.

9.4   CONCLUSIONS ON THE PRESENT SITUATION

Concentrating, for the time being, on dumping cases initiated by developed countries, or regions such as the EU, the great majority of these have been against low-cost or relatively low-cost countries. It has been argued above that such countries often have considerably lower wage levels, and generally lower costs of production, than in the EU, for example, and might therefore have little need or incentive to sell their exports at unprofitable prices.

To prove dumping in these circumstances the developed country or region has to establish that export prices have been below 'normal value'. But in many of these cases normal value cannot, for a number of reasons, be based on actual domestic prices, and has to be artificially constructed. As has been seen in earlier chapters, several of the methods used for the construction of normal value are open to objection.

It follows from this that, in a large number of cases brought by the EU, for example, the finding that dumping has occurred has only been made possible by the construction of a 'normal value' that may have relatively little foundation in economic reality. In addition, many calculations on injury and its causation have similarly been controversial from an economic point of view. In these circumstances, grave doubts must arise on the legitimacy of much of the dumping operation of developed countries or regions.

Doubts must also arise on many of the dumping cases brought by third countries against the EU itself, for example.[7] In particular, both the USA and India have been criticized by the EU for their methods of investigating dumping cases.

Some economists have expressed the view that all anti-dumping provisions are unjustified. If a country wishes to give its exports away, the importing country should relax and enjoy the resulting cheap imports. Others have stressed the danger of allowing domestic industries to be ruined by temporarily low-priced imports. But if the above analysis is broadly correct, low priced imports into high-cost markets such as the EU are, more often than not, likely to be based on genuine low costs of production. There are doubts also about how far dumping is likely to occur in the case of exports from countries with no, or low, import barriers.

It does not therefore follow, in the circumstances of today, and given practical experience of the existing anti-dumping rules, that the application of the present rules is now the best way of tackling cases of what might be called 'unfair trade'. If properly applied, the rules may not in themselves be greatly objectionable, but the manner in which they have been applied in practice can be strongly criticized.

It is interesting that Peter Mandelson, the EU Trade Commissioner, reflected in May and June 2006 on the EU's stance on anti-dumping.[8] He strongly defended anti-dumping rules as necessary to ensure public confidence in fair trade and a fair deal for European businesses. But it was important, he said, to adapt such rules to the complexity of global markets, where manufacturers in the EU may compete with European distributors who have outsourced production, and where consumers and other manufacturers expect the benefits of wider choice and lower prices. Mandelson announced that he would seek to launch a formal reflection on the use of anti-dumping measures, probably in the second half of 2006.

It is not clear what exactly Mandelson had in mind, but it seems likely that a more liberal interpretation of the Community interest provision may be one

---

[7]   'Overview of Third Country Trade Defence Actions Against the Community', Report for 133 Committee, DG Trade B.2. 30 April 2002.

[8]   Speech to political and business leaders, Wolfsberg, Switzerland, 4 May 2006, and *Financial Times*, 8 June and 15 June 2006. This was followed by a Green Paper, 'Global Europe', Brussels, 6 December 2006, COM (2006) final

of the questions that he was considering. An attempt to widen the interpretation of this clause, a decade earlier, by Sir Leon Brittan, a former trade commissioner, did not result in an increase in the number of cases terminated on the grounds of the Community interest.

Pending the reaction to Mandelson's proposals, it is worth considering here a number of proposals for change in the anti-dumping rules have been made from time to time.

9.5   SOME PROPOSALS FOR CHANGE

The outlawing of anti-dumping action is not a practical possibility. It would, however, obviously be preferable for the anti-dumping rules themselves, and especially for their manner of implementation, to be such as to avoid damaging confrontations at the WTO, or to give rise to strongly felt criticisms. A number of proposals to amend the rules can be suggested which, it has been argued, might avoid some of the present difficulties.

Export Prices

What causes injury to the domestic industries of importing countries is low prices for its imports. The prices of the relevant commodities in their country of origin have no direct impact on these import prices. Low export prices may have been made possible by monopoly pricing in the home market of the exporter, but in other cases low export prices may have been made possible for other reasons, such as low costs. But whatever the reason for low export prices, it is their existence which gives rise to the problem for importing countries.

Consider a situation where export prices are low enough to cause injury in the importing country, yet these export prices cover the full long-term costs of producing the commodity concerned in the exporting country. Whatever the dumping rules say, why should such exports be subject to anti-dumping duties just because domestic prices in the exporting country may be higher than its export prices? The export prices concerned are low because costs are low. If these costs are lower over a significant period of time than costs in the importing countries, then not only is there a clear benefit for consumers in the importing countries, but producers there should have no long-term future in the industries concerned.

In these circumstances, it is better for the welfare of the importing country for resources to be taken out of the uncompetitive industries concerned and relocated to other, more competitive, sectors. The producers and workers in the uncompetitive industries are likely to suffer, particularly in the short to medium term, but if such changes in industrial structure were to be systematically impeded, the growth in welfare of the country concerned would be seriously hindered. It is a feature of all successful economies that their industrial structure is subject to considerable change over time.

Consider now a situation where export prices are based, not on full long-term costs of production, but on variable costs only, or on short-run marginal costs, as economists would put it. Prices set at this level are sometimes called predatory prices, reference being made in this case to a policy adopted in order to drive out the relevant industry in an importing country, while raising prices again in the long term. In practice, there are very few examples of such policies being pursued by exporting countries. They may price their exports at marginal cost, but for other reasons than to pursue such a predatory policy.

Pricing at variable cost is particularly prevalent at times of depressed demand. This may occur in domestic as well as export markets. But if domestic markets have some degree of protection, prices there may stay at above variable costs, even in slump conditions. In general, therefore, it is exports which tend to bear the brunt of marginal pricing.

It has been argued elsewhere that variable costs may not be far below full costs in most industries.[9] In such cases, pricing exports at variable cost will not be pricing them much below full cost, and to that extent the effect of low export prices (based on variable costs) on industries in importing countries may be little more objectionable than if exports were priced at full cost.

It may be the case, however, that exports are priced at variable costs which are significantly below full costs. A relevant question in this case is for how long these low export prices are likely to prevail. If they occur temporarily, at times of depressed world demand, only to be raised again at times of high demand, then this would not seem to be highly objectionable from the point of view of importing countries (where at such times variable cost pricing may well prevail on the part of their own exporting industries). If, however, low export prices based on variable costs were to persist indefinitely, then importing countries would have a legitimate cause of grievance, since their domestic industries could be seriously injured by such behaviour.

Regardless of domestic prices in exporting countries, then, there can be few legitimate objections to exports which are priced to cover full long-run costs of production. These exports might injure competing industries in importing countries, but this is all part of the process of establishing the importance of comparative advantage in world trade, and should lead to an all-round improvement in welfare in the long run.

Exports at variable cost may well be a relatively short-term phenomenon.

---

[9]   See Aubrey Silberston, 'Anti-dumping rules – time for change?', *Journal of World Trade*, December 2003.

Provided that periods of variable cost export pricing last for no more than a short period – perhaps for a few months, or for no longer than a year – there may be little justification for anti-dumping action to be taken against exports at such prices.

What this analysis comes down to, therefore, is primarily to suggest that the level of costs in exporting countries is what is relevant to the acceptability of their export prices. If their exports are priced at full long-run costs of production, no objection should be raised to these, even if domestic prices are higher than this. If their exports are priced at, or somewhat above, variable costs of production, there can be no strong objection to this, provided that such prices do not persist for long periods of time. In both these cases, the domestic price of like products in the exporting countries should be irrelevant.

Under the present rules, anti-dumping investigations always involve an investigation of costs of production in countries accused of dumping. An examination of costs would continue to be made under a system which concentrated on export prices alone. Little would apparently change, therefore, if anti-dumping actions were confined to an examination of export prices alone. The difference from the present system, however, would be that the level of the domestic price would no longer be relevant. If high import tariffs enable domestic prices to be high in the exporting country, so be it. What would matter, under this criterion, is the level of export prices, in relation to the level of costs in producing these exports, regardless of how the exporting country sustains these prices.

Having said this, it has to be recognized that, to change the rules, so that they ignore domestic prices, and concentrate on export prices alone, would be far removed from the existing system. In seeking possible changes to that system, therefore, it is probably more realistic to suggest changes that lie within the framework of the present rules. The first such change that might be considered is to concentrate anti-dumping action against what have been called cases of predatory intent.

Predatory Intent

It has been suggested that the rules should permit anti-dumping to be established only if it has been shown that there has been predatory intent on the part of the exporting country. Even if injury can be shown to have taken place, and causation has been established, action could not be taken unless predatory intent had been established also; that is, unless it has been shown that firms in the country concerned have been exporting in a manner deliberately intended to drive out rivals in the importing countries, with the implication that export prices would rise thereafter.

This is at first sight an appealing suggestion. However, as has been said, many exporting countries export at low prices because their costs are low. They hope thereby to gain new markets, but they may have no deliberate intention of behaving in a predatory manner, in the sense defined above. The effect of exporting products at low prices may of course have the consequence of driving firms in importing countries out of existence, but this may often be a normal consequence of free international trade.

The problem with the suggestion that deliberate predation should be outlawed would be the difficulty of proving whether predatory intent had been present or not. To prove injury, for example, involves some study of the relevant statistics, even though controversial conclusions may be drawn from these. But predatory intent cannot be proved from statistics. It can only be inferred from behaviour, and behaviour can be subject to many interpretations.

This is not perhaps a hopeless cause, since establishing the criterion of predatory behaviour would bear some relation to the problem of establishing abuse of a dominant position in anti-trust cases. The tests used to approve mergers could also be helpful. Possibly, therefore, it could be argued, the introduction of predatory intent into the anti-dumping regulations might introduce a hurdle of some value, and prevent some dubious decisions from being made.[10]

There is an alternative method of tackling this issue. The notion of predatory intent could be taken to mean that exports are being made at prices which cover variable costs only, or which leave only a small margin above variable costs. When the term is used in this sense, predatory intent could be demonstrated without difficulty, by a simple examination of the relevant costs. But, as has been argued above, exporting at prices based on variable costs should not necessarily be subject to anti-dumping action if such pricing occurs for a relatively short period of time.

There would be point in outlawing predatory intent, therefore, only if this were defined more generally, that is, action aimed at short term aggression to gain long-term advantage. But in view of the difficult problems of proof that would arise in such a case, the conclusion must be that it scarcely seems worthwhile for a general predatory intent provision to be added to the anti-dumping regulations.

Statistical Tests

Another suggestion is that anti-dumping action should not be taken unless certain statistical tests had been satisfied. In particular, relatively small market

---

[10]   For an account of recent economic theories of predation, see: Miguel de la Mano and Benoit Durand, *A Three-Step Structured Rule of Reason to Assess Predation under Article 82*, Office of the Chief Economist, Discussion Paper, Directorate General for Competition, European Commission, 12 December 2005.

penetration of an import market over a given period, by a single exporting country, might not be regarded as injury.

There is already provision to exclude low market penetration, in Article 5.8 of the AD Agreement. There it is stated that the volume of dumped imports should normally be regarded as negligible if the volume of imports from a particular country is found to account for less than 3 per cent of imports of the like product in the importing Member (unless countries which individually account for less than 3 per cent collectively account for more than 7 per cent of imports of the like product). The EU, on the other hand, has a *de minimis* provision relating to imports which represent 1 per cent or less (or 3 per cent collectively) of market penetration in the importing country.

These provisions could possibly be widened. For example, in the EU case the first 2 per cent of market penetration by an exporting country, during the period under review, might be ignored. Or, simply, any 2 per cent increase in penetration, over a given period, by an exporting country, might not be regarded as injury. The 3 per cent import figure of the AD Agreement could similarly be increased.

Whether the market in the importing country is a new one might also be regarded as relevant. It could be that, from the beginning, imports make up the bulk of market supply. It can be argued that in cases of this sort domestic manufacturers have been prevented from taking a substantial share of the new market, and have therefore been injured by the imports. But it could be the case that the imports are inherently cheaper, or technically better, than the potential domestic product. In such a situation, domestic manufacturers would be inherently uncompetitive. It could reasonably be argued therefore that the imports have not caused injury to the (scarcely existent) domestic industry.

Another relevant consideration might be whether the domestic market is expanding or declining. If it is expanding, then both domestic manufacturers and importers have the opportunity to expand with it. If imports represent a roughly constant share of the expanding market then it might be thought appropriate for any dumping on the part of exporters to be ignored. If, on the other hand, the domestic market is declining, then both domestic manufacturers and importers have to recognize the situation. If the total market is declining at a rapid rate – say 10 per cent per annum or more – then dumping is likely to be almost irrelevant to the declining health of the industry concerned. In such a case also, dumping by an exporter might be treated leniently.

There is, however, an obvious problem if statistical tests were to be applied more widely. This is that it would probably be difficult to reach general agreement on what changes in import or market shares should be ignored for anti-dumping purposes. A different test might therefore be more likely to be acceptable. Such a test might concern not import or market shares but the level of import barriers in exporting countries.

Low Import Barriers

Where import barriers in a country are low, it has been argued earlier, there will not be the opportunity to keep out low-priced imports in order to maintain high domestic prices. The opportunity to charge high domestic prices, in order to subsidize dumped exports, will not therefore exist. Domestic prices are likely to be largely based on costs of production. Export prices are unlikely to be far below the domestic price level, if they are below it at all.

It is suggested, therefore, that consideration should be given to amending the anti-dumping rules to add a provision requiring an investigation of the level of tariffs on the product concerned in the exporting country. Where the level of tariffs (or other barriers to imports) is relatively low, and no subsidies have been involved, the presumption should be that both domestic and export prices are likely to be 'fair', and should therefore be exempt from anti-dumping measures.

If the rules were amended in this way, there would of course have to be a definition of a tariff which was 'low'. It should not, however, be difficult to obtain agreement on this. Any level below, say, 10 per cent, might perhaps be held to qualify as a low tariff. The advantage of such a regulation would be to remove from consideration a number of cases which objective observers might barely regard as dumping. In addition, and more important, it would put considerable pressure on exporting countries to lower their tariff levels. The EU now puts much emphasis on market access, and complains, reasonably enough, that many major exporters to the EU maintain high tariffs, thus denying access to EU products. If, however, the level of tariffs in exporting countries became an issue in anti-dumping cases, this might prove a powerful weapon in helping to transform their market access situation.

A new rule of this sort would of course bring about a radical change. It would simplify many anti-dumping investigations and make them more transparent. It would also help to bring the anti-dumping rules into line with the economic realities of the whole process, and align them more closely with the often expressed desire for trade to be 'fair'. It should remove from consideration several of the cases that are at present widely regarded as unfair by countries accused of dumping, and should help the exports of low-wage countries, once they have brought down their levels of import tariffs.

It is no doubt unrealistic to hope that this particular change, or indeed any of the other proposals for change outlined above, will be incorporated in the anti-dumping rules in the foreseeable future. But even if they are not, the arguments that have been adduced in favour of the various changes might usefully be borne in mind when anti-dumping investigations are taking place. In particular, for both political and diplomatic reasons, it is desirable that anti-dumping action be approached with hesitancy when exporters with low costs of production are concerned, or when action is contemplated against exports from low-tariff countries.

10. Conclusions and recommendations

The bulk of this study has concerned problems that arise in connection with the present rules and practices relating to subsidies and countervailing action, on the one hand, and anti-dumping action, on the other. The light thrown on many of these problems may help the authorities concerned, and also those accused of dumping or of receiving subsidies, to structure their cases more satisfactorily than at present. A number of the problems that have been highlighted cannot, however, be solved readily within the existing framework of laws and regulations.

Considering that the existing laws and regulations were last enacted or amended as a result of the Uruguay Round, that is in 1995 or 1996, the likelihood that further changes can be contemplated in the comparatively near future is probably not high. Even so, it is worth suggesting changes to the existing situation that would be desirable, in the light of the analysis that has been carried out in this study, especially in Chapters 5, 6, 7 and 9. The explanations given there will be rehearsed only briefly in the present chapter.

10.1 ANTI-DUMPING ACTION

The regulations concerning anti-dumping action are contained in the AD Agreement and in the national measures implementing this in the different WTO members, of which the EU AD Regulation is a leading example. The presentation in the AD Agreement, and in most implementing legislation, begins with a consideration of normal value and of export price, leading to the calculation of the dumping margin. Then follows a consideration of injury, and (in the case of the EU) of Community interest. Each of these major headings raises questions that might best be addressed by changes to the AD Agreement and the national legislation which implements this Agreement. Only the most important of these questions give rise to the recommendations that follow.

10.1.1 Normal Value and Export Price

The determination of normal value raises a number of problems. In particular, the question arises whether a similar product to that allegedly being dumped in export markets, is being manufactured in the exporting country. It is frequently found that such a like product is not being manufactured domestically, or is being manufactured only in small quantities. In these circumstances the normal value may be established on the basis of the prices of other sellers or producers, usually in the domestic market concerned.

This procedure may give some guidance as to normal value, but it is clearly not very convincing. Where, however, there are no sales, or insufficient sales, of the like product, the normal value must be calculated on the basis of the costs of production of the exports concerned in the country of origin, plus a reasonable amount for SG&A (selling, general and administrative costs) and profit.

What this amounts to in practice therefore is to rule out costs of production of domestic sales as a measure of normal value, and to concentrate on the costs of production of export sales. Surely this is in any event the logical procedure? It leads to our first recommendation.

Recommendation I: concentrate only on the costs of production for export sales.

This would apply whether or not a like product was being produced domestically. It focuses attention on what really matters: whether or not export sales are at prices which cover their full costs of production. The domestic price is irrelevant to this, however high or low it may be. If export prices cover full production costs, then no anti-dumping action should be possible.

If, however, full costs are not being covered by exports the question of pricing at variable costs arises. The pricing of exports at variable costs is sometimes called pricing with 'predatory intent'. Whatever this pricing practice is called, however, there are periods when the state of the world market is such that competition is fierce. Exports from many countries can only be made at prices based on variable costs, plus a small profit margin. During other periods the world market is strong, and export prices which cover full costs can be charged.

If, over a period of time, the prices of export sales cover full costs of production, then, it is suggested, pricing at variable costs should not give rise to anti-dumping action. This means that the investigation period, although confined for most purposes to the normal 12 months, should also include consideration of a longer period of time as regards pricing. Putting this another way, pricing at variable costs for relatively short periods of time – possibly six months or a year – should be exempt from anti-dumping action, as long as experience shows that prices are likely to rise again over a longer period of time.

Recommendation II: pricing exports at variable costs is acceptable for relatively short periods of time.

It has been suggested in Chapter 9 that exporting territories which have low import barriers, or none at all, such as Hong Kong, are unlikely to be able to export at dumped prices. This is because they are unlikely to be able to charge monopolistic prices in their domestic markets for most commodities. Domestic prices will not normally yield high profit margins, because of the pressure of imports. Exports will therefore have to make their own contribution to profitability, and will not be able to rely on domestic sales to make the bulk of profits. Their prices are unlikely to be far below the domestic price level, if they are below it at all, and in particular are normally likely to cover full costs of production.

It is suggested therefore that consideration should be given to amending the anti-dumping rules to add a provision requiring an investigation of the level of tariffs (or other barriers) on the product concerned in the exporting country. Where there are no other barriers and no subsidies, and the level of tariffs is low (say, below 10 per cent), the presumption should be that the exports concerned should be exempt from anti-dumping measures.

Recommendation III: countries with low import barriers should not be subject to anti-dumping action.

Even in the absence of such a change in the rules, it would be desirable, for the reasons given, for the authorities in the importing country or countries to have regard, in the course of their investigations, to the existence of low import barriers in the exporting country.

10.1.2 The Dumping Margin

There are three methods laid down in the rules for calculating the dumping margin, that is, the difference between normal value and the export price. These can be summarized as the First Symmetrical Method (comparing weighted average normal value with weighted average export price), the Second Symmetrical Method (comparing individual normal values and individual export prices) and the Asymmetrical Method (comparing weighted average normal value with the prices of individual export transactions).

It was pointed out in Chapter 6 that, in considering the merits of each of these methods, the question of zeroing arises: whether to give cases of negative dumping a value of zero. The First Symmetrical Method does not distinguish between cases of positive and negative dumping, so the question of zeroing does not arise in this case. In any event, the WTO, in the *Indian bedlinen case*, ruled out zeroing when the First Symmetrical Method is employed to calculate the dumping margin.

Recommendation IV: zeroing should not be employed to calculate the dumping margin when the First Symmetrical Method is used.

It has also been pointed out, however (see Chapter 6) that the possibility, in the AD Agreement, of using the Asymmetrical Method to calculate the dumping margin implies that zeroing is acceptable in this case. There is otherwise no point in differentiating this method from the First Symmetrical Method. In addition, there is a good theoretical case, when using the Asymmetrical Method, to employ zeroing when it appears that certain markets are being targeted to yield either high or low prices. There has, however, been no WTO ruling regarding the question of employing zeroing in circumstances when the use of the Asymmetrical Method is justified.

Recommendation V: the employment of zeroing should be considered only when the use of the Asymmetrical Method is justified.

There has been a recent WTO ruling[1] regarding the Second Symmetrical Method, but this method is used so rarely that it does not seem to call for any recommendation at this stage.

10.1.3   Non-market Economy Countries

As explained in Chapters 2 and 5, the EU AD Regulation lays down that, in the case of imports from non-market economy countries, normal value shall be determined on the basis of the price or constructed value in a market economy third country. There are other possibilities (for example, the price of exports from such a third country), but these are rarely called upon.

The inclusion of this provision is understandable, since non-market economy countries present a real problem. This applies to any attempt to determine the full cost of their exports as well as to the determination of the appropriate normal value. Nevertheless, in spite of efforts by the EU Authorities and other authorities, inappropriate market economy third countries have frequently been selected as analogues. The problem is less serious than it was, since Russia is now treated as a market economy country, and some Chinese firms are granted market economy status, but the core problem remains.

Even if a country such as China were granted market economy status a number of problems would remain, and on occasions an analogue country might have to be called upon. But nevertheless the analogue country procedure is inherently unsatisfactory. This has been shown in the case of Chinese firms given market economy treatment, where the dumping margin has usually been

---

[1]   See p. 88 (note 22).

found to be much lower than when an analogue country has been selected to provide normal value. There is no easy solution, but, in spite of all the problems involved, it would seem to be a better solution to abandon the analogue country method altogether. It would be more satisfactory to use what records exist, in non-market economy cases, and build on these to construct an appropriate normal value. In particular, regard should be had to the situation of firms selling a like product in the same country, where they exist, which have been granted market economy status.

> Recommendation VI: the analogue method of determining normal value, in the case of non-market economies, should be abandoned in favour of building on what records exist in these countries, particularly those relating to comparable firms in the same country which have been granted market economy status.

10.1.4 Injury

As was pointed out in Chapter 4, the determination that the relevant industry in the importing country has been injured raises a number of problems. In addition, the determination that only part of any injury found has been caused by dumping raises yet more problems. There is, however, no solution to this situation, other than for the investigating authority to approach the issue of injury with great care. For example, as recent studies have shown, macroeconomic conditions in importing countries may stimulate anti-dumping action, rather than any actual dumping by exporters, and this needs to be borne in mind in injury investigations.

It is to the credit of some investigating authorities, including the EU Authorities, that they normally employ considerable care in their injury investigations.

A finding of injury may trigger the imposition of anti-dumping duties. Anti-dumping duties, or countervailing measures, are intended to raise import prices sufficiently to prevent further injury on account of dumped or subsidized imports. Such measures have regard to the lesser duty rule, where this is employed. It has been pointed out in Chapter 4, however, that the calculation of the appropriate level of duties normally takes no account of the effect of these duties on capacity utilization in the relevant industry in the importing country. The *Cellulose acetate yarn case* was an exception, in that this effect was considered, since it was acknowledged in this case that the imposition of duties would raise capacity utilization in the Community industry concerned. Costs of production would therefore be lowered, since overheads would be spread over a larger output than formerly.

It is desirable that this practice normally be used in considering the level of duties to be imposed.

Recommendation VII: take the effect on capacity utilization in the injured industry into account when deciding on the level of duties to be imposed.

10.1.5   Community interest

The application of the Community interest clause in the EU AD Regulation and the EU AS Regulation has rarely modified conclusions regarding the desirability or otherwise of introducing anti-dumping or countervailing measures. This has led to criticism of the EU Authorities on the grounds that they favour, over other interests (notably those of consumers) the interests of the Community industry that has been injured by the dumped or subsidized imports. In 1997, Sir Leon Brittan, then Vice-President of the Commission, tried to get the Community interest clause applied more widely. This appears to have had only a minor effect. The Commission goes through the motions of considering the effect of any contemplated duties on processing industries and also on consumers, but even so it appears to give much the greatest weight to the Community industry that has been injured.

The Community interest clause sounds liberal and impressive, therefore, and is often appealed to by the more liberal Member States, but in practice it is virtually a dead letter.

Recommendation VIII: in EU anti-dumping and anti-subsidy investigations the EU Authorities must take fully into account all affected interests, and not just those of the injured Community industry. The same recommendation could be made, *mutatis mutandis*, for all investigating authorities that apply a general public interest test similar to the EU Community interest test. It is also highly desirable that a formal general public interest test be instituted in those countries which do not yet have one.

10.2   SUBSIDIES AND COUNTERVAILING ACTION

The definition of injury for the purposes of countervailing action is the same as for anti-dumping action and no further comment need be made about this here.

For the purposes of countervailing investigations, the determination of the amount of the subsidy raises various difficulties. Our recommendations in this area are all designed to introduce objectivity and coherence into the calculation. We have seen, in Chapter 7, how there is a close interrelation between the determination of the amount of dumping and the determination of the amount of subsidy. This close relationship argues in favour of conducting anti-dumping and countervailing proceedings at the same time. This is generally the practice of the European Commission, but not always. In the case of *PET film from India*, a countervailing duty was imposed in 1999 and then an anti-dumping duty was imposed in 2001. For the purposes of determining the anti-dumping duty the total dumping margin was calculated, and then the margin of subsidization was deducted, pursuant to Article VI(5) of GATT 1947. However, the margin of subsidization deducted was not that calculated contemporaneously with the margin of dumping, but that determined in the earlier investigation in 1999. This was inconsistent with the principle that the amount of the anti-dumping duty must be determined by reference to all the information available in the investigation period. The degree of subsidization could have changed since 1999, but the Commission did not look into this. As a result, it determined the amount of the anti-dumping duty by reference, in part, to information from a prior investigation period. The effect of this is that the five-year reviews of the anti-dumping and the countervailing duties have been out of phase with each other, and so the problem continues. It is recommended as follows:

> Recommendation IX: anti-dumping and countervailing proceedings against the same country should be run contemporaneously. If, for any reason, an anti-dumping (or countervailing) duty is already in place when an anti-subsidy (or anti-dumping) investigation is opened, a review of the already existing countervailing (or anti-dumping) duty should be opened at the same time, so that the determinations of dumping and subsidization should be based on contemporaneous data.

Related to this recommendation, and following on from the discussion in Chapter 7, it is also recommended as follows:

> Recommendation X: when dumping and subsidization exist contemporaneously, care needs to be taken in applying Article VI(5) of GATT 1995. Although, as a general rule, the margin of export subsidization should be deducted from the total dumping margin in order to determine the amount of anti-dumping duty, this rule should not be applied blindly. In each case the methodology used in the anti-dumping investigation must be examined carefully to ensure that there is neither double imposition of duties nor double deduction of the subsidy margin.

Two issues which we discussed in Chapter 7 were the allocation of subsidies on a per unit basis rather than in proportion to turnover, and the possibility that certain subsidies are of a hybrid nature. In both cases our objective was to show that there is no universally right or wrong way of allocating subsidies. It is necessary to examine the facts of each individual case. We saw how the allocation of subsidies on a per unit basis takes into account differences in unit pricing, and so is perhaps more appropriate in cases where anti-dumping duties are also imposed. We also saw how certain export subsidies can nevertheless benefit production for the domestic market and so should more appropriately be allocated over total production rather than just over export sales. Our objective each time has been to inquire into the most appropriate method of allocation, while recognizing that the answer to this question can depend very much on the precise nature of the subsidy. We will therefore limit ourselves to a general recommendation:

Recommendation XI: there should be no immutable rule that all subsidies which are contingent on export performance should be allocated over export sales. It is necessary to examine the nature of the subsidy in question and the way it is likely to affect the exporter's behaviour in order to determine which is the most appropriate basis of allocation. The same approach applies to the question whether subsidies should be allocated on a per unit or per value basis. The fact that anti-dumping action is also envisaged may be relevant in this respect.

Last of all, for the reasons argued at length in Chapter 7, and in a spirit of financial and economic correctness, the following has to be recommended:

Recommendation XII: no interest charge should be added to subsidies accruing in respect of exports or purchases which are expensed in the year, that is to say, which are not amortized over two or more years. In the case of subsidies linked to the acquisition of fixed assets which are depreciated over more than one year, the amount of the subsidy to be allocated to the investigation period should be determined using discounted cash flow techniques and an appropriate rate of interest.

10.3   FINAL THOUGHTS

In the light of these recommendations, a number of amendments might usefully be made in the long run to the WTO Anti-Dumping and Subsidies Agreements (and hence to the EU, US and other national measures implementing these agreements). In the short run, it is unlikely that substantial changes in the legislation will be made. In the meanwhile, it is hoped that those authorities having recourse to anti-dumping or countervailing actions might take into consideration in their analyses, as far as this is possible, the recommendations that we have made in this study.

Appendix 1 Article VI of GATT 1947

ANTI-DUMPING AND COUNTERVAILING DUTIES

1. The contracting parties recognize that dumping, by which products of one country are introduced into the commerce of another country at less than the normal value of the products, is to be condemned if it causes or threatens material injury to an established industry in the territory of a contracting party or materially retards the establishment of a domestic industry. For the purposes of this Article, a product is to be considered as being introduced into the commerce of an importing country at less than its normal value, if the price of the product exported from one country to another:

(a) is less than the comparable price, in the ordinary course of trade, for the like product when destined for consumption in the exporting country, or,

(b) in the absence of such domestic price, is less than either

 (i) the highest comparable price for the like product for export to any third country in the ordinary course of trade, or

 (ii) the cost of production of the product in the country of origin plus a reasonable addition for selling cost and profit.

Due allowance shall be made in each case for differences in conditions and terms of sale, for differences in taxation, and for other differences affecting price comparability.

2. In order to offset or prevent dumping, a contracting party may levy on any dumped product an anti-dumping duty not greater in amount than the margin of dumping in respect of such product. For the purposes of this Article, the margin of dumping is the price difference determined in accordance with the provisions of paragraph 1.

3. No countervailing duty shall be levied on any product of the territory of any contracting party imported into the territory of another contracting party in excess of an amount equal to the estimated bounty or subsidy determined to have been granted, directly or indirectly, on the manufacture, production or export of such product in the country of origin or exportation, including any special subsidy to the transportation of a particular product.

The term 'countervailing duty' shall be understood to mean a special duty levied for the purpose of offsetting any bounty or subsidy bestowed, directly, or indirectly, upon the manufacture, production or export of any merchandise.

4. No product of the territory of any contracting party imported into the territory of any other contracting party shall be subject to anti-dumping or countervailing duty by reason of the exemption of such product from duties or taxes borne by the like product when destined for consumption in the country of origin or exportation, or by reason of the refund of such duties or taxes.

5. No product of the territory of any contracting party imported into the territory of any other contracting party shall be subject to both anti-dumping and countervailing duties to compensate for the same situation of dumping or export subsidization.

6. (a) No contracting party shall levy any anti-dumping or countervailing duty on the importation of any product of the territory of another contracting party unless it determines that the effect of the dumping or subsidization, as the case may be, is such as to cause or threaten material injury to an established domestic industry, or is such as to retard materially the establishment of a domestic industry.

(b) The CONTRACTING PARTIES may waive the requirement of subparagraph (a) of this paragraph so as to permit a contracting party to levy an anti-dumping or countervailing duty on the importation of any product for the purpose of offsetting dumping or subsidization which causes or threatens material injury to an industry in the territory of another contracting party exporting the product concerned to the territory of the importing contracting party. The CONTRACTING PARTIES shall waive the requirements of subparagraph (a) of this paragraph, so as to permit the levying of a countervailing duty, in cases in which they find that a subsidy is causing or threatening material injury to an industry in the territory of another contracting party exporting the product concerned to the territory of the importing contracting party.

(c) In exceptional circumstances, however, where delay might cause damage which would be difficult to repair, a contracting party may levy a countervailing duty for the purpose referred to in subparagraph (b) of this paragraph without the prior approval of the CONTRACTING PARTIES; Provided that such action shall be reported immediately to the CONTRACTING PARTIES and that the countervailing duty shall be withdrawn promptly if the CONTRACTING PARTIES disapprove.

7. A system for the stabilization of the domestic price or of the return to domestic producers of a primary commodity, independently of the movements of export prices, which results at times in the sale of the commodity for export at a price lower than the comparable price charged for the like

commodity to buyers in the domestic market, shall be presumed not to result in material injury within the meaning of paragraph 6 if it is determined by consultation among the contracting parties substantially interested in the commodity concerned that:

(a) the system has also resulted in the sale of the commodity for export at a price higher than the comparable price charged for the like commodity to buyers in the domestic market, and

(b) the system is so operated, either because of the effective regulation of production, or otherwise, as not to stimulate exports unduly or otherwise seriously prejudice the interests of other contracting parties.

NOTES TO ARTICLE VI

Paragraph 1

1. Hidden dumping by associated houses (that is, the sale by an importer at a price below that corresponding to the price invoiced by an exporter with whom the importer is associated, and also below the price in the exporting country) constitutes a form of price dumping with respect to which the margin of dumping may be calculated on the basis of the price at which the goods are resold by the importer.

2. It is recognised that, in the case of imports from a country which has a complete or substantially complete monopoly of its trade and where all domestic prices are fixed by the State, special difficulties may exist in determining price comparability for the purposes of paragraph 1, and in such cases importing contracting parties may find it necessary to take into account the possibility that a strict comparison with domestic prices in such a country may not always be appropriate.

Paragraphs 2 and 3

1. As in many other cases in customs administration, a contracting party may require reasonable security (bond or cash deposit) for the payment of anti-dumping or countervailing duty pending final determination of the facts in any case of suspected dumping or subsidisation.

2. Multiple currency practices can in certain circumstances constitute a subsidy to exports which may be met by countervailing duties under paragraph 3 or can constitute a form of dumping by means of a partial depreciation of a country's currency which may be met by action under paragraph 2. By 'multiple currency practices' is meant practices by governments or sanctioned by governments.

Paragraph 6 (b)

Waivers under the provisions of this subparagraph shall be granted only on application by the contracting party proposing to levy an anti-dumping or countervailing duty, as the case may be.

Appendix 2 Agreement on Implementation of Article VI of GATT 1994 (AD Agreement)

Members hereby agree as follows:

PART I

Article 1

Principles

An anti-dumping measure shall be applied only under the circumstances provided for in Article VI of GATT 1994 and pursuant to investigations initiated[1] and conducted in accordance with the provisions of this Agreement. The following provisions govern the application of Article VI of GATT 1994 in so far as action is taken under anti-dumping legislation or regulations.

Article 2

Determination of Dumping

2.1 For the purpose of this Agreement, a product is to be considered as being dumped, i.e. introduced into the commerce of another country at less than its normal value, if the export price of the product exported from one country to another is less than the comparable price, in the ordinary course of trade, for the like product when destined for consumption in the exporting country.

2.2 When there are no sales of the like product in the ordinary course of trade in the domestic market of the exporting country or when, because of the particular market situation or the low volume of the sales in the domestic market of the exporting country,[2] such sales do not permit a proper comparison,

---

[1] The term 'initiated' as used in this Agreement means the procedural action by which a Member formally commences an investigation as provided in Article 5.

[2] Sales of the like product destined for consumption in the domestic market of the exporting country shall normally be considered a sufficient quantity for the

the margin of dumping shall be determined by comparison with a comparable price of the like product when exported to an appropriate third country, provided that this price is representative, or with the cost of production in the country of origin plus a reasonable amount for administrative, selling and general costs and for profits.

2.2.1 Sales of the like product in the domestic market of the exporting country or sales to a third country at prices below per unit (fixed and variable) costs of production plus administrative, selling and general costs may be treated as not being in the ordinary course of trade by reason of price and may be disregarded in determining normal value only if the authorities[3] determine that such sales are made within an extended period of time[4] in substantial quantities[5] and are at prices which do not provide for the recovery of all costs within a reasonable period of time. If prices which are below per unit costs at the time of sale are above weighted average per unit costs for the period of investigation, such prices shall be considered to provide for recovery of costs within a reasonable period of time.

2.2.1.1 For the purpose of paragraph 2, costs shall normally be calculated on the basis of records kept by the exporter or producer under investigation, provided that such records are in accordance with the generally accepted accounting principles of the exporting country and reasonably reflect the costs associated with the production and sale of the product under consideration. Authorities shall consider all available evidence on the proper allocation of costs, including that which is made available by the exporter or producer in the course of the investigation provided that such allocations have been histori-cally utilized by the exporter or producer, in particular in relation to establish-ing appropriate amortization and depreciation periods and allowances for capital expenditures and other development costs. Unless already reflected in the cost allocations under this subparagraph, costs shall be adjusted appropri-ately for those non-recurring items of cost which benefit future and/or current

---

determination of the normal value if such sales constitute 5 per cent or more of the sales of the product under consideration to the importing Member, provided that a lower ratio should be acceptable where the evidence demonstrates that domestic sales at such lower ratio are nonetheless of sufficient magnitude to provide for a proper comparison.

   [3]   When in this Agreement the term 'authorities' is used, it shall be interpreted as meaning authorities at an appropriate senior level.

   [4]   The extended period of time should normally be one year but shall in no case be less than six months.

   [5]   Sales below per unit costs are made in substantial quantities when the author-ities establish that the weighted average selling price of the transactions under consid-eration for the determination of the normal value is below the weighted average per unit costs, or that the volume of sales below per unit costs represents not less than 20 per cent of the volume sold in transactions under consideration for the determination of the normal value.

production, or for circumstances in which costs during the period of investigation are affected by start-up operations.[6]

2.2.2 For the purpose of paragraph 2, the amounts for administrative, selling and general costs and for profits shall be based on actual data pertaining to production and sales in the ordinary course of trade of the like product by the exporter or producer under investigation. When such amounts cannot be determined on this basis, the amounts may be determined on the basis of:

(i) the actual amounts incurred and realised by the exporter or producer in question in respect of production and sales in the domestic market of the country of origin of the same general category of products;

(ii) the weighted average of the actual amounts incurred and realised by other exporters or producers subject to investigation in respect of production and sales of the like product in the domestic market of the country of origin;

(iii) any other reasonable method, provided that the amount for profit so established shall not exceed the profit normally realised by other exporters or producers on sales of products of the same general category in the domestic market of the country of origin.

2.3 In cases where there is no export price or where it appears to the authorities concerned that the export price is unreliable because of association or a compensatory arrangement between the exporter and the importer or a third party, the export price may be constructed on the basis of the price at which the imported products are first resold to an independent buyer, or if the products are not resold to an independent buyer, or not resold in the condition as imported, on such reasonable basis as the authorities may determine.

2.4 A fair comparison shall be made between the export price and the normal value. This comparison shall be made at the same level of trade, normally at the ex-factory level, and in respect of sales made at as nearly as possible the same time. Due allowance shall be made in each case, on its merits, for differences which affect price comparability, including differences in conditions and terms of sale, taxation, levels of trade, quantities, physical characteristics, and any other differences which are also demonstrated to affect price comparability.[7] In the cases referred to in paragraph 3, allowances for costs, including duties and taxes, incurred between importation and resale, and for profits accruing, should also be made. If in these cases price comparability has been affected, the

---

[6] The adjustment made for start-up operations shall reflect the costs at the end of the start-up period or, if that period extends beyond the period of investigation, the most recent costs which can reasonably be taken into account by the authorities during the investigation.

[7] It is understood that some of the above factors may overlap, and authorities shall ensure that they do not duplicate adjustments that have been already made under this provision.

authorities shall establish the normal value at a level of trade equivalent to the level of trade of the constructed export price, or shall make due allowance as warranted under this paragraph. The authorities shall indicate to the parties in question what information is necessary to ensure a fair comparison and shall not impose an unreasonable burden of proof on those parties.

2.4.1 When the comparison under paragraph 4 requires a conversion of currencies, such conversion should be made using the rate of exchange on the date of sale,[8] provided that when a sale of foreign currency on forward markets is directly linked to the export sale involved, the rate of exchange in the forward sale shall be used. Fluctuations in exchange rates shall be ignored and in an investigation the authorities shall allow exporters at least 60 days to have adjusted their export prices to reflect sustained movements in exchange rates during the period of investigation.

2.4.2 Subject to the provisions governing fair comparison in paragraph 4, the existence of margins of dumping during the investigation phase shall normally be established on the basis of a comparison of a weighted average normal value with a weighted average of prices of all comparable export transactions or by a comparison of normal value and export prices on a transaction-to-transaction basis. A normal value established on a weighted average basis may be compared to prices of individual export transactions if the authorities find a pattern of export prices which differ significantly among different purchasers, regions or time periods, and if an explanation is provided as to why such differences cannot be taken into account appropriately by the use of a weighted average-to-weighted average or transaction-to-transaction comparison.

2.5 In the case where products are not imported directly from the country of origin but are exported to the importing Member from an intermediate country, the price at which the products are sold from the country of export to the importing Member shall normally be compared with the comparable price in the country of export. However, comparison may be made with the price in the country of origin, if, for example, the products are merely transshipped through the country of export, or such products are not produced in the country of export, or there is no comparable price for them in the country of export.

2.6 Throughout this Agreement the term 'like product' ('produit similaire') shall be interpreted to mean a product which is identical, i.e. alike in all respects to the product under consideration, or in the absence of such a product, another product which, although not alike in all respects, has characteristics closely resembling those of the product under consideration.

---

8   Normally, the date of sale would be the date of contract, purchase order, order confirmation, or invoice, whichever establishes the material terms of sale.

2.7 This Article is without prejudice to the second Supplementary Provision to paragraph 1 of Article VI in Annex I to GATT 1994.

Article 3

Determination of Injury[9]

3.1 A determination of injury for purposes of Article VI of GATT 1994 shall be based on positive evidence and involve an objective examination of both (a) the volume of the dumped imports and the effect of the dumped imports on prices in the domestic market for like products, and (b) the consequent impact of these imports on domestic producers of such products.

3.2 With regard to the volume of the dumped imports, the investigating authorities shall consider whether there has been a significant increase in dumped imports, either in absolute terms or relative to production or consumption in the importing Member. With regard to the effect of the dumped imports on prices, the investigating authorities shall consider whether there has been a significant price undercutting by the dumped imports as compared with the price of a like product of the importing Member, or whether the effect of such imports is otherwise to depress prices to a significant degree or prevent price increases, which otherwise would have occurred, to a significant degree. No one or several of these factors can necessarily give decisive guidance.

3.3 Where imports of a product from more than one country are simultaneously subject to anti-dumping investigations, the investigating authorities may cumulatively assess the effects of such imports only if they determine that (a) the margin of dumping established in relation to the imports from each country is more than *de minimis* as defined in paragraph 8 of Article 5 and the volume of imports from each country is not negligible and (b) a cumulative assessment of the effects of the imports is appropriate in light of the conditions of competition between the imported products and the conditions of competition between the imported products and the like domestic product.

3.4 The examination of the impact of the dumped imports on the domestic industry concerned shall include an evaluation of all relevant economic factors and indices having a bearing on the state of the industry, including actual and potential decline in sales, profits, output, market share, productivity, return on investments, or utilization of capacity; factors affecting domestic prices; the magnitude of the margin of dumping; actual and potential negative effects on

---

[9]   Under this Agreement the term 'injury' shall, unless otherwise specified, be taken to mean material injury to a domestic industry, threat of material injury to a domestic industry or material retardation of the establishment of such an industry and shall be interpreted in accordance with the provisions of this Article.

cash flow, inventories, employment, wages, growth, ability to raise capital or investments. This list is not exhaustive, nor can one or several of these factors necessarily give decisive guidance.

3.5 It must be demonstrated that the dumped imports are, through the effects of dumping, as set forth in paragraphs 2 and 4, causing injury within the meaning of this Agreement. The demonstration of a causal relationship between the dumped imports and the injury to the domestic industry shall be based on an examination of all relevant evidence before the authorities. The authorities shall also examine any known factors other than the dumped imports which at the same time are injuring the domestic industry, and the injuries caused by these other factors must not be attributed to the dumped imports. Factors which may be relevant in this respect include, inter alia, the volume and prices of imports not sold at dumping prices, contraction in demand or changes in the patterns of consumption, trade restrictive practices of and competition between the foreign and domestic producers, developments in technology and the export performance and productivity of the domestic industry.

3.6 The effect of the dumped imports shall be assessed in relation to the domestic production of the like product when available data permit the separate identification of that production on the basis of such criteria as the production process, producers' sales and profits. If such separate identification of that production is not possible, the effects of the dumped imports shall be assessed by the examination of the production of the narrowest group or range of products, which includes the like product, for which the necessary information can be provided.

3.7 A determination of a threat of material injury shall be based on facts and not merely on allegation, conjecture or remote possibility. The change in circumstances which would create a situation in which the dumping would cause injury must be clearly foreseen and imminent.[10] In making a determination regarding the existence of a threat of material injury, the authorities should consider, inter alia, such factors as:

(i) a significant rate of increase of dumped imports into the domestic market indicating the likelihood of substantially increased importation;

(ii) sufficient freely disposable, or an imminent, substantial increase in, capacity of the exporter indicating the likelihood of substantially increased dumped exports to the importing Member's market, taking into account the availability of other export markets to absorb any additional exports;

(iii) whether imports are entering at prices that will have a significant

---

[10] One example, though not an exclusive one, is that there is convincing reason to believe that there will be, in the near future, substantially increased importation of the product at dumped prices.

depressing or suppressing effect on domestic prices, and would likely increase demand for further imports; and

(iv) inventories of the product being investigated.

No one of these factors by itself can necessarily give decisive guidance but the totality of the factors considered must lead to the conclusion that further dumped exports are imminent and that, unless protective action is taken, material injury would occur.

3.8 With respect to cases where injury is threatened by dumped imports, the application of anti-dumping measures shall be considered and decided with special care.

Article 4

Definition of Domestic Industry

4.1 For the purposes of this Agreement, the term 'domestic industry' shall be interpreted as referring to the domestic producers as a whole of the like products or to those of them whose collective output of the products constitutes a major proportion of the total domestic production of those products, except that:

(i) when producers are related[11] to the exporters or importers or are themselves importers of the allegedly dumped product, the term 'domestic industry' may be interpreted as referring to the rest of the producers;

(ii) in exceptional circumstances the territory of a Member may, for the production in question, be divided into two or more competitive markets and the producers within each market may be regarded as a separate industry if (a) the producers within such market sell all or almost all of their production of the product in question in that market, and (b) the demand in that market is not to any substantial degree supplied by producers of the product in question located elsewhere in the territory. In such circumstances, injury may be found to exist even where a major portion of the total domestic industry is not injured, provided there is a concentration of dumped imports into such an isolated market and provided further that the dumped imports are causing injury to the producers of all or almost all of the production within such market.

---

[11]   For the purpose of this paragraph, producers shall be deemed to be related to exporters or importers only if *(a)* one of them directly or indirectly controls the other; or *(b)* both of them are directly or indirectly controlled by a third person; or *(c)* together they directly or indirectly control a third person, provided that there are grounds for believing or suspecting that the effect of the relationship is such as to cause the producer concerned to behave differently from non-related producers. For the purpose of this paragraph, one shall be deemed to control another when the former is legally or operationally in a position to exercise restraint or direction over the latter.

4.2 When the domestic industry has been interpreted as referring to the producers in a certain area, i.e. a market as defined in paragraph 1(ii), anti-dumping duties shall be levied[12] only on the products in question consigned for final consumption to that area. When the constitutional law of the importing Member does not permit the levying of anti-dumping duties on such a basis, the importing Member may levy the anti-dumping duties without limitation only if (a) the exporters shall have been given an opportunity to cease exporting at dumped prices to the area concerned or otherwise give assurances pursuant to Article 8 and adequate assurances in this regard have not been promptly given, and (b) such duties cannot be levied only on products of specific producers which supply the area in question.

4.3 Where two or more countries have reached under the provisions of paragraph 8(a) of Article XXIV of GATT 1994 such a level of integration that they have the characteristics of a single, unified market, the industry in the entire area of integration shall be taken to be the domestic industry referred to in paragraph 1.

4.4 The provisions of paragraph 6 of Article 3 shall be applicable to this Article.

Article 5

Initiation and Subsequent Investigation

5.1 Except as provided for in paragraph 6, an investigation to determine the existence, degree and effect of any alleged dumping shall be initiated upon a written application by or on behalf of the domestic industry.

5.2 An application under paragraph 1 shall include evidence of (a) dumping, (b) injury within the meaning of Article VI of GATT 1994 as interpreted by this Agreement and (c) a causal link between the dumped imports and the alleged injury. Simple assertion, unsubstantiated by relevant evidence, cannot be considered sufficient to meet the requirements of this paragraph. The application shall contain such information as is reasonably available to the applicant on the following:

(i) the identity of the applicant and a description of the volume and value of the domestic production of the like product by the applicant. Where a written application is made on behalf of the domestic industry, the application shall identify the industry on behalf of which the application is made by a list of all known domestic producers of the like product (or associations of domestic producers of the like product) and, to the extent possible, a description of

---

[12]   As used in this Agreement 'levy' shall mean the definitive or final legal assessment or collection of a duty or tax.

the volume and value of domestic production of the like product accounted for by such producers;

(ii) a complete description of the allegedly dumped product, the names of the country or countries of origin or export in question, the identity of each known exporter or foreign producer and a list of known persons importing the product in question;

(iii) information on prices at which the product in question is sold when destined for consumption in the domestic markets of the country or countries of origin or export (or, where appropriate, information on the prices at which the product is sold from the country or countries of origin or export to a third country or countries, or on the constructed value of the product) and information on export prices or, where appropriate, on the prices at which the product is first resold to an independent buyer in the territory of the importing Member;

(iv) information on the evolution of the volume of the allegedly dumped imports, the effect of these imports on prices of the like product in the domestic market and the consequent impact of the imports on the domestic industry, as demonstrated by relevant factors and indices having a bearing on the state of the domestic industry, such as those listed in paragraphs 2 and 4 of Article 3.

5.3 The authorities shall examine the accuracy and adequacy of the evidence provided in the application to determine whether there is sufficient evidence to justify the initiation of an investigation.

5.4 An investigation shall not be initiated pursuant to paragraph 1 unless the authorities have determined, on the basis of an examination of the degree of support for, or opposition to, the application expressed[13] by domestic producers of the like product, that the application has been made by or on behalf of the domestic industry.[14] The application shall be considered to have been made 'by or on behalf of the domestic industry' if it is supported by those domestic producers whose collective output constitutes more than 50 per cent of the total production of the like product produced by that portion of the domestic industry expressing either support for or opposition to the application. However, no investigation shall be initiated when domestic producers expressly supporting the application account for less than 25 per cent of total production of the like product produced by the domestic industry.

---

[13]   In the case of fragmented industries involving an exceptionally large number of producers, authorities may determine support and opposition by using statistically valid sampling techniques.

[14]   Members are aware that in the territory of certain Members employees of domestic producers of the like product or representatives of those employees may make or support an application for an investigation under paragraph 1.

5.5 The authorities shall avoid, unless a decision has been made to initiate an investigation, any publicizing of the application for the initiation of an investigation. However, after receipt of a properly documented application and before proceeding to initiate an investigation, the authorities shall notify the government of the exporting Member concerned.

5.6 If, in special circumstances, the authorities concerned decide to initiate an investigation without having received a written application by or on behalf of a domestic industry for the initiation of such investigation, they shall proceed only if they have sufficient evidence of dumping, injury and a causal link, as described in paragraph 2, to justify the initiation of an investigation.

5.7 The evidence of both dumping and injury shall be considered simultaneously (a) in the decision whether or not to initiate an investigation, and (b) thereafter, during the course of the investigation, starting on a date not later than the earliest date on which in accordance with the provisions of this Agreement provisional measures may be applied.

5.8 An application under paragraph 1 shall be rejected and an investigation shall be terminated promptly as soon as the authorities concerned are satisfied that there is not sufficient evidence of either dumping or of injury to justify proceeding with the case. There shall be immediate termination in cases where the authorities determine that the margin of dumping is *de minimis*, or that the volume of dumped imports, actual or potential, or the injury, is negligible. The margin of dumping shall be considered to be *de minimis* if this margin is less than 2 per cent, expressed as a percentage of the export price. The volume of dumped imports shall normally be regarded as negligible if the volume of dumped imports from a particular country is found to account for less than 3 per cent of imports of the like product in the importing Member, unless countries which individually account for less than 3 per cent of the imports of the like product in the importing Member collectively account for more than 7 per cent of imports of the like product in the importing Member.

5.9 An anti-dumping proceeding shall not hinder the procedures of customs clearance.

5.10 Investigations shall, except in special circumstances, be concluded within one year, and in no case more than 18 months, after their initiation.

Article 6

Evidence

6.1 All interested parties in an anti-dumping investigation shall be given notice of the information which the authorities require and ample opportunity to present in writing all evidence which they consider relevant in respect of the investigation in question.

6.1.1 Exporters or foreign producers receiving questionnaires used in an anti-dumping investigation shall be given at least 30 days for reply.[15] Due consideration should be given to any request for an extension of the 30-day period and, upon cause shown, such an extension should be granted whenever practicable.

6.1.2 Subject to the requirement to protect confidential information, evidence presented in writing by one interested party shall be made available promptly to other interested parties participating in the investigation.

6.1.3 As soon as an investigation has been initiated, the authorities shall provide the full text of the written application received under paragraph 1 of Article 5 to the known exporters[16] and to the authorities of the exporting Member and shall make it available, upon request, to other interested parties involved. Due regard shall be paid to the requirement for the protection of confidential information, as provided for in paragraph 5.

6.2 Throughout the anti-dumping investigation all interested parties shall have a full opportunity for the defence of their interests. To this end, the authorities shall, on request, provide opportunities for all interested parties to meet those parties with adverse interests, so that opposing views may be presented and rebuttal arguments offered. Provision of such opportunities must take account of the need to preserve confidentiality and of the convenience to the parties. There shall be no obligation on any party to attend a meeting, and failure to do so shall not be prejudicial to that party's case. Interested parties shall also have the right, on justification, to present other information orally.

6.3 Oral information provided under paragraph 2 shall be taken into account by the authorities only in so far as it is subsequently reproduced in writing and made available to other interested parties, as provided for in subparagraph 1.2.

6.4 The authorities shall whenever practicable provide timely opportunities for all interested parties to see all information that is relevant to the presentation of their cases, that is not confidential as defined in paragraph 5, and that is used by the authorities in an anti-dumping investigation, and to prepare presentations on the basis of this information.

---

[15] As a general rule, the time-limit for exporters shall be counted from the date of receipt of the questionnaire, which for this purpose shall be deemed to have been received one week from the date on which it was sent to the respondent or transmitted to the appropriate diplomatic representative of the exporting Member or, in the case of a separate customs territory Member of the WTO, an official representative of the exporting territory.

[16] It being understood that, where the number of exporters involved is particularly high, the full text of the written application should instead be provided only to the authorities of the exporting Member or to the relevant trade association.

6.5 Any information which is by nature confidential (for example, because its disclosure would be of significant competitive advantage to a competitor or because its disclosure would have a significantly adverse effect upon a person supplying the information or upon a person from whom that person acquired the information), or which is provided on a confidential basis by parties to an investigation shall, upon good cause shown, be treated as such by the authorities. Such information shall not be disclosed without specific permission of the party submitting it.[17]

6.5.1 The authorities shall require interested parties providing confidential information to furnish non-confidential summaries thereof. These summaries shall be in sufficient detail to permit a reasonable understanding of the substance of the information submitted in confidence. In exceptional circumstances, such parties may indicate that such information is not susceptible of summary. In such exceptional circumstances, a statement of the reasons why summarisation is not possible must be provided.

6.5.2 If the authorities find that a request for confidentiality is not warranted and if the supplier of the information is either unwilling to make the information public or to authorize its disclosure in generalized or summary form, the authorities may disregard such information unless it can be demonstrated to their satisfaction from appropriate sources that the information is correct.[18]

6.6 Except in circumstances provided for in paragraph 8, the authorities shall during the course of an investigation satisfy themselves as to the accuracy of the information supplied by interested parties upon which their findings are based.

6.7 In order to verify information provided or to obtain further details, the authorities may carry out investigations in the territory of other Members as required, provided they obtain the agreement of the firms concerned and notify the representatives of the government of the Member in question, and unless that Member objects to the investigation. The procedures described in Annex I shall apply to investigations carried out in the territory of other Members. Subject to the requirement to protect confidential information, the authorities shall make the results of any such investigations available, or shall provide disclosure thereof pursuant to paragraph 9, to the firms to which they pertain and may make such results available to the applicants.

6.8 In cases in which any interested party refuses access to, or otherwise does not provide, necessary information within a reasonable period or signifi-

---

17   Members are aware that in the territory of certain Members disclosure pursuant to a narrowly-drawn protective order may be required.
18   Members agree that requests for confidentiality should not be arbitrarily rejected.

cantly impedes the investigation, preliminary and final determinations, affirmative or negative, may be made on the basis of the facts available. The provisions of Annex II shall be observed in the application of this paragraph.

6.9 The authorities shall, before a final determination is made, inform all interested parties of the essential facts under consideration which form the basis for the decision whether to apply definitive measures. Such disclosure should take place in sufficient time for the parties to defend their interests.

6.10 The authorities shall, as a rule, determine an individual margin of dumping for each known exporter or producer concerned of the product under investigation. In cases where the number of exporters, producers, importers or types of products involved is so large as to make such a determination impracticable, the authorities may limit their examination either to a reasonable number of interested parties or products by using samples which are statistically valid on the basis of information available to the authorities at the time of the selection, or to the largest percentage of the volume of the exports from the country in question which can reasonably be investigated.

6.10.1 Any selection of exporters, producers, importers or types of products made under this paragraph shall preferably be chosen in consultation with and with the consent of the exporters, producers or importers concerned.

6.10.2 In cases where the authorities have limited their examination, as provided for in this paragraph, they shall nevertheless determine an individual margin of dumping for any exporter or producer not initially selected who submits the necessary information in time for that information to be considered during the course of the investigation, except where the number of exporters or producers is so large that individual examinations would be unduly burdensome to the authorities and prevent the timely completion of the investigation. Voluntary responses shall not be discouraged.

6.11 For the purposes of this Agreement, 'interested parties' shall include:

(i) an exporter or foreign producer or the importer of a product subject to investigation, or a trade or business association a majority of the members of which are producers, exporters or importers of such product;

(ii) the government of the exporting Member; and

(iii) a producer of the like product in the importing Member or a trade and business association a majority of the members of which produce the like product in the territory of the importing Member.

This list shall not preclude Members from allowing domestic or foreign parties other than those mentioned above to be included as interested parties.

6.12 The authorities shall provide opportunities for industrial users of the product under investigation, and for representative consumer organizations in cases where the product is commonly sold at the retail level, to provide information which is relevant to the investigation regarding dumping, injury and causality.

6.13 The authorities shall take due account of any difficulties experienced by interested parties, in particular small companies, in supplying information requested, and shall provide any assistance practicable.

6.14 The procedures set out above are not intended to prevent the authorities of a Member from proceeding expeditiously with regard to initiating an investigation, reaching preliminary or final determinations, whether affirmative or negative, or from applying provisional or final measures, in accordance with relevant provisions of this Agreement.

Article 7

Provisional Measures

7.1 Provisional measures may be applied only if:

(i) an investigation has been initiated in accordance with the provisions of Article 5, a public notice has been given to that effect and interested parties have been given adequate opportunities to submit information and make comments;

(ii) a preliminary affirmative determination has been made of dumping and consequent injury to a domestic industry; and

(iii) the authorities concerned judge such measures necessary to prevent injury being caused during the investigation.

7.2 Provisional measures may take the form of a provisional duty or, preferably, a security – by cash deposit or bond – equal to the amount of the anti-dumping duty provisionally estimated, being not greater than the provisionally estimated margin of dumping. Withholding of appraisement is an appropriate provisional measure, provided that the normal duty and the estimated amount of the anti-dumping duty be indicated and as long as the withholding of appraisement is subject to the same conditions as other provisional measures.

7.3 Provisional measures shall not be applied sooner than 60 days from the date of initiation of the investigation.

7.4 The application of provisional measures shall be limited to as short a period as possible, not exceeding four months or, on decision of the authorities concerned, upon request by exporters representing a significant percentage of the trade involved, to a period not exceeding six months. When authorities, in the course of an investigation, examine whether a duty lower than the margin of dumping would be sufficient to remove injury, these periods may be six and nine months, respectively.

7.5 The relevant provisions of Article 9 shall be followed in the application of provisional measures.

Article 8

Price Undertakings

8.1 Proceedings may[19] be suspended or terminated without the imposition of provisional measures or anti-dumping duties upon receipt of satisfactory voluntary undertakings from any exporter to revise its prices or to cease exports to the area in question at dumped prices so that the authorities are satisfied that the injurious effect of the dumping is eliminated. Price increases under such undertakings shall not be higher than necessary to eliminate the margin of dumping. It is desirable that the price increases be less than the margin of dumping if such increases would be adequate to remove the injury to the domestic industry.

8.2 Price undertakings shall not be sought or accepted from exporters unless the authorities of the importing Member have made a preliminary affirmative determination of dumping and injury caused by such dumping.

8.3 Undertakings offered need not be accepted if the authorities consider their acceptance impractical, for example, if the number of actual or potential exporters is too great, or for other reasons, including reasons of general policy. Should the case arise and where practicable, the authorities shall provide to the exporter the reasons which have led them to consider acceptance of an undertaking as inappropriate, and shall, to the extent possible, give the exporter an opportunity to make comments thereon.

8.4 If an undertaking is accepted, the investigation of dumping and injury shall nevertheless be completed if the exporter so desires or the authorities so decide. In such a case, if a negative determination of dumping or injury is made, the undertaking shall automatically lapse, except in cases where such a determination is due in large part to the existence of a price undertaking. In such cases, the authorities may require that an undertaking be maintained for a reasonable period consistent with the provisions of this Agreement. In the event that an affirmative determination of dumping and injury is made, the undertaking shall continue consistent with its terms and the provisions of this Agreement.

8.5 Price undertakings may be suggested by the authorities of the importing Member, but no exporter shall be forced to enter into such undertakings. The fact that exporters do not offer such undertakings, or do not accept an invitation to do so, shall in no way prejudice the consideration of the case. However, the authorities are free to determine that a threat of injury is more likely to be realised if the dumped imports continue.

8.6 Authorities of an importing Member may require any exporter from

---

[19] The word 'may' shall not be interpreted to allow the simultaneous continuation of proceedings with the implementation of price undertakings except as provided in paragraph 4.

whom an undertaking has been accepted to provide periodically information relevant to the fulfilment of such an undertaking and to permit verification of pertinent data. In case of violation of an undertaking, the
authorities of the importing Member may take, under this Agreement in
conformity with its provisions, expeditious actions which may constitute
immediate application of provisional measures using the best information
available. In such cases, definitive duties may be levied in accordance with
this Agreement on products entered for consumption not more than 90 days
before the application of such provisional measures, except that any such
retroactive assessment shall not apply to imports entered before the violation of the undertaking.

Article 9

Imposition and Collection of Anti-Dumping Duties
   9.1 The decision whether or not to impose an anti-dumping duty in cases
where all requirements for the imposition have been fulfilled, and the decision whether the amount of the anti-dumping duty to be imposed shall be
the full margin of dumping or less, are decisions to be made by the authorities of the importing Member. It is desirable that the imposition be permissive in the territory of all Members, and that the duty be less than the
margin if such lesser duty would be adequate to remove the injury to the
domestic industry.
   9.2 When an anti-dumping duty is imposed in respect of any product,
such anti-dumping duty shall be collected in the appropriate amounts in each
case, on a non-discriminatory basis on imports of such product from all
sources found to be dumped and causing injury, except as to imports from
those sources from which price undertakings under the terms of this
Agreement have been accepted. The authorities shall name the supplier or
suppliers of the product concerned. If, however, several suppliers from the
same country are involved, and it is impracticable to name all these suppliers, the authorities may name the supplying country concerned. If several
suppliers from more than one country are involved, the authorities may
name either all the suppliers involved, or, if this is impracticable, all the
supplying countries involved.
   9.3 The amount of the anti-dumping duty shall not exceed the margin of
dumping as established under Article 2.
   9.3.1 When the amount of the anti-dumping duty is assessed on a retrospective basis, the determination of the final liability for payment of anti-
dumping duties shall take place as soon as possible, normally within
12 months, and in no case more than 18 months, after the date on which a
request for a final assessment of the amount of the anti-dumping duty has been

made.[20] Any refund shall be made promptly and normally in not more than 90 days following the determination of final liability made pursuant to this subparagraph. In any case, where a refund is not made within 90 days, the authorities shall provide an explanation if so requested.

9.3.2 When the amount of the anti-dumping duty is assessed on a prospective basis, provision shall be made for a prompt refund, upon request, of any duty paid in excess of the margin of dumping. A refund of any such duty paid in excess of the actual margin of dumping shall normally take place within 12 months, and in no case more than 18 months, after the date on which a request for a refund, duly supported by evidence, has been made by an importer of the product subject to the anti-dumping duty. The refund authorized should normally be made within 90 days of the above-noted decision.

9.3.3 In determining whether and to what extent a reimbursement should be made when the export price is constructed in accordance with paragraph 3 of Article 2, authorities should take account of any change in normal value, any change in costs incurred between importation and resale, and any movement in the resale price which is duly reflected in subsequent selling prices, and should calculate the export price with no deduction for the amount of anti-dumping duties paid when conclusive evidence of the above is provided.

9.4 When the authorities have limited their examination in accordance with the second sentence of paragraph 10 of Article 6, any anti-dumping duty applied to imports from exporters or producers not included in the examination shall not exceed:

(i) the weighted average margin of dumping established with respect to the selected exporters or producers or,

(ii) where the liability for payment of anti-dumping duties is calculated on the basis of a prospective normal value, the difference between the weighted average normal value of the selected exporters or producers and the export prices of exporters or producers not individually examined, provided that the authorities shall disregard for the purpose of this paragraph any zero and *de minimis* margins and margins established under the circumstances referred to in paragraph 8 of Article 6. The authorities shall apply individual duties or normal values to imports from any exporter or producer not included in the examination who has provided the necessary information during the course of the investigation, as provided for in subparagraph 10.2 of Article 6.

9.5 If a product is subject to anti-dumping duties in an importing Member, the authorities shall promptly carry out a review for the purpose of determining

---

[20]   It is understood that the observance of the time-limits mentioned in this subparagraph and in subparagraph 3.2 may not be possible where the product in question is subject to judicial review proceedings.

individual margins of dumping for any exporters or producers in the exporting country in question who have not exported the product to the importing Member during the period of investigation, provided that these exporters or producers can show that they are not related to any of the exporters or producers in the exporting country who are subject to the anti-dumping duties on the product. Such a review shall be initiated and carried out on an accelerated basis, compared to normal duty assessment and review proceedings in the importing Member. No anti-dumping duties shall be levied on imports from such exporters or producers while the review is being carried out. The authorities may, however, withhold appraisement and/or request guarantees to ensure that, should such a review result in a determination of dumping in respect of such producers or exporters, anti-dumping duties can be levied retroactively to the date of the initiation of the review.

Article 10

Retroactivity

10.1 Provisional measures and anti-dumping duties shall only be applied to products which enter for consumption after the time when the decision taken under paragraph 1 of Article 7 and paragraph 1 of Article 9, respectively, enters into force, subject to the exceptions set out in this Article.

10.2 Where a final determination of injury (but not of a threat thereof or of a material retardation of the establishment of an industry) is made or, in the case of a final determination of a threat of injury, where the effect of the dumped imports would, in the absence of the provisional measures, have led to a determination of injury, anti-dumping duties may be levied retroactively for the period for which provisional measures, if any, have been applied.

10.3 If the definitive anti-dumping duty is higher than the provisional duty paid or payable, or the amount estimated for the purpose of the security, the difference shall not be collected. If the definitive duty is lower than the provisional duty paid or payable, or the amount estimated for the purpose of the security, the difference shall be reimbursed or the duty recalculated, as the case may be.

10.4 Except as provided in paragraph 2, where a determination of threat of injury or material retardation is made (but no injury has yet occurred) a definitive anti-dumping duty may be imposed only from the date of the determination of threat of injury or material retardation, and any cash deposit made during the period of the application of provisional measures shall be refunded and any bonds released in an expeditious manner.

10.5 Where a final determination is negative, any cash deposit made during the period of the application of provisional measures shall be refunded and any bonds released in an expeditious manner.

10.6 A definitive anti-dumping duty may be levied on products which were entered for consumption not more than 90 days prior to the date of application of provisional measures, when the authorities determine for the dumped product in question that:

(i) there is a history of dumping which caused injury or that the importer was, or should have been, aware that the exporter practises dumping and that such dumping would cause injury, and

(ii) the injury is caused by massive dumped imports of a product in a relatively short time which in light of the timing and the volume of the dumped imports and other circumstances (such as a rapid build-up of inventories of the imported product) is likely to seriously undermine the remedial effect of the definitive anti-dumping duty to be applied, provided that the importers concerned have been given an opportunity to comment.

10.7 The authorities may, after initiating an investigation, take such measures as the withholding of appraisement or assessment as may be necessary to collect anti-dumping duties retroactively, as provided for in paragraph 6, once they have sufficient evidence that the conditions set forth in that paragraph are satisfied.

10.8 No duties shall be levied retroactively pursuant to paragraph 6 on products entered for consumption prior to the date of initiation of the investigation.

Article 11

Duration and Review of Anti-Dumping Duties and Price Undertakings

11.1 An anti-dumping duty shall remain in force only as long as and to the extent necessary to counteract dumping which is causing injury.

11.2 The authorities shall review the need for the continued imposition of the duty, where warranted, on their own initiative or, provided that a reasonable period of time has elapsed since the imposition of the definitive anti-dumping duty, upon request by any interested party which submits positive information substantiating the need for a review.[21] Interested parties shall have the right to request the authorities to examine whether the continued imposition of the duty is necessary to offset dumping, whether the injury would be likely to continue or recur if the duty were removed or varied, or both. If, as a result of the review under this paragraph, the authorities determine that the anti-dumping duty is no longer warranted, it shall be terminated immediately.

---

[21] A determination of final liability for payment of anti-dumping duties, as provided for in paragraph 3 of Article 9, does not by itself constitute a review within the meaning of this Article.

11.3 Notwithstanding the provisions of paragraphs 1 and 2, any definitive anti-dumping duty shall be terminated on a date not later than five years from its imposition (or from the date of the most recent review under paragraph 2 if that review has covered both dumping and injury, or under this paragraph), unless the authorities determine, in a review initiated before that date on their own initiative or upon a duly substantiated request made by or on behalf of the domestic industry within a reasonable period of time prior to that date, that the expiry of the duty would be likely to lead to continuation or recurrence of dumping and injury.[22] The duty may remain in force pending the outcome of such a review.

11.4 The provisions of Article 6 regarding evidence and procedure shall apply to any review carried out under this Article. Any such review shall be carried out expeditiously and shall normally be concluded within 12 months of the date of initiation of the review.

11.5 The provisions of this Article shall apply *mutatis mutandis* to price undertakings accepted under Article 8.

Article 12

Public Notice and Explanation of Determinations

12.1 When the authorities are satisfied that there is sufficient evidence to justify the initiation of an anti-dumping investigation pursuant to Article 5, the Member or Members the products of which are subject to such investigation and other interested parties known to the investigating authorities to have an interest therein shall be notified and a public notice shall be given.

12.1.1 A public notice of the initiation of an investigation shall contain, or otherwise make available through a separate report,[23] adequate information on the following:

(i) the name of the exporting country or countries and the product involved;

(ii) the date of initiation of the investigation;

(iii) the basis on which dumping is alleged in the application;

(iv) a summary of the factors on which the allegation of injury is based;

(v) the address to which representations by interested parties should be directed;

(vi) the time-limits allowed to interested parties for making their views known.

---

[22] When the amount of the anti-dumping duty is assessed on a retrospective basis, a finding in the most recent assessment proceeding under subparagraph 3.1 of Article 9 that no duty is to be levied shall not by itself require the authorities to terminate the definitive duty.

[23] Where authorities provide information and explanations under the provisions of this Article in a separate report, they shall ensure that such report is readily available to the public.

12.2 Public notice shall be given of any preliminary or final determination, whether affirmative or negative, of any decision to accept an undertaking pursuant to Article 8, of the termination of such an undertaking, and of the termination of a definitive anti-dumping duty. Each such notice shall set forth, or otherwise make available through a separate report, in sufficient detail the findings and conclusions reached on all issues of fact and law considered material by the investigating authorities. All such notices and reports shall be forwarded to the Member or Members the products of which are subject to such determination or undertaking and to other interested parties known to have an interest therein.

12.2.1 A public notice of the imposition of provisional measures shall set forth, or otherwise make available through a separate report, sufficiently detailed explanations for the preliminary determinations on dumping and injury and shall refer to the matters of fact and law which have led to arguments being accepted or rejected. Such a notice or report shall, due regard being paid to the requirement for the protection of confidential information, contain in particular:

(i) the names of the suppliers, or when this is impracticable, the supplying countries involved;

(ii) a description of the product which is sufficient for customs purposes;

(iii) the margins of dumping established and a full explanation of the reasons for the methodology used in the establishment and comparison of the export price and the normal value under Article 2;

(iv) considerations relevant to the injury determination as set out in Article 3;

(v) the main reasons leading to the determination.

12.2.2 A public notice of conclusion or suspension of an investigation in the case of an affirmative determination providing for the imposition of a definitive duty or the acceptance of a price undertaking shall contain, or otherwise make available through a separate report, all relevant information on the matters of fact and law and reasons which have led to the imposition of final measures or the acceptance of a price undertaking, due regard being paid to the requirement for the protection of confidential information. In particular, the notice or report shall contain the information described in subparagraph 2.1, as well as the reasons for the acceptance or rejection of relevant arguments or claims made by the exporters and importers, and the basis for any decision made under subparagraph 10.2 of Article 6.

12.2.3 A public notice of the termination or suspension of an investigation following the acceptance of an undertaking pursuant to Article 8 shall include, or otherwise make available through a separate report, the non-confidential part of this undertaking.

12.3 The provisions of this Article shall apply *mutatis mutandis* to the initiation and completion of reviews pursuant to Article 11 and to decisions under Article 10 to apply duties retroactively.

Article 13

Judicial Review

Each Member whose national legislation contains provisions on anti-dumping measures shall maintain judicial, arbitral or administrative tribunals or procedures for the purpose, inter alia, of the prompt review of administrative actions relating to final determinations and reviews of determinations within the meaning of Article 11. Such tribunals or procedures shall be independent of the authorities responsible for the determination or review in question.

Article 14

Anti-Dumping Action on Behalf of a Third Country

14.1 An application for anti-dumping action on behalf of a third country shall be made by the authorities of the third country requesting action.

14.2 Such an application shall be supported by price information to show that the imports are being dumped and by detailed information to show that the alleged dumping is causing injury to the domestic industry concerned in the third country. The government of the third country shall afford all assistance to the authorities of the importing country to obtain any further information which the latter may require.

14.3 In considering such an application, the authorities of the importing country shall consider the effects of the alleged dumping on the industry concerned as a whole in the third country; that is to say, the injury shall not be assessed in relation only to the effect of the alleged dumping on the industry's exports to the importing country or even on the industry's total exports.

14.4 The decision whether or not to proceed with a case shall rest with the importing country. If the importing country decides that it is prepared to take action, the initiation of the approach to the Council for Trade in Goods seeking its approval for such action shall rest with the importing country.

Article 15

Developing Country Members

It is recognised that special regard must be given by developed country Members to the special situation of developing country Members when considering the application of anti-dumping measures under this Agreement. Possibilities of constructive remedies provided for by this Agreement shall be explored before applying anti-dumping duties where they would affect the essential interests of developing country Members.

PART II

Article 16

Committee on Anti-Dumping Practices

16.1 There is hereby established a Committee on Anti-Dumping Practices (referred to in this Agreement as the 'Committee') composed of representatives from each of the Members. The Committee shall elect its own Chairman and shall meet not less than twice a year and otherwise as envisaged by relevant provisions of this Agreement at the request of any Member. The Committee shall carry out responsibilities as assigned to it under this Agreement or by the Members and it shall afford Members the opportunity of consulting on any matters relating to the operation of the Agreement or the furtherance of its objectives. The WTO Secretariat shall act as the secretariat to the Committee.

16.2 The Committee may set up subsidiary bodies as appropriate.

16.3 In carrying out their functions, the Committee and any subsidiary bodies may consult with and seek information from any source they deem appropriate. However, before the Committee or a subsidiary body seeks such information from a source within the jurisdiction of a Member, it shall inform the Member involved. It shall obtain the consent of the Member and any firm to be consulted.

16.4 Members shall report without delay to the Committee all preliminary or final anti-dumping actions taken. Such reports shall be available in the Secretariat for inspection by other Members. Members shall also submit, on a semi-annual basis, reports of any anti-dumping actions taken within the preceding six months. The semi-annual reports shall be submitted on an agreed standard form.

16.5 Each Member shall notify the Committee (a) which of its authorities are competent to initiate and conduct investigations referred to in Article 5 and (b) its domestic procedures governing the initiation and conduct of such investigations.

Article 17

Consultation and Dispute Settlement

17.1 Except as otherwise provided herein, the Dispute Settlement Understanding is applicable to consultations and the settlement of disputes under this Agreement.

17.2 Each Member shall afford sympathetic consideration to, and shall afford adequate opportunity for consultation regarding, representations made by another Member with respect to any matter affecting the operation of this Agreement.

17.3 If any Member considers that any benefit accruing to it, directly or indirectly, under this Agreement is being nullified or impaired, or that the achievement of any objective is being impeded, by another Member or Members, it may, with a view to reaching a mutually satisfactory resolution of the matter, request in writing consultations with the Member or Members in question. Each Member shall afford sympathetic consideration to any request from another Member for consultation.

17.4 If the Member that requested consultations considers that the consultations pursuant to paragraph 3 have failed to achieve a mutually agreed solution, and if final action has been taken by the administering authorities of the importing Member to levy definitive anti-dumping duties or to accept price undertakings, it may refer the matter to the Dispute Settlement Body ('DSB'). When a provisional measure has a significant impact and the Member that requested consultations considers that the measure was taken contrary to the provisions of paragraph 1 of Article 7, that Member may also refer such matter to the DSB.

17.5 The DSB shall, at the request of the complaining party, establish a panel to examine the matter based upon:

(i) a written statement of the Member making the request indicating how a benefit accruing to it, directly or indirectly, under this Agreement has been nullified or impaired, or that the achieving of the objectives of the Agreement is being impeded, and

(ii) the facts made available in conformity with appropriate domestic procedures to the authorities of the importing Member.

17.6 In examining the matter referred to in paragraph 5:

(i) in its assessment of the facts of the matter, the panel shall determine whether the authorities' establishment of the facts was proper and whether their evaluation of those facts was unbiased and objective. If the establishment of the facts was proper and the evaluation was unbiased and objective, even though the panel might have reached a different conclusion, the evaluation shall not be overturned;

(ii) the panel shall interpret the relevant provisions of the Agreement in accordance with customary rules of interpretation of public international law. Where the panel finds that a relevant provision of the Agreement admits of more than one permissible interpretation, the panel shall find the authorities' measure to be in conformity with the Agreement if it rests upon one of those permissible interpretations.

17.7 Confidential information provided to the panel shall not be disclosed without formal authorization from the person, body or authority providing such information. Where such information is requested from the panel but release of such information by the panel is not authorized, a non-confidential summary of the information, authorized by the person, body or authority providing the information, shall be provided.

PART III

Article 18

Final Provisions

18.1 No specific action against dumping of exports from another Member can be taken except in accordance with the provisions of GATT 1994, as interpreted by this Agreement.[24]

18.2 Reservations may not be entered in respect of any of the provisions of this Agreement without the consent of the other Members.

18.3 Subject to subparagraphs 3.1 and 3.2, the provisions of this Agreement shall apply to investigations, and reviews of existing measures, initiated pursuant to applications which have been made on or after the date of entry into force for a Member of the WTO Agreement.

18.3.1 With respect to the calculation of margins of dumping in refund procedures under paragraph 3 of Article 9, the rules used in the most recent determination or review of dumping shall apply.

18.3.2 For the purposes of paragraph 3 of Article 11, existing anti-dumping measures shall be deemed to be imposed on a date not later than the date of entry into force for a Member of the WTO Agreement, except in cases in which the domestic legislation of a Member in force on that date already included a clause of the type provided for in that paragraph.

18.4 Each Member shall take all necessary steps, of a general or particular character, to ensure, not later than the date of entry into force of the WTO Agreement for it, the conformity of its laws, regulations and administrative procedures with the provisions of this Agreement as they may apply for the Member in question.

18.5 Each Member shall inform the Committee of any changes in its laws and regulations relevant to this Agreement and in the administration of such laws and regulations.

18.6 The Committee shall review annually the implementation and operation of this Agreement taking into account the objectives thereof. The

---

[24] This is not intended to preclude action under other relevant provisions of GATT 1994, as appropriate.

Committee shall inform annually the Council for Trade in Goods of developments during the period covered by such reviews.

18.7 The Annexes to this Agreement constitute an integral part thereof.

ANNEX I   PROCEDURES FOR ON-THE-SPOT INVESTIGATIONS PURSUANT TO PARAGRAPH 7 OF ARTICLE 6

1. Upon initiation of an investigation, the authorities of the exporting Member and the firms known to be concerned should be informed of the intention to carry out on-the-spot investigations.

2. If in exceptional circumstances it is intended to include non-governmental experts in the investigating team, the firms and the authorities of the exporting Member should be so informed. Such non-governmental experts should be subject to effective sanctions for breach of confidentiality requirements.

3. It should be standard practice to obtain explicit agreement of the firms concerned in the exporting Member before the visit is finally scheduled.

4. As soon as the agreement of the firms concerned has been obtained, the investigating authorities should notify the authorities of the exporting Member of the names and addresses of the firms to be visited and the dates agreed.

5. Sufficient advance notice should be given to the firms in question before the visit is made.

6. Visits to explain the questionnaire should only be made at the request of an exporting firm. Such a visit may only be made if (a) the authorities of the importing Member notify the representatives of the Member in question and (b) the latter do not object to the visit.

7. As the main purpose of the on-the-spot investigation is to verify information provided or to obtain further details, it should be carried out after the response to the questionnaire has been received unless the firm agrees to the contrary and the government of the exporting Member is informed by the investigating authorities of the anticipated visit and does not object to it; further, it should be standard practice prior to the visit to advise the firms concerned of the general nature of the information to be verified and of any further information which needs to be provided, though this should not preclude requests to be made on the spot for further details to be provided in the light of information obtained.

8. Enquiries or questions put by the authorities or firms of the exporting Members and essential to a successful on-the-spot investigation should, whenever possible, be answered before the visit is made.

ANNEX II BEST INFORMATION AVAILABLE IN TERMS OF PARAGRAPH 8 OF ARTICLE 6

1. As soon as possible after the initiation of the investigation, the investigating authorities should specify in detail the information required from any interested party, and the manner in which that information should be structured by the interested party in its response. The authorities should also ensure that the party is aware that if information is not supplied within a reasonable time, the authorities will be free to make determinations on the basis of the facts available, including those contained in the application for the initiation of the investigation by the domestic industry.

2. The authorities may also request that an interested party provide its response in a particular medium (e.g. computer tape) or computer language. Where such a request is made, the authorities should consider the reasonable ability of the interested party to respond in the preferred medium or computer language, and should not request the party to use for its response a computer system other than that used by the party. The authority should not maintain a request for a computerized response if the interested party does not maintain computerized accounts and if presenting the response as requested would result in an unreasonable extra burden on the interested party, e.g., it would entail unreasonable additional cost and trouble. The authorities should not maintain a request for a response in a particular medium or computer language if the interested party does not maintain its computerized accounts in such medium or computer language and if presenting the response as requested would result in an unreasonable extra burden on the interested party, e.g., it would entail unreasonable additional cost and trouble.

3. All information which is verifiable, which is appropriately submitted so that it can be used in the investigation without undue difficulties, which is supplied in a timely fashion, and, where applicable, which is supplied in a medium or computer language requested by the authorities, should be taken into account when determinations are made. If a party does not respond in the preferred medium or computer language but the authorities find that the circumstances set out in paragraph 2 have been satisfied, the failure to respond in the preferred medium or computer language should not be considered to significantly impede the investigation.

4. Where the authorities do not have the ability to process information if provided in a particular medium (e.g. computer tape), the information should be supplied in the form of written material or any other form acceptable to the authorities.

5. Even though the information provided may not be ideal in all respects, this should not justify the authorities from disregarding it, provided the interested party has acted to the best of its ability.

6. If evidence or information is not accepted, the supplying party should be informed forthwith of the reasons therefor, and should have an opportunity to provide further explanations within a reasonable period, due account being taken of the time-limits of the investigation. If the explanations are considered by the authorities as not being satisfactory, the reasons for the rejection of such evidence or information should be given in any published determinations.

7. If the authorities have to base their findings, including those with respect to normal value, on information from a secondary source, including the information supplied in the application for the initiation of the investigation, they should do so with special circumspection. In such cases, the authorities should, where practicable, check the information from other independent sources at their disposal, such as published price lists, official import statistics and customs returns, and from the information obtained from other interested parties during the investigation. It is clear, however, that if an interested party does not cooperate and thus relevant information is being withheld from the authorities, this situation could lead to a result which is less favourable to the party than if the party did cooperate.

Appendix 3   Agreement on Subsidies and Countervailing Measures

Members hereby agree as follows:

PART I: GENERAL PROVISIONS

Article 1

Definition of a Subsidy

1.1 For the purpose of this Agreement, a subsidy shall be deemed to exist if:

(a)(1) there is a financial contribution by a government or any public body within the territory of a Member (referred to in this Agreement as 'government'), i.e. where:

(i) a government practice involves a direct transfer of funds (e.g. grants, loans, and equity infusion), potential direct transfers of funds or liabilities (e.g. loan guarantees);

(ii) government revenue that is otherwise due is foregone or not collected (e.g. fiscal incentives such as tax credits);[1]

(iii) a government provides goods or services other than general infrastructure, or purchases goods;

(iv) a government makes payments to a funding mechanism, or entrusts or directs a private body to carry out one or more of the type of functions illustrated in (i) to (iii) above which would normally be vested in the government and the practice, in no real sense, differs from practices normally followed by governments;

or

---

[1]   In accordance with the provisions of Article XVI of GATT 1994 (Note to Article XVI) and the provisions of Annexes I through III of this Agreement, the exemption of an exported product from duties or taxes borne by the like product when destined for domestic consumption, or the remission of such duties or taxes in amounts not in excess of those which have accrued, shall not be deemed to be a subsidy.

(a)(2) there is any form of income or price support in the sense of Article XVI of GATT 1994;
and

(b) a benefit is thereby conferred.

1.2 A subsidy as defined in paragraph 1 shall be subject to the provisions of Part II or shall be subject to the provisions of Part III or V only if such a subsidy is specific in accordance with the provisions of Article 2.

Article 2

Specificity

2.1 In order to determine whether a subsidy, as defined in paragraph 1 of Article 1, is specific to an enterprise or industry or group of enterprises or industries (referred to in this Agreement as 'certain enterprises') within the jurisdiction of the granting authority, the following principles shall apply:

(a) Where the granting authority, or the legislation pursuant to which the granting authority operates, explicitly limits access to a subsidy to certain enterprises, such subsidy shall be specific.

(b) Where the granting authority, or the legislation pursuant to which the granting authority operates, establishes objective criteria or conditions[2] governing the eligibility for, and the amount of, a subsidy, specificity shall not exist, provided that the eligibility is automatic and that such criteria and conditions are strictly adhered to. The criteria or conditions must be clearly spelled out in law, regulation, or other official document, so as to be capable of verification.

(c) If, notwithstanding any appearance of non-specificity resulting from the application of the principles laid down in subparagraphs (a) and (b), there are reasons to believe that the subsidy may in fact be specific, other factors may be considered. Such factors are: use of a subsidy programme by a limited number of certain enterprises, predominant use by certain enterprises, the granting of disproportionately large amounts of subsidy to certain enterprises, and the manner in which discretion has been exercised by the granting authority in the decision to grant a subsidy.[3] In applying this subparagraph, account shall be taken of the extent of diversification of economic activities within the

---

[2]   Objective criteria or conditions, as used herein, mean criteria or conditions which are neutral, which do not favour certain enterprises over others, and which are economic in nature and horizontal in application, such as number of employees or size of enterprise.

[3]   In this regard, in particular, information on the frequency with which applications for a subsidy are refused or approved and the reasons for such decisions shall be considered.

jurisdiction of the granting authority, as well as of the length of time during which the subsidy programme has been in operation.

2.2 A subsidy which is limited to certain enterprises located within a designated geographical region within the jurisdiction of the granting authority shall be specific. It is understood that the setting or change of generally applicable tax rates by all levels of government entitled to do so shall not be deemed to be a specific subsidy for the purposes of this Agreement.

2.3 Any subsidy falling under the provisions of Article 3 shall be deemed to be specific.

2.4 Any determination of specificity under the provisions of this Article shall be clearly substantiated on the basis of positive evidence.

PART II: PROHIBITED SUBSIDIES

Article 3

Prohibition

3.1 Except as provided in the Agreement on Agriculture, the following subsidies, within the meaning of Article 1, shall be prohibited:

(a) subsidies contingent, in law or in fact,[4] whether solely or as one of several other conditions, upon export performance, including those illustrated in Annex I;[5]

(b) subsidies contingent, whether solely or as one of several other conditions, upon the use of domestic over imported goods.

3.2 A Member shall neither grant nor maintain subsidies referred to in paragraph 1.

Article 4

Remedies

4.1 Whenever a Member has reason to believe that a prohibited subsidy is being granted or maintained by another Member, such Member may request consultations with such other Member.

---

[4]   This standard is met when the facts demonstrate that the granting of a subsidy, without having been made legally contingent upon export performance, is in fact tied to actual or anticipated exportation or export earnings. The mere fact that a subsidy is granted to enterprises which export shall not for that reason alone be considered to be an export subsidy within the meaning of this provision.

[5]   Measures referred to in Annex I as not constituting export subsidies shall not be prohibited under this or any other provision of this Agreement.

4.2 A request for consultations under paragraph 1 shall include a statement of available evidence with regard to the existence and nature of the subsidy in question.

4.3 Upon request for consultations under paragraph 1, the Member believed to be granting or maintaining the subsidy in question shall enter into such consultations as quickly as possible. The purpose of the consultations shall be to clarify the facts of the situation and to arrive at a mutually agreed solution.

4.4 If no mutually agreed solution has been reached within 30 days[6] of the request for consultations, any Member party to such consultations may refer the matter to the Dispute Settlement Body ('DSB') for the immediate establishment of a panel, unless the DSB decides by consensus not to establish a panel.

4.5 Upon its establishment, the panel may request the assistance of the Permanent Group of Experts[7] (referred to in this Agreement as the 'PGE') with regard to whether the measure in question is a prohibited subsidy. If so requested, the PGE shall immediately review the evidence with regard to the existence and nature of the measure in question and shall provide an opportunity for the Member applying or maintaining the measure to demonstrate that the measure in question is not a prohibited subsidy. The PGE shall report its conclusions to the panel within a time-limit determined by the panel. The PGE's conclusions on the issue of whether or not the measure in question is a prohibited subsidy shall be accepted by the panel without modification.

4.6 The panel shall submit its final report to the parties to the dispute. The report shall be circulated to all Members within 90 days of the date of the composition and the establishment of the panel's terms of reference.

4.7 If the measure in question is found to be a prohibited subsidy, the panel shall recommend that the subsidising Member withdraw the subsidy without delay. In this regard, the panel shall specify in its recommendation the time-period within which the measure must be withdrawn.

4.8 Within 30 days of the issuance of the panel's report to all Members, the report shall be adopted by the DSB unless one of the parties to the dispute formally notifies the DSB of its decision to appeal or the DSB decides by consensus not to adopt the report.

4.9 Where a panel report is appealed, the Appellate Body shall issue its decision within 30 days from the date when the party to the dispute formally notifies its intention to appeal. When the Appellate Body considers that it cannot provide its report within 30 days, it shall inform the DSB in writing of the reasons for the delay together with an estimate of the period within which

---

[6] Any time-periods mentioned in this Article may be extended by mutual agreement.

[7] As established in Article 24.

it will submit its report. In no case shall the proceedings exceed 60 days. The appellate report shall be adopted by the DSB and unconditionally accepted by the parties to the dispute unless the DSB decides by consensus not to adopt the appellate report within 20 days following its issuance to the Members.[8]

4.10 In the event the recommendation of the DSB is not followed within the time-period specified by the panel, which shall commence from the date of adoption of the panel's report or the Appellate Body's report, the DSB shall grant authorization to the complaining Member to take appropriate[9] counter-measures, unless the DSB decides by consensus to reject the request.

4.11 In the event a party to the dispute requests arbitration under paragraph 6 of Article 22 of the Dispute Settlement Understanding ('DSU'), the arbitrator shall determine whether the countermeasures are appropriate.[10]

4.12 For purposes of disputes conducted pursuant to this Article, except for time-periods specifically prescribed in this Article, time-periods applicable under the DSU for the conduct of such disputes shall be half the time prescribed therein.

PART III: ACTIONABLE SUBSIDIES

Article 5

Adverse Effects
No Member should cause, through the use of any subsidy referred to in paragraphs 1 and 2 of Article 1, adverse effects to the interests of other Members, i.e.:

(a) injury to the domestic industry of another Member;[11]

(b) nullification or impairment of benefits accruing directly or indirectly to other Members under GATT 1994, in particular the benefits of concessions bound under Article II of GATT 1994;[12]

---

[8] If a meeting of the DSB is not scheduled during this period, such a meeting shall be held for this purpose.

[9] This expression is not meant to allow countermeasures that are disproportionate in light of the fact that the subsidies dealt with under these provisions are prohibited.

[10] This expression is not meant to allow countermeasures that are disproportionate in light of the fact that the subsidies dealt with under these provisions are prohibited.

[11] The term 'injury to the domestic industry' is used here in the same sense as it is used in Part V.

[12] The term 'nullification or impairment' is used in this Agreement in the same sense as it is used in the relevant provisions of GATT 1994, and the existence of such

(c) serious prejudice to the interests of another Member.[13]

This Article does not apply to subsidies maintained on agricultural products as provided in Article 13 of the Agreement on Agriculture.

Article 6

Serious Prejudice

6.1 Serious prejudice in the sense of paragraph (c) of Article 5 shall be deemed to exist in the case of:

(a) the total *ad valorem* subsidisation[14] of a product exceeding 5 per cent;[15]

(b) subsidies to cover operating losses sustained by an industry;

(c) subsidies to cover operating losses sustained by an enterprise, other than one-time measures which are non-recurrent and cannot be repeated for that enterprise and which are given merely to provide time for the development of long-term solutions and to avoid acute social problems;

(d) direct forgiveness of debt, i.e. forgiveness of government-held debt, and grants to cover debt repayment.[16]

6.2 Notwithstanding the provisions of paragraph 1, serious prejudice shall not be found if the subsidising Member demonstrates that the subsidy in question has not resulted in any of the effects enumerated in paragraph 3.

6.3 Serious prejudice in the sense of paragraph (c) of Article 5 may arise in any case where one or several of the following apply:

(a) the effect of the subsidy is to displace or impede the imports of a like product of another Member into the market of the subsidising Member;

(b) the effect of the subsidy is to displace or impede the exports of a like product of another Member from a third country market;

(c) the effect of the subsidy is a significant price undercutting by the subsidised product as compared with the price of a like product of another Member in the same market or significant price suppression, price depression or lost sales in the same market;

---

nullification or impairment shall be established in accordance with the practice of application of these provisions.

[13] The term 'serious prejudice to the interests of another Member' is used in this Agreement in the same sense as it is used in paragraph 1 of Article XVI of GATT 1994, and includes threat of serious prejudice.

[14] The total *ad valorem* subsidisation shall be calculated in accordance with the provisions of Annex IV.

[15] Since it is anticipated that civil aircraft will be subject to specific multilateral rules, the threshold in this subparagraph does not apply to civil aircraft.

[16] Members recognize that where royalty-based financing for a civil aircraft programme is not being fully repaid due to the level of actual sales falling below the level of forecast sales, this does not in itself constitute serious prejudice for the purposes of this subparagraph.

(d) the effect of the subsidy is an increase in the world market share of the subsidising Member in a particular subsidised primary product or commodity[17] as compared to the average share it had during the previous period of three years and this increase follows a consistent trend over a period when subsidies have been granted.

6.4 For the purpose of paragraph 3(b), the displacement or impeding of exports shall include any case in which, subject to the provisions of paragraph 7, it has been demonstrated that there has been a change in relative shares of the market to the disadvantage of the non-subsidised like product (over an appropriately representative period sufficient to demonstrate clear trends in the development of the market for the product concerned, which, in normal circumstances, shall be at least one year). 'Change in relative shares of the market' shall include any of the following situations: (a) there is an increase in the market share of the subsidised product; (b) the market share of the subsidised product remains constant in circumstances in which, in the absence of the subsidy, it would have declined; (c) the market share of the subsidised product declines, but at a slower rate than would have been the case in the absence of the subsidy.

6.5 For the purpose of paragraph 3(c), price undercutting shall include any case in which such price undercutting has been demonstrated through a comparison of prices of the subsidised product with prices of a non-subsidised like product supplied to the same market. The comparison shall be made at the same level of trade and at comparable times, due account being taken of any other factor affecting price comparability. However, if such a direct comparison is not possible, the existence of price undercutting may be demonstrated on the basis of export unit values.

6.6 Each Member in the market of which serious prejudice is alleged to have arisen shall, subject to the provisions of paragraph 3 of Annex V, make available to the parties to a dispute arising under Article 7, and to the panel established pursuant to paragraph 4 of Article 7, all relevant information that can be obtained as to the changes in market shares of the parties to the dispute as well as concerning prices of the products involved.

6.7 Displacement or impediment resulting in serious prejudice shall not arise under paragraph 3 where any of the following circumstances exist[18] during the relevant period:

---

[17] Unless other multilaterally agreed specific rules apply to the trade in the product or commodity in question.

[18] The fact that certain circumstances are referred to in this paragraph does not, in itself, confer upon them any legal status in terms of either GATT 1994 or this Agreement. These circumstances must not be isolated, sporadic or otherwise insignificant.

(a) prohibition or restriction on exports of the like product from the complaining Member or on imports from the complaining Member into the third country market concerned;

(b) decision by an importing government operating a monopoly of trade or state trading in the product concerned to shift, for non-commercial reasons, imports from the complaining Member to another country or countries;

(c) natural disasters, strikes, transport disruptions or other force majeure substantially affecting production, qualities, quantities or prices of the product available for export from the complaining Member;

(d) existence of arrangements limiting exports from the complaining Member;

(e) voluntary decrease in the availability for export of the product concerned from the complaining Member (including, inter alia, a situation where firms in the complaining Member have been autonomously reallocating exports of this product to new markets);

(f) failure to conform to standards and other regulatory requirements in the importing country.

6.8 In the absence of circumstances referred to in paragraph 7, the existence of serious prejudice should be determined on the basis of the information submitted to or obtained by the panel, including information submitted in accordance with the provisions of Annex V.

6.9 This Article does not apply to subsidies maintained on agricultural products as provided in Article 13 of the Agreement on Agriculture.

Article 7

Remedies

7.1 Except as provided in Article 13 of the Agreement on Agriculture, whenever a Member has reason to believe that any subsidy referred to in Article 1, granted or maintained by another Member, results in injury to its domestic industry, nullification or impairment or serious prejudice, such Member may request consultations with such other Member.

7.2 A request for consultations under paragraph 1 shall include a statement of available evidence with regard to (a) the existence and nature of the subsidy in question, and (b) the injury caused to the domestic industry, or the nullification or impairment, or serious prejudice[19] caused to the interests of the Member requesting consultations.

---

[19]   In the event that the request relates to a subsidy deemed to result in serious prejudice in terms of paragraph 1 of Article 6, the available evidence of serious prejudice may be limited to the available evidence as to whether the conditions of paragraph 1 of Article 6 have been met or not.

7.3 Upon request for consultations under paragraph 1, the Member believed to be granting or maintaining the subsidy practice in question shall enter into such consultations as quickly as possible. The purpose of the consultations shall be to clarify the facts of the situation and to arrive at a mutually agreed solution.

7.4 If consultations do not result in a mutually agreed solution within 60 days,[20] any Member party to such consultations may refer the matter to the DSB for the establishment of a panel, unless the DSB decides by consensus not to establish a panel. The composition of the panel and its terms of reference shall be established within 15 days from the date when it is established.

7.5 The panel shall review the matter and shall submit its final report to the parties to the dispute. The report shall be circulated to all Members within 120 days of the date of the composition and establishment of the panel's terms of reference.

7.6 Within 30 days of the issuance of the panel's report to all Members, the report shall be adopted by the DSB[21] unless one of the parties to the dispute formally notifies the DSB of its decision to appeal or the DSB decides by consensus not to adopt the report.

7.7 Where a panel report is appealed, the Appellate Body shall issue its decision within 60 days from the date when the party to the dispute formally notifies its intention to appeal. When the Appellate Body considers that it cannot provide its report within 60 days, it shall inform the DSB in writing of the reasons for the delay together with an estimate of the period within which it will submit its report. In no case shall the proceedings exceed 90 days. The appellate report shall be adopted by the DSB and unconditionally accepted by the parties to the dispute unless the DSB decides by consensus not to adopt the appellate report within 20 days following its issuance to the Members.[22]

7.8 Where a panel report or an Appellate Body report is adopted in which it is determined that any subsidy has resulted in adverse effects to the interests of another Member within the meaning of Article 5, the Member granting or maintaining such subsidy shall take appropriate steps to remove the adverse effects or shall withdraw the subsidy.

7.9 In the event the Member has not taken appropriate steps to remove the adverse effects of the subsidy or withdraw the subsidy within six months from the date when the DSB adopts the panel report or the Appellate Body report,

---

[20] Any time-periods mentioned in this Article may be extended by mutual agreement.
[21] If a meeting of the DSB is not scheduled during this period, such a meeting shall be held for this purpose.
[22] If a meeting of the DSB is not scheduled during this period, such a meeting shall be held for this purpose.

and in the absence of agreement on compensation, the DSB shall grant authorization to the complaining Member to take countermeasures, commensurate with the degree and nature of the adverse effects determined to exist, unless the DSB decides by consensus to reject the request.

7.10 In the event that a party to the dispute requests arbitration under paragraph 6 of Article 22 of the DSU, the arbitrator shall determine whether the countermeasures are commensurate with the degree and nature of the adverse effects determined to exist.

PART IV: NON-ACTIONABLE SUBSIDIES

Article 8

Identification of Non-Actionable Subsidies

8.1 The following subsidies shall be considered as non-actionable:[23]

(a) subsidies which are not specific within the meaning of Article 2;

(b) subsidies which are specific within the meaning of Article 2 but which meet all of the conditions provided for in paragraphs 2(a), 2(b) or 2(c) below.

8.2 Notwithstanding the provisions of Parts III and V, the following subsidies shall be non-actionable:

(a) assistance for research activities conducted by firms or by higher education or research establishments on a contract basis with firms if:[24,25,26]

the assistance covers[27] not more than 75 per cent of the costs of industrial

---

[23]   It is recognized that government assistance for various purposes is widely provided by Members and that the mere fact that such assistance may not qualify for non-actionable treatment under the provisions of this Article does not in itself restrict the ability of Members to provide such assistance.

[24]   Since it is anticipated that civil aircraft will be subject to specific multilateral rules, the provisions of this subparagraph do not apply to that product.

[25]   Not later than 18 months after the date of entry into force of the WTO Agreement, the Committee on Subsidies and Countervailing Measures provided for in Article 24 (referred to in this Agreement as 'the Committee') shall review the operation of the provisions of subparagraph 2(a) with a view to making all necessary modifications to improve the operation of these provisions. In its consideration of possible modifications, the Committee shall carefully review the definitions of the categories set forth in this subparagraph in the light of the experience of Members in the operation of research programmes and the work in other relevant international institutions.

[26]   The provisions of this Agreement do not apply to fundamental research activities independently conducted by higher education or research establishments. The term 'fundamental research' means an enlargement of general scientific and technical knowledge not linked to industrial or commercial objectives.

[27]   The allowable levels of non-actionable assistance referred to in this subparagraph shall be established by reference to the total eligible costs incurred over the duration of an individual project.

research[28] or 50 per cent of the costs of pre-competitive development activity,[29,30]; and provided that such assistance is limited exclusively to:

(i) costs of personnel (researchers, technicians and other supporting staff employed exclusively in the research activity);

(ii) costs of instruments, equipment, land and buildings used exclusively and permanently (except when disposed of on a commercial basis) for the research activity;

(iii) costs of consultancy and equivalent services used exclusively for the research activity, including bought-in research, technical knowledge, patents, etc.;

(iv) additional overhead costs incurred directly as a result of the research activity;

(v) other running costs (such as those of materials, supplies and the like), incurred directly as a result of the research activity.

(b) assistance to disadvantaged regions within the territory of a Member given pursuant to a general framework of regional development[31] and non-specific (within the meaning of Article 2) within eligible regions provided that:

(i) each disadvantaged region must be a clearly designated contiguous geographical area with a definable economic and administrative identity;

---

[28] The term 'industrial research' means planned search or critical investigation aimed at discovery of new knowledge, with the objective that such knowledge may be useful in developing new products, processes or services, or in bringing about a significant improvement to existing products, processes or services.

[29] The term 'pre-competitive development activity' means the translation of industrial research findings into a plan, blueprint or design for new, modified or improved products, processes or services whether intended for sale or use, including the creation of a first prototype which would not be capable of commercial use. It may further include the conceptual formulation and design of products, processes or services alternatives and initial demonstration or pilot projects, provided that these same projects cannot be converted or used for industrial application or commercial exploitation. It does not include routine or periodic alterations to existing products, production lines, manufacturing processes, services, and other on-going operations even though those alterations may represent improvements.

[30] In the case of programmes which span industrial research and pre-competitive development activity, the allowable level of non-actionable assistance shall not exceed the simple average of the allowable levels of non-actionable assistance applicable to the above two categories, calculated on the basis of all eligible costs as set forth in items (i) to (v) of this subparagraph.

[31] A 'general framework of regional development' means that regional subsidy programmes are part of an internally consistent and generally applicable regional development policy and that regional development subsidies are not granted in isolated geographical points having no, or virtually no, influence on the development of a region.

(ii) the region is considered as disadvantaged on the basis of neutral and objective criteria,[32] indicating that the region's difficulties arise out of more than temporary circumstances; such criteria must be clearly spelled out in law, regulation, or other official document, so as to be capable of verification;

(iii) the criteria shall include a measurement of economic development which shall be based on at least one of the following factors:

– one of either income per capita or household income per capita, or GDP per capita, which must not be above 85 per cent of the average for the territory concerned;

– unemployment rate, which must be at least 110 per cent of the average for the territory concerned;

as measured over a three-year period; such measurement, however, may be a composite one and may include other factors.

(c) assistance to promote adaptation of existing facilities[33] to new environmental requirements imposed by law and/or regulations which result in greater constraints and financial burden on firms, provided that the assistance:

(i) is a one-time non-recurring measure; and

(ii) is limited to 20 per cent of the cost of adaptation; and

(iii) does not cover the cost of replacing and operating the assisted investment, which must be fully borne by firms; and

(iv) is directly linked to and proportionate to a firm's planned reduction of nuisances and pollution, and does not cover any manufacturing cost savings which may be achieved; and

(v) is available to all firms which can adopt the new equipment and/or production processes.

8.3 A subsidy programme for which the provisions of paragraph 2 are invoked shall be notified in advance of its implementation to the Committee in accordance with the provisions of Part VII. Any such notification shall be sufficiently precise to enable other Members to evaluate the consistency of the programme with the conditions and criteria provided for in the relevant provi-

---

[32] 'Neutral and objective criteria' means criteria which do not favour certain regions beyond what is appropriate for the elimination or reduction of regional disparities within the framework of the regional development policy. In this regard, regional subsidy programmes shall include ceilings on the amount of assistance which can be granted to each subsidised project. Such ceilings must be differentiated according to the different levels of development of assisted regions and must be expressed in terms of investment costs or cost of job creation. Within such ceilings, the distribution of assistance shall be sufficiently broad and even to avoid the predominant use of a subsidy by, or the granting of disproportionately large amounts of subsidy to, certain enterprises as provided for in Article 2.

[33] The term 'existing facilities' means facilities which have been in operation for at least two years at the time when new environmental requirements are imposed.

sions of paragraph 2. Members shall also provide the Committee with yearly updates of such notifications, in particular by supplying information on global expenditure for each programme, and on any modification of the programme. Other Members shall have the right to request information about individual cases of subsidisation under a notified programme.[34]

8.4 Upon request of a Member, the Secretariat shall review a notification made pursuant to paragraph 3 and, where necessary, may require additional information from the subsidising Member concerning the notified programme under review. The Secretariat shall report its findings to the Committee. The Committee shall, upon request, promptly review the findings of the Secretariat (or, if a review by the Secretariat has not been requested, the notification itself), with a view to determining whether the conditions and criteria laid down in paragraph 2 have not been met. The procedure provided for in this paragraph shall be completed at the latest at the first regular meeting of the Committee following the notification of a subsidy programme, provided that at least two months have elapsed between such notification and the regular meeting of the Committee. The review procedure described in this paragraph shall also apply, upon request, to substantial modifications of a programme notified in the yearly updates referred to in paragraph 3.

8.5 Upon the request of a Member, the determination by the Committee referred to in paragraph 4, or a failure by the Committee to make such a determination, as well as the violation, in individual cases, of the conditions set out in a notified programme, shall be submitted to binding arbitration. The arbitration body shall present its conclusions to the Members within 120 days from the date when the matter was referred to the arbitration body. Except as otherwise provided in this paragraph, the DSU shall apply to arbitrations conducted under this paragraph.

Article 9

Consultations and Authorized Remedies

9.1 If, in the course of implementation of a programme referred to in paragraph 2 of Article 8, notwithstanding the fact that the programme is consistent with the criteria laid down in that paragraph, a Member has reasons to believe that this programme has resulted in serious adverse effects to the domestic industry of that Member, such as to cause damage which would be difficult to repair, such Member may request consultations with the Member granting or maintaining the subsidy.

---

[34] It is recognised that nothing in this notification provision requires the provision of confidential information, including confidential business information.

9.2 Upon request for consultations under paragraph 1, the Member granting or maintaining the subsidy programme in question shall enter into such consultations as quickly as possible. The purpose of the consultations shall be to clarify the facts of the situation and to arrive at a mutually acceptable solution.

9.3 If no mutually acceptable solution has been reached in consultations under paragraph 2 within 60 days of the request for such consultations, the requesting Member may refer the matter to the Committee.

9.4 Where a matter is referred to the Committee, the Committee shall immediately review the facts involved and the evidence of the effects referred to in paragraph 1. If the Committee determines that such effects exist, it may recommend to the subsidising Member to modify this programme in such a way as to remove these effects. The Committee shall present its conclusions within 120 days from the date when the matter is referred to it under paragraph 3. In the event the recommendation is not followed within six months, the Committee shall authorize the requesting Member to take appropriate countermeasures commensurate with the nature and degree of the effects determined to exist.

PART V: COUNTERVAILING MEASURES

Article 10

Application of Article VI of GATT 1994[35]

Members shall take all necessary steps to ensure that the imposition of a countervailing duty[36] on any product of the territory of any Member imported into

---

[35]   The provisions of Part II or III may be invoked in parallel with the provisions of Part V; however, with regard to the effects of a particular subsidy in the domestic market of the importing Member, only one form of relief (either a countervailing duty, if the requirements of Part V are met, or a countermeasure under Articles 4 or 7) shall be available. The provisions of Parts III and V shall not be invoked regarding measures considered non-actionable in accordance with the provisions of Part IV. However, measures referred to in paragraph 1(a) of Article 8 may be investigated in order to determine whether or not they are specific within the meaning of Article 2. In addition, in the case of a subsidy referred to in paragraph 2 of Article 8 conferred pursuant to a programme which has not been notified in accordance with paragraph 3 of Article 8, the provisions of Part III or V may be invoked, but such subsidy shall be treated as non-actionable if it is found to conform to the standards set forth in paragraph 2 of Article 8.

[36]   The term 'countervailing duty' shall be understood to mean a special duty levied for the purpose of offsetting any subsidy bestowed directly or indirectly upon the manufacture, production or export of any merchandise, as provided for in paragraph 3 of Article VI of GATT 1994.

the territory of another Member is in accordance with the provisions of Article VI of GATT 1994 and the terms of this Agreement. Countervailing duties may only be imposed pursuant to investigations initiated[37] and conducted in accordance with the provisions of this Agreement and the Agreement on Agriculture.

Article 11

Initiation and Subsequent Investigation

11.1 Except as provided in paragraph 6, an investigation to determine the existence, degree and effect of any alleged subsidy shall be initiated upon a written application by or on behalf of the domestic industry.

11.2 An application under paragraph 1 shall include sufficient evidence of the existence of (a) a subsidy and, if possible, its amount, (b) injury within the meaning of Article VI of GATT 1994 as interpreted by this Agreement, and (c) a causal link between the subsidised imports and the alleged injury. Simple assertion, unsubstantiated by relevant evidence, cannot be considered sufficient to meet the requirements of this paragraph. The application shall contain such information as is reasonably available to the applicant on the following:

(i) the identity of the applicant and a description of the volume and value of the domestic production of the like product by the applicant. Where a written application is made on behalf of the domestic industry, the application shall identify the industry on behalf of which the application is made by a list of all known domestic producers of the like product (or associations of domestic producers of the like product) and, to the extent possible, a description of the volume and value of domestic production of the like product accounted for by such producers;

(ii) a complete description of the allegedly subsidised product, the names of the country or countries of origin or export in question, the identity of each known exporter or foreign producer and a list of known persons importing the product in question;

(iii) evidence with regard to the existence, amount and nature of the subsidy in question;

(iv) evidence that alleged injury to a domestic industry is caused by subsidised imports through the effects of the subsidies; this evidence includes information on the evolution of the volume of the allegedly subsidised imports, the effect of these imports on prices of the like product in the domestic market and the consequent impact of the imports on the domestic industry,

---

[37] The term 'initiated' as used hereinafter means procedural action by which a Member formally commences an investigation as provided in Article 11.

as demonstrated by relevant factors and indices having a bearing on the state of the domestic industry, such as those listed in paragraphs 2 and 4 of Article 15.

11.3 The authorities shall review the accuracy and adequacy of the evidence provided in the application to determine whether the evidence is sufficient to justify the initiation of an investigation.

11.4 An investigation shall not be initiated pursuant to paragraph 1 unless the authorities have determined, on the basis of an examination of the degree of support for, or opposition to, the application expressed[38] by domestic producers of the like product, that the application has been made by or on behalf of the domestic industry.[39] The application shall be considered to have been made 'by or on behalf of the domestic industry' if it is supported by those domestic producers whose collective output constitutes more than 50 per cent of the total production of the like product produced by that portion of the domestic industry expressing either support for or opposition to the application. However, no investigation shall be initiated when domestic producers expressly supporting the application account for less than 25 per cent of total production of the like product produced by the domestic industry.

11.5 The authorities shall avoid, unless a decision has been made to initiate an investigation, any publicising of the application for the initiation of an investigation.

11.6 If, in special circumstances, the authorities concerned decide to initiate an investigation without having received a written application by or on behalf of a domestic industry for the initiation of such investigation, they shall proceed only if they have sufficient evidence of the existence of a subsidy, injury and causal link, as described in paragraph 2, to justify the initiation of an investigation.

11.7 The evidence of both subsidy and injury shall be considered simultaneously (a) in the decision whether or not to initiate an investigation and (b) thereafter, during the course of the investigation, starting on a date not later than the earliest date on which in accordance with the provisions of this Agreement provisional measures may be applied.

11.8 In cases where products are not imported directly from the country of origin but are exported to the importing Member from an intermediate country, the provisions of this Agreement shall be fully applicable and the transac-

---

[38] In the case of fragmented industries involving an exceptionally large number of producers, authorities may determine support and opposition by using statistically valid sampling techniques.

[39] Members are aware that in the territory of certain Members employees of domestic producers of the like product or representatives of those employees may make or support an application for an investigation under paragraph 1.

tion or transactions shall, for the purposes of this Agreement, be regarded as having taken place between the country of origin and the importing Member.

11.9 An application under paragraph 1 shall be rejected and an investigation shall be terminated promptly as soon as the authorities concerned are satisfied that there is not sufficient evidence of either subsidisation or of injury to justify proceeding with the case. There shall be immediate termination in cases where the amount of a subsidy is *de minimis*, or where the volume of subsidised imports, actual or potential, or the injury, is negligible. For the purpose of this paragraph, the amount of the subsidy shall be considered to be *de minimis* if the subsidy is less than 1 per cent *ad valorem*.

11.10 An investigation shall not hinder the procedures of customs clearance.

11.11 Investigations shall, except in special circumstances, be concluded within one year, and in no case more than 18 months, after their initiation.

Article 12

Evidence

12.1 Interested Members and all interested parties in a countervailing duty investigation shall be given notice of the information which the authorities require and ample opportunity to present in writing all evidence which they consider relevant in respect of the investigation in question.

12.1.1 Exporters, foreign producers or interested Members receiving questionnaires used in a countervailing duty investigation shall be given at least 30 days for reply.[40] Due consideration should be given to any request for an extension of the 30-day period and, upon cause shown, such an extension should be granted whenever practicable.

12.1.2 Subject to the requirement to protect confidential information, evidence presented in writing by one interested Member or interested party shall be made available promptly to other interested Members or interested parties participating in the investigation.

12.1.3 As soon as an investigation has been initiated, the authorities shall provide the full text of the written application received under paragraph 1 of Article 11 to the known exporters[41] and to the authorities of the exporting

---

[40]   As a general rule, the time-limit for exporters shall be counted from the date of receipt of the questionnaire, which for this purpose shall be deemed to have been received one week from the date on which it was sent to the respondent or transmitted to the appropriate diplomatic representatives of the exporting Member or, in the case of a separate customs territory Member of the WTO, an official representative of the exporting territory.

[41]   It being understood that where the number of exporters involved is particularly

Member and shall make it available, upon request, to other interested parties involved. Due regard shall be paid to the protection of confidential information, as provided for in paragraph 4.

12.2 Interested Members and interested parties also shall have the right, upon justification, to present information orally. Where such information is provided orally, the interested Members and interested parties subsequently shall be required to reduce such submissions to writing. Any decision of the investigating authorities can only be based on such information and arguments as were on the written record of this authority and which were available to interested Members and interested parties participating in the investigation, due account having been given to the need to protect confidential information.

12.3 The authorities shall whenever practicable provide timely opportunities for all interested Members and interested parties to see all information that is relevant to the presentation of their cases, that is not confidential as defined in paragraph 4, and that is used by the authorities in a countervailing duty investigation, and to prepare presentations on the basis of this information.

12.4 Any information which is by nature confidential (for example, because its disclosure would be of significant competitive advantage to a competitor or because its disclosure would have a significantly adverse effect upon a person supplying the information or upon a person from whom the supplier acquired the information), or which is provided on a confidential basis by parties to an investigation shall, upon good cause shown, be treated as such by the authorities. Such information shall not be disclosed without specific permission of the party submitting it.[42]

12.4.1 The authorities shall require interested Members or interested parties providing confidential information to furnish non-confidential summaries thereof. These summaries shall be in sufficient detail to permit a reasonable understanding of the substance of the information submitted in confidence. In exceptional circumstances, such Members or parties may indicate that such information is not susceptible of summary. In such exceptional circumstances, a statement of the reasons why summarization is not possible must be provided.

12.4.2 If the authorities find that a request for confidentiality is not warranted and if the supplier of the information is either unwilling to make the information public or to authorize its disclosure in generalized or summary form, the authorities may disregard such information unless it can be demon-

---

high, the full text of the application should instead be provided only to the authorities of the exporting Member or to the relevant trade association who then should forward copies to the exporters concerned.

[42]   Members are aware that in the territory of certain Members disclosure pursuant to a narrowly-drawn protective order may be required.

strated to their satisfaction from appropriate sources that the information is correct.[43]

12.5 Except in circumstances provided for in paragraph 7, the authorities shall during the course of an investigation satisfy themselves as to the accuracy of the information supplied by interested Members or interested parties upon which their findings are based.

12.6 The investigating authorities may carry out investigations in the territory of other Members as required, provided that they have notified in good time the Member in question and unless that Member objects to the investigation. Further, the investigating authorities may carry out investigations on the premises of a firm and may examine the records of a firm if (a) the firm so agrees and (b) the Member in question is notified and does not object. The procedures set forth in Annex VI shall apply to investigations on the premises of a firm. Subject to the requirement to protect confidential information, the authorities shall make the results of any such investigations available, or shall provide disclosure thereof pursuant to paragraph 8, to the firms to which they pertain and may make such results available to the applicants.

12.7 In cases in which any interested Member or interested party refuses access to, or otherwise does not provide, necessary information within a reasonable period or significantly impedes the investigation, preliminary and final determinations, affirmative or negative, may be made on the basis of the facts available.

12.8 The authorities shall, before a final determination is made, inform all interested Members and interested parties of the essential facts under consideration which form the basis for the decision whether to apply definitive measures. Such disclosure should take place in sufficient time for the parties to defend their interests.

12.9 For the purposes of this Agreement, 'interested parties' shall include:

(i) an exporter or foreign producer or the importer of a product subject to investigation, or a trade or business association a majority of the members of which are producers, exporters or importers of such product; and

(ii) a producer of the like product in the importing Member or a trade and business association a majority of the members of which produce the like product in the territory of the importing Member.

This list shall not preclude Members from allowing domestic or foreign parties other than those mentioned above to be included as interested parties.

12.10 The authorities shall provide opportunities for industrial users of the product under investigation, and for representative consumer organizations in

---

[43] Members agree that requests for confidentiality should not be arbitrarily rejected. Members further agree that the investigating authority may request the waiving of confidentiality only regarding information relevant to the proceedings.

cases where the product is commonly sold at the retail level, to provide information which is relevant to the investigation regarding subsidisation, injury and causality.

12.11 The authorities shall take due account of any difficulties experienced by interested parties, in particular small companies, in supplying information requested, and shall provide any assistance practicable.

12.12 The procedures set out above are not intended to prevent the authorities of a Member from proceeding expeditiously with regard to initiating an investigation, reaching preliminary or final determinations, whether affirmative or negative, or from applying provisional or final measures, in accordance with relevant provisions of this Agreement.

Article 13

Consultations

13.1 As soon as possible after an application under Article 11 is accepted, and in any event before the initiation of any investigation, Members the products of which may be subject to such investigation shall be invited for consultations with the aim of clarifying the situation as to the matters referred to in paragraph 2 of Article 11 and arriving at a mutually agreed solution.

13.2 Furthermore, throughout the period of investigation, Members the products of which are the subject of the investigation shall be afforded a reasonable opportunity to continue consultations, with a view to clarifying the factual situation and to arriving at a mutually agreed solution.[44]

13.3 Without prejudice to the obligation to afford reasonable opportunity for consultation, these provisions regarding consultations are not intended to prevent the authorities of a Member from proceeding expeditiously with regard to initiating the investigation, reaching preliminary or final determinations, whether affirmative or negative, or from applying provisional or final measures, in accordance with the provisions of this Agreement.

13.4 The Member which intends to initiate any investigation or is conducting such an investigation shall permit, upon request, the Member or Members the products of which are subject to such investigation access to non-confidential evidence, including the non-confidential summary of confidential data being used for initiating or conducting the investigation.

---

[44] It is particularly important, in accordance with the provisions of this paragraph, that no affirmative determination whether preliminary or final be made without reasonable opportunity for consultations having been given. Such consultations may establish the basis for proceeding under the provisions of Part II, III or X.

Article 14

Calculation of the Amount of a Subsidy in Terms of the Benefit to the Recipient

For the purpose of Part V, any method used by the investigating authority to calculate the benefit to the recipient conferred pursuant to paragraph 1 of Article 1 shall be provided for in the national legislation or implementing regulations of the Member concerned and its application to each particular case shall be transparent and adequately explained. Furthermore, any such method shall be consistent with the following guidelines:

(a) government provision of equity capital shall not be considered as conferring a benefit, unless the investment decision can be regarded as inconsistent with the usual investment practice (including for the provision of risk capital) of private investors in the territory of that Member;

(b) a loan by a government shall not be considered as conferring a benefit, unless there is a difference between the amount that the firm receiving the loan pays on the government loan and the amount the firm would pay on a comparable commercial loan which the firm could actually obtain on the market. In this case the benefit shall be the difference between these two amounts;

(c) a loan guarantee by a government shall not be considered as conferring a benefit, unless there is a difference between the amount that the firm receiving the guarantee pays on a loan guaranteed by the government and the amount that the firm would pay on a comparable commercial loan absent the government guarantee. In this case the benefit shall be the difference between these two amounts adjusted for any differences in fees;

(d) the provision of goods or services or purchase of goods by a government shall not be considered as conferring a benefit unless the provision is made for less than adequate remuneration, or the purchase is made for more than adequate remuneration. The adequacy of remuneration shall be determined in relation to prevailing market conditions for the good or service in question in the country of provision or purchase (including price, quality, availability, marketability, transportation and other conditions of purchase or sale).

Article 15

Determination of Injury[45]

15.1 A determination of injury for purposes of Article VI of GATT 1994 shall be based on positive evidence and involve an objective examination of

---

[45] Under this Agreement the term 'injury' shall, unless otherwise specified, be taken to mean material injury to a domestic industry, threat of material injury to a

both (a) the volume of the subsidised imports and the effect of the subsidised imports on prices in the domestic market for like products[46] and (b) the consequent impact of these imports on the domestic producers of such products.

15.2 With regard to the volume of the subsidised imports, the investigating authorities shall consider whether there has been a significant increase in subsidised imports, either in absolute terms or relative to production or consumption in the importing Member. With regard to the effect of the subsidised imports on prices, the investigating authorities shall consider whether there has been a significant price undercutting by the subsidised imports as compared with the price of a like product of the importing Member, or whether the effect of such imports is otherwise to depress prices to a significant degree or to prevent price increases, which otherwise would have occurred, to a significant degree. No one or several of these factors can necessarily give decisive guidance.

15.3 Where imports of a product from more than one country are simultaneously subject to countervailing duty investigations, the investigating authorities may cumulatively assess the effects of such imports only if they determine that (a) the amount of subsidisation established in relation to the imports from each country is more than *de minimis* as defined in paragraph 9 of Article 11 and the volume of imports from each country is not negligible and (b) a cumulative assessment of the effects of the imports is appropriate in light of the conditions of competition between the imported products and the conditions of competition between the imported products and the like domestic product.

15.4 The examination of the impact of the subsidised imports on the domestic industry shall include an evaluation of all relevant economic factors and indices having a bearing on the state of the industry, including actual and potential decline in output, sales, market share, profits, productivity, return on investments, or utilization of capacity; factors affecting domestic prices; actual and potential negative effects on cash flow, inventories, employment, wages, growth, ability to raise capital or investments and, in the case of agriculture, whether there has been an increased burden on government support programmes. This list is not exhaustive, nor can one or several of these factors necessarily give decisive guidance.

---

domestic industry or material retardation of the establishment of such an industry and shall be interpreted in accordance with the provisions of this Article.

[46]   Throughout this Agreement the term 'like product' ('produit similaire') shall be interpreted to mean a product which is identical, i.e. alike in all respects to the product under consideration, or in the absence of such a product, another product which, although not alike in all respects, has characteristics closely resembling those of the product under consideration.

15.5 It must be demonstrated that the subsidised imports are, through the effects[47] of subsidies, causing injury within the meaning of this Agreement. The demonstration of a causal relationship between the subsidised imports and the injury to the domestic industry shall be based on an examination of all relevant evidence before the authorities. The authorities shall also examine any known factors other than the subsidised imports which at the same time are injuring the domestic industry, and the injuries caused by these other factors must not be attributed to the subsidised imports. Factors which may be relevant in this respect include, inter alia, the volumes and prices of non-subsidised imports of the product in question, contraction in demand or changes in the patterns of consumption, trade restrictive practices of and competition between the foreign and domestic producers, developments in technology and the export performance and productivity of the domestic industry.

15.6 The effect of the subsidised imports shall be assessed in relation to the domestic production of the like product when available data permit the separate identification of that production on the basis of such criteria as the production process, producers' sales and profits. If such separate identification of that production is not possible, the effects of the subsidised imports shall be assessed by the examination of the production of the narrowest group or range of products, which includes the like product, for which the necessary information can be provided.

15.7 A determination of a threat of material injury shall be based on facts and not merely on allegation, conjecture or remote possibility. The change in circumstances which would create a situation in which the subsidy would cause injury must be clearly foreseen and imminent. In making a determination regarding the existence of a threat of material injury, the investigating authorities should consider, inter alia, such factors as:

(i) nature of the subsidy or subsidies in question and the trade effects likely to arise therefrom;

(ii) a significant rate of increase of subsidised imports into the domestic market indicating the likelihood of substantially increased importation;

(iii) sufficient freely disposable, or an imminent, substantial increase in, capacity of the exporter indicating the likelihood of substantially increased subsidised exports to the importing Member's market, taking into account the availability of other export markets to absorb any additional exports;

(iv) whether imports are entering at prices that will have a significant depressing or suppressing effect on domestic prices, and would likely increase demand for further imports; and

---

[47]   As set forth in paragraphs 2 and 4.

(v) inventories of the product being investigated.

No one of these factors by itself can necessarily give decisive guidance but the totality of the factors considered must lead to the conclusion that further subsidised exports are imminent and that, unless protective action is taken, material injury would occur.

15.8 With respect to cases where injury is threatened by subsidised imports, the application of countervailing measures shall be considered and decided with special care.

Article 16

Definition of Domestic Industry

16.1 For the purposes of this Agreement, the term 'domestic industry' shall, except as provided in paragraph 2, be interpreted as referring to the domestic producers as a whole of the like products or to those of them whose collective output of the products constitutes a major proportion of the total domestic production of those products, except that when producers are related[48] to the exporters or importers or are themselves importers of the allegedly subsidised product or a like product from other countries, the term 'domestic industry' may be interpreted as referring to the rest of the producers.

16.2 In exceptional circumstances, the territory of a Member may, for the production in question, be divided into two or more competitive markets and the producers within each market may be regarded as a separate industry if (a) the producers within such market sell all or almost all of their production of the product in question in that market, and (b) the demand in that market is not to any substantial degree supplied by producers of the product in question located elsewhere in the territory. In such circumstances, injury may be found to exist even where a major portion of the total domestic industry is not injured, provided there is a concentration of subsidised imports into such an isolated market and provided further that the subsidised imports are causing injury to the producers of all or almost all of the production within such market.

---

[48] For the purpose of this paragraph, producers shall be deemed to be related to exporters or importers only if *(a)* one of them directly or indirectly controls the other; or *(b)* both of them are directly or indirectly controlled by a third person; or *(c)* together they directly or indirectly control a third person, provided that there are grounds for believing or suspecting that the effect of the relationship is such as to cause the producer concerned to behave differently from non-related producers. For the purpose of this paragraph, one shall be deemed to control another when the former is legally or operationally in a position to exercise restraint or direction over the latter.

16.3 When the domestic industry has been interpreted as referring to the producers in a certain area, i.e. a market as defined in paragraph 2, counter-vailing duties shall be levied only on the products in question consigned for final consumption to that area. When the constitutional law of the importing Member does not permit the levying of countervailing duties on such a basis, the importing Member may levy the countervailing duties without limitation only if (a) the exporters shall have been given an opportunity to cease export-ing at subsidised prices to the area concerned or otherwise give assurances pursuant to Article 18, and adequate assurances in this regard have not been promptly given, and (b) such duties cannot be levied only on products of specific producers which supply the area in question.

16.4 Where two or more countries have reached under the provisions of paragraph 8(a) of Article XXIV of GATT 1994 such a level of integration that they have the characteristics of a single, unified market, the industry in the entire area of integration shall be taken to be the domestic industry referred to in paragraphs 1 and 2.

16.5 The provisions of paragraph 6 of Article 15 shall be applicable to this Article.

Article 17

Provisional Measures

17.1 Provisional measures may be applied only if:

(a) an investigation has been initiated in accordance with the provisions of Article 11, a public notice has been given to that effect and interested Members and interested parties have been given adequate opportunities to submit information and make comments;

(b) a preliminary affirmative determination has been made that a subsidy exists and that there is injury to a domestic industry caused by subsidised imports; and

(c) the authorities concerned judge such measures necessary to prevent injury being caused during the investigation.

17.2 Provisional measures may take the form of provisional countervailing duties guaranteed by cash deposits or bonds equal to the amount of the provi-sionally calculated amount of subsidisation.

17.3 Provisional measures shall not be applied sooner than 60 days from the date of initiation of the investigation.

17.4 The application of provisional measures shall be limited to as short a period as possible, not exceeding four months.

17.5 The relevant provisions of Article 19 shall be followed in the applica-tion of provisional measures.

Article 18

Undertakings

18.1 Proceedings may[49] be suspended or terminated without the imposition of provisional measures or countervailing duties upon receipt of satisfactory voluntary undertakings under which:

(a) the government of the exporting Member agrees to eliminate or limit the subsidy or take other measures concerning its effects; or

(b) the exporter agrees to revise its prices so that the investigating authorities are satisfied that the injurious effect of the subsidy is eliminated. Price increases under such undertakings shall not be higher than necessary to eliminate the amount of the subsidy. It is desirable that the price increases be less than the amount of the subsidy if such increases would be adequate to remove the injury to the domestic industry.

18.2 Undertakings shall not be sought or accepted unless the authorities of the importing Member have made a preliminary affirmative determination of subsidisation and injury caused by such subsidisation and, in case of undertakings from exporters, have obtained the consent of the exporting Member.

18.3 Undertakings offered need not be accepted if the authorities of the importing Member consider their acceptance impractical, for example if the number of actual or potential exporters is too great, or for other reasons, including reasons of general policy. Should the case arise and where practicable, the authorities shall provide to the exporter the reasons which have led them to consider acceptance of an undertaking as inappropriate, and shall, to the extent possible, give the exporter an opportunity to make comments thereon.

18.4 If an undertaking is accepted, the investigation of subsidisation and injury shall nevertheless be completed if the exporting Member so desires or the importing Member so decides. In such a case, if a negative determination of subsidisation or injury is made, the undertaking shall automatically lapse, except in cases where such a determination is due in large part to the existence of an undertaking. In such cases, the authorities concerned may require that an undertaking be maintained for a reasonable period consistent with the provisions of this Agreement. In the event that an affirmative determination of subsidisation and injury is made, the undertaking shall continue consistent with its terms and the provisions of this Agreement.

---

[49] The word 'may' shall not be interpreted to allow the simultaneous continuation of proceedings with the implementation of undertakings, except as provided in paragraph 4.

18.5 Price undertakings may be suggested by the authorities of the importing Member, but no exporter shall be forced to enter into such undertakings. The fact that governments or exporters do not offer such undertakings, or do not accept an invitation to do so, shall in no way prejudice the consideration of the case. However, the authorities are free to determine that a threat of injury is more likely to be realized if the subsidised imports continue.

18.6 Authorities of an importing Member may require any government or exporter from whom an undertaking has been accepted to provide periodically information relevant to the fulfilment of such an undertaking, and to permit verification of pertinent data. In case of violation of an undertaking, the authorities of the importing Member may take, under this Agreement in conformity with its provisions, expeditious actions which may constitute immediate application of provisional measures using the best information available. In such cases, definitive duties may be levied in accordance with this Agreement on products entered for consumption not more than 90 days before the application of such provisional measures, except that any such retroactive assessment shall not apply to imports entered before the violation of the undertaking.

Article 19

Imposition and Collection of Countervailing Duties

19.1 If, after reasonable efforts have been made to complete consultations, a Member makes a final determination of the existence and amount of the subsidy and that, through the effects of the subsidy, the subsidised imports are causing injury, it may impose a countervailing duty in accordance with the provisions of this Article unless the subsidy or subsidies are withdrawn.

19.2 The decision whether or not to impose a countervailing duty in cases where all requirements for the imposition have been fulfilled, and the decision whether the amount of the countervailing duty to be imposed shall be the full amount of the subsidy or less, are decisions to be made by the authorities of the importing Member. It is desirable that the imposition should be permissive in the territory of all Members, that the duty should be less than the total amount of the subsidy if such lesser duty would be adequate to remove the injury to the domestic industry, and that procedures should be established which would allow the authorities concerned to take due account of representations made by domestic interested parties[50] whose interests might be adversely affected by the imposition of a countervailing duty.

---

[50] For the purpose of this paragraph, the term 'domestic interested parties' shall include consumers and industrial users of the imported product subject to investigation.

19.3 When a countervailing duty is imposed in respect of any product, such countervailing duty shall be levied, in the appropriate amounts in each case, on a non-discriminatory basis on imports of such product from all sources found to be subsidised and causing injury, except as to imports from those sources which have renounced any subsidies in question or from which undertakings under the terms of this Agreement have been accepted. Any exporter whose exports are subject to a definitive countervailing duty but who was not actually investigated for reasons other than a refusal to cooperate, shall be entitled to an expedited review in order that the investigating authorities promptly establish an individual countervailing duty rate for that exporter.

19.4 No countervailing duty shall be levied[51] on any imported product in excess of the amount of the subsidy found to exist, calculated in terms of subsidisation per unit of the subsidised and exported product.

Article 20

Retroactivity

20.1 Provisional measures and countervailing duties shall only be applied to products which enter for consumption after the time when the decision under paragraph 1 of Article 17 and paragraph 1 of Article 19, respectively, enters into force, subject to the exceptions set out in this Article.

20.2 Where a final determination of injury (but not of a threat thereof or of a material retardation of the establishment of an industry) is made or, in the case of a final determination of a threat of injury, where the effect of the subsidised imports would, in the absence of the provisional measures, have led to a determination of injury, countervailing duties may be levied retroactively for the period for which provisional measures, if any, have been applied.

20.3 If the definitive countervailing duty is higher than the amount guaranteed by the cash deposit or bond, the difference shall not be collected. If the definitive duty is less than the amount guaranteed by the cash deposit or bond, the excess amount shall be reimbursed or the bond released in an expeditious manner.

20.4 Except as provided in paragraph 2, where a determination of threat of injury or material retardation is made (but no injury has yet occurred) a definitive countervailing duty may be imposed only from the date of the determination of threat of injury or material retardation, and any cash deposit made during the period of the application of provisional measures shall be refunded and any bonds released in an expeditious manner.

---

[51]   As used in this Agreement 'levy' shall mean the definitive or final legal assessment or collection of a duty or tax.

20.5 Where a final determination is negative, any cash deposit made during the period of the application of provisional measures shall be refunded and any bonds released in an expeditious manner.

20.6 In critical circumstances where for the subsidised product in question the authorities find that injury which is difficult to repair is caused by massive imports in a relatively short period of a product benefiting from subsidies paid or bestowed inconsistently with the provisions of GATT 1994 and of this Agreement and where it is deemed necessary, in order to preclude the recurrence of such injury, to assess countervailing duties retroactively on those imports, the definitive countervailing duties may be assessed on imports which were entered for consumption not more than 90 days prior to the date of application of provisional measures.

Article 21

Duration and Review of Countervailing Duties and Undertakings

21.1 A countervailing duty shall remain in force only as long as and to the extent necessary to counteract subsidisation which is causing injury.

21.2 The authorities shall review the need for the continued imposition of the duty, where warranted, on their own initiative or, provided that a reasonable period of time has elapsed since the imposition of the definitive countervailing duty, upon request by any interested party which submits positive information substantiating the need for a review. Interested parties shall have the right to request the authorities to examine whether the continued imposition of the duty is necessary to offset subsidisation, whether the injury would be likely to continue or recur if the duty were removed or varied, or both. If, as a result of the review under this paragraph, the authorities determine that the countervailing duty is no longer warranted, it shall be terminated immediately.

21.3 Notwithstanding the provisions of paragraphs 1 and 2, any definitive countervailing duty shall be terminated on a date not later than five years from its imposition (or from the date of the most recent review under paragraph 2 if that review has covered both subsidisation and injury, or under this paragraph), unless the authorities determine, in a review initiated before that date on their own initiative or upon a duly substantiated request made by or on behalf of the domestic industry within a reasonable period of time prior to that date, that the expiry of the duty would be likely to lead to continuation or recurrence of subsidisation and injury.[52] The duty may remain in force pending the outcome of such a review.

---

[52]   When the amount of the countervailing duty is assessed on a retrospective basis, a finding in the most recent assessment proceeding that no duty is to be levied shall not by itself require the authorities to terminate the definitive duty.

21.4 The provisions of Article 12 regarding evidence and procedure shall apply to any review carried out under this Article. Any such review shall be carried out expeditiously and shall normally be concluded within 12 months of the date of initiation of the review.

21.5 The provisions of this Article shall apply *mutatis mutandis* to undertakings accepted under Article 18.

Article 22

Public Notice and Explanation of Determinations

22.1 When the authorities are satisfied that there is sufficient evidence to justify the initiation of an investigation pursuant to Article 11, the Member or Members the products of which are subject to such investigation and other interested parties known to the investigating authorities to have an interest therein shall be notified and a public notice shall be given.

22.2 A public notice of the initiation of an investigation shall contain, or otherwise make available through a separate report,[53] adequate information on the following:

(i) the name of the exporting country or countries and the product involved;

(ii) the date of initiation of the investigation;

(iii) a description of the subsidy practice or practices to be investigated;

(iv) a summary of the factors on which the allegation of injury is based;

(v) the address to which representations by interested Members and interested parties should be directed; and

(vi) the time-limits allowed to interested Members and interested parties for making their views known.

22.3 Public notice shall be given of any preliminary or final determination, whether affirmative or negative, of any decision to accept an undertaking pursuant to Article 18, of the termination of such an undertaking, and of the termination of a definitive countervailing duty. Each such notice shall set forth, or otherwise make available through a separate report, in sufficient detail the findings and conclusions reached on all issues of fact and law considered material by the investigating authorities. All such notices and reports shall be forwarded to the Member or Members the products of which are subject to such determination or undertaking and to other interested parties known to have an interest therein.

22.4 A public notice of the imposition of provisional measures shall set forth, or otherwise make available through a separate report, sufficiently detailed explanations for the preliminary determinations on the existence of a

---

[53]   Where authorities provide information and explanations under the provisions of this Article in a separate report, they shall ensure that such report is readily available to the public.

subsidy and injury and shall refer to the matters of fact and law which have led to arguments being accepted or rejected. Such a notice or report shall, due regard being paid to the requirement for the protection of confidential information, contain in particular:

(i) the names of the suppliers or, when this is impracticable, the supplying countries involved;

(ii) a description of the product which is sufficient for customs purposes;

(iii) the amount of subsidy established and the basis on which the existence of a subsidy has been determined;

(iv) considerations relevant to the injury determination as set out in Article 15;

(v) the main reasons leading to the determination.

22.5 A public notice of conclusion or suspension of an investigation in the case of an affirmative determination providing for the imposition of a definitive duty or the acceptance of an undertaking shall contain, or otherwise make available through a separate report, all relevant information on the matters of fact and law and reasons which have led to the imposition of final measures or the acceptance of an undertaking, due regard being paid to the requirement for the protection of confidential information. In particular, the notice or report shall contain the information described in paragraph 4, as well as the reasons for the acceptance or rejection of relevant arguments or claims made by interested Members and by the exporters and importers.

22.6 A public notice of the termination or suspension of an investigation following the acceptance of an undertaking pursuant to Article 18 shall include, or otherwise make available through a separate report, the non-confidential part of this undertaking.

22.7 The provisions of this Article shall apply *mutatis mutandis* to the initiation and completion of reviews pursuant to Article 21 and to decisions under Article 20 to apply duties retroactively.

Article 23

Judicial Review

Each Member whose national legislation contains provisions on countervailing duty measures shall maintain judicial, arbitral or administrative tribunals or procedures for the purpose, inter alia, of the prompt review of administrative actions relating to final determinations and reviews of determinations within the meaning of Article 21. Such tribunals or procedures shall be independent of the authorities responsible for the determination or review in question, and shall provide all interested parties who participated in the administrative proceeding and are directly and individually affected by the administrative actions with access to review.

PART VI: INSTITUTIONS

Article 24

Committee on Subsidies and Countervailing Measures and Subsidiary Bodies

24.1 There is hereby established a Committee on Subsidies and Countervailing Measures composed of representatives from each of the Members. The Committee shall elect its own Chairman and shall meet not less than twice a year and otherwise as envisaged by relevant provisions of this Agreement at the request of any Member. The Committee shall carry out responsibilities as assigned to it under this Agreement or by the Members and it shall afford Members the opportunity of consulting on any matter relating to the operation of the Agreement or the furtherance of its objectives. The WTO Secretariat shall act as the secretariat to the Committee.

24.2 The Committee may set up subsidiary bodies as appropriate.

24.3 The Committee shall establish a Permanent Group of Experts composed of five independent persons, highly qualified in the fields of subsidies and trade relations. The experts will be elected by the Committee and one of them will be replaced every year. The PGE may be requested to assist a panel, as provided for in paragraph 5 of Article 4. The Committee may also seek an advisory opinion on the existence and nature of any subsidy.

24.4 The PGE may be consulted by any Member and may give advisory opinions on the nature of any subsidy proposed to be introduced or currently maintained by that Member. Such advisory opinions will be confidential and may not be invoked in proceedings under Article 7.

24.5 In carrying out their functions, the Committee and any subsidiary bodies may consult with and seek information from any source they deem appropriate. However, before the Committee or a subsidiary body seeks such information from a source within the jurisdiction of a Member, it shall inform the Member involved.

PART VII: NOTIFICATION AND SURVEILLANCE

Article 25

Notifications

25.1 Members agree that, without prejudice to the provisions of paragraph 1 of Article XVI of GATT 1994, their notifications of subsidies shall be submitted not later than 30 June of each year and shall conform to the provisions of paragraphs 2 through 6.

25.2 Members shall notify any subsidy as defined in paragraph 1 of Article 1, which is specific within the meaning of Article 2, granted or maintained within their territories.

25.3 The content of notifications should be sufficiently specific to enable other Members to evaluate the trade effects and to understand the operation of notified subsidy programmes. In this connection, and without prejudice to the contents and form of the questionnaire on subsidies,[54] Members shall ensure that their notifications contain the following information:

(i) form of a subsidy (i.e. grant, loan, tax concession, etc.);

(ii) subsidy per unit or, in cases where this is not possible, the total amount or the annual amount budgeted for that subsidy (indicating, if possible, the average subsidy per unit in the previous year);

(iii) policy objective and/or purpose of a subsidy;

(iv) duration of a subsidy and/or any other time-limits attached to it;

(v) statistical data permitting an assessment of the trade effects of a subsidy.

25.4 Where specific points in paragraph 3 have not been addressed in a notification, an explanation shall be provided in the notification itself.

25.5 If subsidies are granted to specific products or sectors, the notifications should be organized by product or sector.

25.6 Members which consider that there are no measures in their territories requiring notification under paragraph 1 of Article XVI of GATT 1994 and this Agreement shall so inform the Secretariat in writing.

25.7 Members recognize that notification of a measure does not prejudge either its legal status under GATT 1994 and this Agreement, the effects under this Agreement, or the nature of the measure itself.

25.8 Any Member may, at any time, make a written request for information on the nature and extent of any subsidy granted or maintained by another Member (including any subsidy referred to in Part IV), or for an explanation of the reasons for which a specific measure has been considered as not subject to the requirement of notification.

25.9 Members so requested shall provide such information as quickly as possible and in a comprehensive manner, and shall be ready, upon request, to provide additional information to the requesting Member. In particular, they shall provide sufficient details to enable the other Member to assess their compliance with the terms of this Agreement. Any Member which considers that such information has not been provided may bring the matter to the attention of the Committee.

25.10 Any Member which considers that any measure of another Member

---

[54] The Committee shall establish a Working Party to review the contents and form of the questionnaire as contained in BISD 9S/193–194.

having the effects of a subsidy has not been notified in accordance with the provisions of paragraph 1 of Article XVI of GATT 1994 and this Article may bring the matter to the attention of such other Member. If the alleged subsidy is not thereafter notified promptly, such Member may itself bring the alleged subsidy in question to the notice of the Committee.

25.11 Members shall report without delay to the Committee all preliminary or final actions taken with respect to countervailing duties. Such reports shall be available in the Secretariat for inspection by other Members. Members shall also submit, on a semi-annual basis, reports on any countervailing duty actions taken within the preceding six months. The semi-annual reports shall be submitted on an agreed standard form.

25.12 Each Member shall notify the Committee (a) which of its authorities are competent to initiate and conduct investigations referred to in Article 11 and (b) its domestic procedures governing the initiation and conduct of such investigations.

Article 26

Surveillance

26.1 The Committee shall examine new and full notifications submitted under paragraph 1 of Article XVI of GATT 1994 and paragraph 1 of Article 25 of this Agreement at special sessions held every third year. Notifications submitted in the intervening years (updating notifications) shall be examined at each regular meeting of the Committee.

26.2 The Committee shall examine reports submitted under paragraph 11 of Article 25 at each regular meeting of the Committee.

PART VIII: DEVELOPING COUNTRY MEMBERS

Article 27

Special and Differential Treatment of Developing Country Members

27.1 Members recognize that subsidies may play an important role in economic development programmes of developing country Members.

27.2 The prohibition of paragraph 1(a) of Article 3 shall not apply to:

(a) developing country Members referred to in Annex VII.

(b) other developing country Members for a period of eight years from the date of entry into force of the WTO Agreement, subject to compliance with the provisions in paragraph 4.

27.3 The prohibition of paragraph 1(b) of Article 3 shall not apply to developing country Members for a period of five years, and shall not apply to least developed country Members for a period of eight years, from the date of entry into force of the WTO Agreement.

27.4 Any developing country Member referred to in paragraph 2(b) shall phase out its export subsidies within the eight-year period, preferably in a progressive manner. However, a developing country Member shall not increase the level of its export subsidies,[55] and shall eliminate them within a period shorter than that provided for in this paragraph when the use of such export subsidies is inconsistent with its development needs. If a developing country Member deems it necessary to apply such subsidies beyond the eight-year period, it shall not later than one year before the expiry of this period enter into consultation with the Committee, which will determine whether an extension of this period is justified, after examining all the relevant economic, financial and development needs of the developing country Member in question. If the Committee determines that the extension is justified, the developing country Member concerned shall hold annual consultations with the Committee to determine the necessity of maintaining the subsidies. If no such determination is made by the Committee, the developing country Member shall phase out the remaining export subsidies within two years from the end of the last authorized period.

27.5 A developing country Member which has reached export competitiveness in any given product shall phase out its export subsidies for such product(s) over a period of two years. However, for a developing country Member which is referred to in Annex VII and which has reached export competitiveness in one or more products, export subsidies on such products shall be gradually phased out over a period of eight years.

27.6 Export competitiveness in a product exists if a developing country Member's exports of that product have reached a share of at least 3.25 per cent in world trade of that product for two consecutive calendar years. Export competitiveness shall exist either (a) on the basis of notification by the developing country Member having reached export competitiveness, or (b) on the basis of a computation undertaken by the Secretariat at the request of any Member. For the purpose of this paragraph, a product is defined as a section heading of the Harmonized System Nomenclature. The Committee shall review the operation of this provision five years from the date of the entry into force of the WTO Agreement.

27.7 The provisions of Article 4 shall not apply to a developing country Member in the case of export subsidies which are in conformity with the provisions of paragraphs 2 through 5. The relevant provisions in such a case shall be those of Article 7.

---

[55] For a developing country Member not granting export subsidies as of the date of entry into force of the WTO Agreement, this paragraph shall apply on the basis of the level of export subsidies granted in 1986.

27.8 There shall be no presumption in terms of paragraph 1 of Article 6 that a subsidy granted by a developing country Member results in serious prejudice, as defined in this Agreement. Such serious prejudice, where applicable under the terms of paragraph 9, shall be demonstrated by positive evidence, in accordance with the provisions of paragraphs 3 through 8 of Article 6.

27.9 Regarding actionable subsidies granted or maintained by a developing country Member other than those referred to in paragraph 1 of Article 6, action may not be authorized or taken under Article 7 unless nullification or impairment of tariff concessions or other obligations under GATT 1994 is found to exist as a result of such a subsidy, in such a way as to displace or impede imports of a like product of another Member into the market of the subsidising developing country Member or unless injury to a domestic industry in the market of an importing Member occurs.

27.10 Any countervailing duty investigation of a product originating in a developing country Member shall be terminated as soon as the authorities concerned determine that:

(a) the overall level of subsidies granted upon the product in question does not exceed 2 per cent of its value calculated on a per unit basis; or

(b) the volume of the subsidised imports represents less than 4 per cent of the total imports of the like product in the importing Member, unless imports from developing country Members whose individual shares of total imports represent less than 4 per cent collectively account for more than 9 per cent of the total imports of the like product in the importing Member.

27.11 For those developing country Members within the scope of paragraph 2(b) which have eliminated export subsidies prior to the expiry of the period of eight years from the date of entry into force of the WTO Agreement, and for those developing country Members referred to in Annex VII, the number in paragraph 10(a) shall be 3 per cent rather than 2 per cent. This provision shall apply from the date that the elimination of export subsidies is notified to the Committee, and for so long as export subsidies are not granted by the notifying developing country Member. This provision shall expire eight years from the date of entry into force of the WTO Agreement.

27.12 The provisions of paragraphs 10 and 11 shall govern any determination of *de minimis* under paragraph 3 of Article 15.

27.13 The provisions of Part III shall not apply to direct forgiveness of debts, subsidies to cover social costs, in whatever form, including relinquishment of government revenue and other transfer of liabilities when such subsidies are granted within and directly linked to a privatization programme of a developing country Member, provided that both such programme and the subsidies involved are granted for a limited period and notified to the Committee and that the programme results in eventual privatization of the enterprise concerned.

27.14 The Committee shall, upon request by an interested Member, undertake a review of a specific export subsidy practice of a developing country Member to examine whether the practice is in conformity with its development needs.

27.15 The Committee shall, upon request by an interested developing country Member, undertake a review of a specific countervailing measure to examine whether it is consistent with the provisions of paragraphs 10 and 11 as applicable to the developing country Member in question.

PART IX: TRANSITIONAL ARRANGEMENTS

Article 28

Existing Programmes

28.1 Subsidy programmes which have been established within the territory of any Member before the date on which such a Member signed the WTO Agreement and which are inconsistent with the provisions of this Agreement shall be:

(a) notified to the Committee not later than 90 days after the date of entry into force of the WTO Agreement for such Member; and

(b) brought into conformity with the provisions of this Agreement within three years of the date of entry into force of the WTO Agreement for such Member and until then shall not be subject to Part II.

28.2 No Member shall extend the scope of any such programme, nor shall such a programme be renewed upon its expiry.

Article 29

Transformation into a Market Economy

29.1 Members in the process of transformation from a centrally-planned into a market, free-enterprise economy may apply programmes and measures necessary for such a transformation.

29.2 For such Members, subsidy programmes falling within the scope of Article 3, and notified according to paragraph 3, shall be phased out or brought into conformity with Article 3 within a period of seven years from the date of entry into force of the WTO Agreement. In such a case, Article 4 shall not apply. In addition during the same period:

(a) Subsidy programmes falling within the scope of paragraph 1(d) of Article 6 shall not be actionable under Article 7;

(b) With respect to other actionable subsidies, the provisions of paragraph 9 of Article 27 shall apply.

29.3 Subsidy programmes falling within the scope of Article 3 shall be notified to the Committee by the earliest practicable date after the date of entry into force of the WTO Agreement. Further notifications of such subsidies may be made up to two years after the date of entry into force of the WTO Agreement.

29.4 In exceptional circumstances Members referred to in paragraph 1 may be given departures from their notified programmes and measures and their time-frame by the Committee if such departures are deemed necessary for the process of transformation.

PART X: DISPUTE SETTLEMENT

Article 30

The provisions of Articles XXII and XXIII of GATT 1994 as elaborated and applied by the Dispute Settlement Understanding shall apply to consultations and the settlement of disputes under this Agreement, except as otherwise specifically provided herein.

PART XI: FINAL PROVISIONS

Article 31

Provisional Application

The provisions of paragraph 1 of Article 6 and the provisions of Article 8 and Article 9 shall apply for a period of five years, beginning with the date of entry into force of the WTO Agreement. Not later than 180 days before the end of this period, the Committee shall review the operation of those provisions, with a view to determining whether to extend their application, either as presently drafted or in a modified form, for a further period.

Article 32

Other Final Provisions

32.1 No specific action against a subsidy of another Member can be taken except in accordance with the provisions of GATT 1994, as interpreted by this Agreement.[56]

---

[56] This paragraph is not intended to preclude action under other relevant provisions of GATT 1994, where appropriate.

32.2 Reservations may not be entered in respect of any of the provisions of this Agreement without the consent of the other Members.

32.3 Subject to paragraph 4, the provisions of this Agreement shall apply to investigations, and reviews of existing measures, initiated pursuant to applications which have been made on or after the date of entry into force for a Member of the WTO Agreement.

32.4 For the purposes of paragraph 3 of Article 21, existing countervailing measures shall be deemed to be imposed on a date not later than the date of entry into force for a Member of the WTO Agreement, except in cases in which the domestic legislation of a Member in force at that date already included a clause of the type provided for in that paragraph.

32.5 Each Member shall take all necessary steps, of a general or particular character, to ensure, not later than the date of entry into force of the WTO Agreement for it, the conformity of its laws, regulations and administrative procedures with the provisions of this Agreement as they may apply to the Member in question.

32.6 Each Member shall inform the Committee of any changes in its laws and regulations relevant to this Agreement and in the administration of such laws and regulations.

32.7 The Committee shall review annually the implementation and operation of this Agreement, taking into account the objectives thereof. The Committee shall inform annually the Council for Trade in Goods of developments during the period covered by such reviews.

32.8 The Annexes to this Agreement constitute an integral part thereof.

ANNEX I ILLUSTRATIVE LIST OF EXPORT SUBSIDIES

(a) The provision by governments of direct subsidies to a firm or an industry contingent upon export performance.

(b) Currency retention schemes or any similar practices which involve a bonus on exports.

(c) Internal transport and freight charges on export shipments, provided or mandated by governments, on terms more favourable than for domestic shipments.

(d) The provision by governments or their agencies either directly or indirectly through government-mandated schemes, of imported or domestic products or services for use in the production of exported goods, on terms or conditions more favourable than for provision of like or directly competitive products or services for use in the production of goods for domestic consumption, if (in the case of products) such terms or conditions are more favourable than those commercially available[57] on world markets to their exporters.

(e) The full or partial exemption remission, or deferral specifically related to exports, of direct taxes[58] or social welfare charges paid or payable by industrial or commercial enterprises.[59]

(f) The allowance of special deductions directly related to exports or export performance, over and above those granted in respect to production for domestic consumption, in the calculation of the base on which direct taxes are charged.

(g) The exemption or remission, in respect of the production and distribution of exported products, of indirect taxes[58] in excess of those levied in respect of the production and distribution of like products when sold for domestic consumption.

(h) The exemption, remission or deferral of prior-stage cumulative indirect taxes[58] on goods or services used in the production of exported products in excess of the exemption, remission or deferral of like prior-stage cumulative

---

[57] The term 'commercially available' means that the choice between domestic and imported products is unrestricted and depends only on commercial considerations.

[58] For the purpose of this Agreement:

The term 'direct taxes' shall mean taxes on wages, profits, interests, rents, royalties, and all other forms of income, and taxes on the ownership of real property;

The term 'import charges' shall mean tariffs, duties, and other fiscal charges not elsewhere enumerated in this note that are levied on imports;

The term 'indirect taxes' shall mean sales, excise, turnover, value added, franchise, stamp, transfer, inventory and equipment taxes, border taxes and all taxes other than direct taxes and import charges;

'Prior-stage' indirect taxes are those levied on goods or services used directly or indirectly in making the product;

'Cumulative' indirect taxes are multi-staged taxes levied where there is no mechanism for subsequent crediting of the tax if the goods or services subject to tax at one stage of production are used in a succeeding stage of production;

'Remission' of taxes includes the refund or rebate of taxes;

'Remission or drawback' includes the full or partial exemption or deferral of import charges.

[59] The Members recognize that deferral need not amount to an export subsidy where, for example, appropriate interest charges are collected. The Members reaffirm the principle that prices for goods in transactions between exporting enterprises and foreign buyers under their or under the same control should for tax purposes be the prices which would be charged between independent enterprises acting at arm's length. Any Member may draw the attention of another Member to administrative or other practices which may contravene this principle and which result in a significant saving of direct taxes in export transactions. In such circumstances the Members shall normally attempt to resolve their differences using the facilities of existing bilateral tax treaties or other specific international mechanisms, without prejudice to the rights and obligations of Members under GATT 1994, including the right of consultation created in the preceding sentence.

indirect taxes on goods or services used in the production of like products when sold for domestic consumption; provided, however, that prior-stage cumulative indirect taxes may be exempted, remitted or deferred on exported products even when not exempted, remitted or deferred on like products when sold for domestic consumption, if the prior-stage cumulative indirect taxes are levied on inputs that are consumed in the production of the exported product (making normal allowance for waste).[60] This item shall be interpreted in accordance with the guidelines on consumption of inputs in the production process contained in Annex II.

(i) The remission or drawback of import charges[58] in excess of those levied on imported inputs that are consumed in the production of the exported product (making normal allowance for waste); provided, however, that in particular cases a firm may use a quantity of home market inputs equal to, and having the same quality and characteristics as, the imported inputs as a substitute for them in order to benefit from this provision if the import and the corresponding export operations both occur within a reasonable time period, not to exceed two years. This item shall be interpreted in accordance with the guidelines on consumption of inputs in the production process contained in Annex II and the guidelines in the determination of substitution drawback systems as export subsidies contained in Annex III.

(j) The provision by governments (or special institutions controlled by governments) of export credit guarantee or insurance programmes, of insurance or guarantee programmes against increases in the cost of exported products or of exchange risk programmes, at premium rates which are inadequate to cover the long-term operating costs and losses of the programmes.

(k) The grant by governments (or special institutions controlled by and/or acting under the authority of governments) of export credits at rates below those which they actually have to pay for the funds so employed (or would have to pay if they borrowed on international capital markets in order to obtain funds of the same maturity and other credit terms and denominated in the same currency as the export credit), or the payment by them of all or part of the costs incurred by exporters or financial institutions in obtaining credits, in so far as they are used to secure a material advantage in the field of export credit terms.

Provided, however, that if a Member is a party to an international undertaking on official export credits to which at least twelve original Members to

---

Paragraph (e) is not intended to limit a Member from taking measures to avoid the double taxation of foreign-source income earned by its enterprises or the enterprises of another Member.

[60] Paragraph (h) does not apply to value-added tax systems and border-tax adjustment in lieu thereof; the problem of the excessive remission of value-added taxes is exclusively covered by paragraph (g).

this Agreement are parties as of 1 January 1979 (or a successor undertaking which has been adopted by those original Members), or if in practice a Member applies the interest rates provisions of the relevant undertaking, an export credit practice which is in conformity with those provisions shall not be considered an export subsidy prohibited by this Agreement.

(l) Any other charge on the public account constituting an export subsidy in the sense of Article XVI of GATT 1994.

ANNEX II   GUIDELINES ON CONSUMPTION OF INPUTS IN THE PRODUCTION PROCESS[61]

I

1. Indirect tax rebate schemes can allow for exemption, remission or deferral of prior-stage cumulative indirect taxes levied on inputs that are consumed in the production of the exported product (making normal allowance for waste). Similarly, drawback schemes can allow for the remission or drawback of import charges levied on inputs that are consumed in the production of the exported product (making normal allowance for waste).

2. The Illustrative List of Export Subsidies in Annex I of this Agreement makes reference to the term 'inputs that are consumed in the production of the exported product' in paragraphs (h) and (i). Pursuant to paragraph (h), indirect tax rebate schemes can constitute an export subsidy to the extent that they result in exemption, remission or deferral of prior-stage cumulative indirect taxes in excess of the amount of such taxes actually levied on inputs that are consumed in the production of the exported product. Pursuant to paragraph (i), drawback schemes can constitute an export subsidy to the extent that they result in a remission or drawback of import charges in excess of those actually levied on inputs that are consumed in the production of the exported product. Both paragraphs stipulate that normal allowance for waste must be made in findings regarding consumption of inputs in the production of the exported product. Paragraph (i) also provides for substitution, where appropriate.

II

In examining whether inputs are consumed in the production of the exported

---

[61] Inputs consumed in the production process are inputs physically incorporated, energy, fuels and oil used in the production process and catalysts which are consumed in the course of their use to obtain the exported product.

product, as part of a countervailing duty investigation pursuant to this Agreement, investigating authorities should proceed on the following basis:

1. Where it is alleged that an indirect tax rebate scheme, or a drawback scheme, conveys a subsidy by reason of over-rebate or excess drawback of indirect taxes or import charges on inputs consumed in the production of the exported product, the investigating authorities should first determine whether the government of the exporting Member has in place and applies a system or procedure to confirm which inputs are consumed in the production of the exported product and in what amounts. Where such a system or procedure is determined to be applied, the investigating authorities should then examine the system or procedure to see whether it is reasonable, effective for the purpose intended, and based on generally accepted commercial practices in the country of export. The investigating authorities may deem it necessary to carry out, in accordance with paragraph 6 of Article 12, certain practical tests in order to verify information or to satisfy themselves that the system or procedure is being effectively applied.

2. Where there is no such system or procedure, where it is not reasonable, or where it is instituted and considered reasonable but is found not to be applied or not to be applied effectively, a further examination by the exporting Member based on the actual inputs involved would need to be carried out in the context of determining whether an excess payment occurred. If the investigating authorities deemed it necessary, a further examination would be carried out in accordance with paragraph 1.

3. Investigating authorities should treat inputs as physically incorporated if such inputs are used in the production process and are physically present in the product exported. The Members note that an input need not be present in the final product in the same form in which it entered the production process.

4. In determining the amount of a particular input that is consumed in the production of the exported product, a 'normal allowance for waste' should be taken into account, and such waste should be treated as consumed in the production of the exported product. The term 'waste' refers to that portion of a given input which does not serve an independent function in the production process, is not consumed in the production of the exported product (for reasons such as inefficiencies) and is not recovered, used or sold by the same manufacturer.

5. The investigating authority's determination of whether the claimed allowance for waste is 'normal' should take into account the production process, the average experience of the industry in the country of export, and other technical factors, as appropriate. The investigating authority should bear in mind that an important question is whether the authorities in the exporting Member have reasonably calculated the amount of waste, when such an amount is intended to be included in the tax or duty rebate or remission.

ANNEX III   GUIDELINES IN THE DETERMINATION OF SUBSTITUTION DRAWBACK SYSTEMS AS EXPORT SUBSIDIES

I

Drawback systems can allow for the refund or drawback of import charges on inputs which are consumed in the production process of another product and where the export of this latter product contains domestic inputs having the same quality and characteristics as those substituted for the imported inputs. Pursuant to paragraph (i) of the Illustrative List of Export Subsidies in Annex I, substitution drawback systems can constitute an export subsidy to the extent that they result in an excess drawback of the import charges levied initially on the imported inputs for which drawback is being claimed.

II

In examining any substitution drawback system as part of a countervailing duty investigation pursuant to this Agreement, investigating authorities should proceed on the following basis:

1. Paragraph (i) of the Illustrative List stipulates that home market inputs may be substituted for imported inputs in the production of a product for export provided such inputs are equal in quantity to, and have the same quality and characteristics as, the imported inputs being substituted. The existence of a verification system or procedure is important because it enables the government of the exporting Member to ensure and demonstrate that the quantity of inputs for which drawback is claimed does not exceed the quantity of similar products exported, in whatever form, and that there is not drawback of import charges in excess of those originally levied on the imported inputs in question.

2. Where it is alleged that a substitution drawback system conveys a subsidy, the investigating authorities should first proceed to determine whether the government of the exporting Member has in place and applies a verification system or procedure. Where such a system or procedure is determined to be applied, the investigating authorities should then examine the verification procedures to see whether they are reasonable, effective for the purpose intended, and based on generally accepted commercial practices in the country of export. To the extent that the procedures are determined to meet this test and are effectively applied, no subsidy should be presumed to exist. It may be deemed necessary by the investigating authorities to carry out, in accordance with paragraph 6 of Article 12, certain practical tests in order to verify infor-

mation or to satisfy themselves that the verification procedures are being effectively applied.

3. Where there are no verification procedures, where they are not reasonable, or where such procedures are instituted and considered reasonable but are found not to be actually applied or not applied effectively, there may be a subsidy. In such cases a further examination by the exporting Member based on the actual transactions involved would need to be carried out to determine whether an excess payment occurred. If the investigating authorities deemed it necessary, a further examination would be carried out in accordance with paragraph 2.

4. The existence of a substitution drawback provision under which exporters are allowed to select particular import shipments on which drawback is claimed should not of itself be considered to convey a subsidy.

5. An excess drawback of import charges in the sense of paragraph (i) would be deemed to exist where governments paid interest on any monies refunded under their drawback schemes, to the extent of the interest actually paid or payable.

ANNEX IV   CALCULATION OF THE TOTAL AD VALOREM SUBSIDISATION (PARAGRAPH 1(A) OF ARTICLE 6)[62]

1. Any calculation of the amount of a subsidy for the purpose of paragraph 1(a) of Article 6 shall be done in terms of the cost to the granting government.

2. Except as provided in paragraphs 3 through 5, in determining whether the overall rate of subsidisation exceeds 5 per cent of the value of the product, the value of the product shall be calculated as the total value of the recipient firm's[63] sales in the most recent 12-month period, for which sales data is available, preceding the period in which the subsidy is granted.[64]

3. Where the subsidy is tied to the production or sale of a given product, the value of the product shall be calculated as the total value of the recipient firm's sales of that product in the most recent 12-month period, for which sales data is available, preceding the period in which the subsidy is granted.

---

[62]   An understanding among Members should be developed, as necessary, on matters which are not specified in this Annex or which need further clarification for the purposes of paragraph 1(a) of Article 6.

[63]   The recipient firm is a firm in the territory of the subsidising Member.

[64]   In the case of tax-related subsidies the value of the product shall be calculated as the total value of the recipient firm's sales in the fiscal year in which the tax-related measure was earned.

4. Where the recipient firm is in a start-up situation, serious prejudice shall be deemed to exist if the overall rate of subsidisation exceeds 15 per cent of the total funds invested. For purposes of this paragraph, a start-up period will not extend beyond the first year of production.[65]

5. Where the recipient firm is located in an inflationary economy country, the value of the product shall be calculated as the recipient firm's total sales (or sales of the relevant product, if the subsidy is tied) in the preceding calendar year indexed by the rate of inflation experienced in the 12 months preceding the month in which the subsidy is to be given.

6. In determining the overall rate of subsidisation in a given year, subsidies given under different programmes and by different authorities in the territory of a Member shall be aggregated.

7. Subsidies granted prior to the date of entry into force of the WTO Agreement, the benefits of which are allocated to future production, shall be included in the overall rate of subsidisation.

8. Subsidies which are non-actionable under relevant provisions of this Agreement shall not be included in the calculation of the amount of a subsidy for the purpose of paragraph 1(a) of Article 6.

ANNEX V   PROCEDURES FOR DEVELOPING INFORMATION CONCERNING SERIOUS PREJUDICE

1. Every Member shall cooperate in the development of evidence to be examined by a panel in procedures under paragraphs 4 through 6 of Article 7. The parties to the dispute and any third-country Member concerned shall notify to the DSB, as soon as the provisions of paragraph 4 of Article 7 have been invoked, the organization responsible for administration of this provision within its territory and the procedures to be used to comply with requests for information.

2. In cases where matters are referred to the DSB under paragraph 4 of Article 7, the DSB shall, upon request, initiate the procedure to obtain such information from the government of the subsidising Member as necessary to establish the existence and amount of subsidisation, the value of total sales of the subsidised firms, as well as information necessary to analyze the adverse effects caused by the subsidised product.[66] This process may include, where

---

[65]   Start-up situations include instances where financial commitments for product development or construction of facilities to manufacture products benefiting from the subsidy have been made, even though production has not begun.

[66]   In cases where the existence of serious prejudice has to be demonstrated.

appropriate, presentation of questions to the government of the subsidising Member and of the complaining Member to collect information, as well as to clarify and obtain elaboration of information available to the parties to a dispute through the notification procedures set forth in Part VII.[67]

3. In the case of effects in third-country markets, a party to a dispute may collect information, including through the use of questions to the government of the third-country Member, necessary to analyse adverse effects, which is not otherwise reasonably available from the complaining Member or the subsidising Member. This requirement should be administered in such a way as not to impose an unreasonable burden on the third-country Member. In particular, such a Member is not expected to make a market or price analysis specially for that purpose. The information to be supplied is that which is already available or can be readily obtained by this Member (e.g. most recent statistics which have already been gathered by relevant statistical services but which have not yet been published, customs data concerning imports and declared values of the products concerned, etc.). However, if a party to a dispute undertakes a detailed market analysis at its own expense, the task of the person or firm conducting such an analysis shall be facilitated by the authorities of the third-country Member and such a person or firm shall be given access to all information which is not normally maintained confidential by the government.

4. The DSB shall designate a representative to serve the function of facilitating the information-gathering process. The sole purpose of the representative shall be to ensure the timely development of the information necessary to facilitate expeditious subsequent multilateral review of the dispute. In particular, the representative may suggest ways to most efficiently solicit necessary information as well as encourage the cooperation of the parties.

5. The information-gathering process outlined in paragraphs 2 through 4 shall be completed within 60 days of the date on which the matter has been referred to the DSB under paragraph 4 of Article 7. The information obtained during this process shall be submitted to the panel established by the DSB in accordance with the provisions of Part X. This information should include, inter alia, data concerning the amount of the subsidy in question (and, where appropriate, the value of total sales of the subsidised firms), prices of the subsidised product, prices of the non-subsidised product, prices of other suppliers to the market, changes in the supply of the subsidised product to the market in question and changes in market shares. It should also include rebuttal

---

[67] The information-gathering process by the DSB shall take into account the need to protect information which is by nature confidential or which is provided on a confidential basis by any Member involved in this process.

evidence, as well as such supplemental information as the panel deems relevant in the course of reaching its conclusions.

6. If the subsidising and/or third-country Member fail to cooperate in the information-gathering process, the complaining Member will present its case of serious prejudice, based on evidence available to it, together with facts and circumstances of the non-cooperation of the subsidising and/or third-country Member. Where information is unavailable due to non-cooperation by the subsidising and/or third-country Member, the panel may complete the record as necessary relying on best information otherwise available.

7. In making its determination, the panel should draw adverse inferences from instances of non-cooperation by any party involved in the information-gathering process.

8. In making a determination to use either best information available or adverse inferences, the panel shall consider the advice of the DSB representative nominated under paragraph 4 as to the reasonableness of any requests for information and the efforts made by parties to comply with these requests in a cooperative and timely manner.

9. Nothing in the information-gathering process shall limit the ability of the panel to seek such additional information it deems essential to a proper resolution to the dispute, and which was not adequately sought or developed during that process. However, ordinarily the panel should not request additional information to complete the record where the information would support a particular party's position and the absence of that information in the record is the result of unreasonable non-cooperation by that party in the information-gathering process.

ANNEX VI PROCEDURES FOR ON-THE-SPOT INVESTIGATIONS PURSUANT TO PARAGRAPH 6 OF ARTICLE 12

1. Upon initiation of an investigation, the authorities of the exporting Member and the firms known to be concerned should be informed of the intention to carry out on-the-spot investigations.

2. If in exceptional circumstances it is intended to include non-governmental experts in the investigating team, the firms and the authorities of the exporting Member should be so informed. Such non-governmental experts should be subject to effective sanctions for breach of confidentiality requirements.

3. It should be standard practice to obtain explicit agreement of the firms concerned in the exporting Member before the visit is finally scheduled.

4. As soon as the agreement of the firms concerned has been obtained, the

investigating authorities should notify the authorities of the exporting Member of the names and addresses of the firms to be visited and the dates agreed.

5. Sufficient advance notice should be given to the firms in question before the visit is made.

6. Visits to explain the questionnaire should only be made at the request of an exporting firm. In case of such a request the investigating authorities may place themselves at the disposal of the firm; such a visit may only be made if (a) the authorities of the importing Member notify the representatives of the government of the Member in question and (b) the latter do not object to the visit.

7. As the main purpose of the on-the-spot investigation is to verify information provided or to obtain further details, it should be carried out after the response to the questionnaire has been received unless the firm agrees to the contrary and the government of the exporting Member is informed by the investigating authorities of the anticipated visit and does not object to it; further, it should be standard practice prior to the visit to advise the firms concerned of the general nature of the information to be verified and of any further information which needs to be provided, though this should not preclude requests to be made on the spot for further details to be provided in the light of information obtained.

8. Enquiries or questions put by the authorities or firms of the exporting Members and essential to a successful on-the-spot investigation should, whenever possible, be answered before the visit is made.

ANNEX VII   DEVELOPING COUNTRY MEMBERS REFERRED TO IN PARAGRAPH 2(A) OF ARTICLE 27

The developing country Members not subject to the provisions of paragraph 1(a) of Article 3 under the terms of paragraph 2(a) of Article 27 are:

(a) Least-developed countries designated as such by the United Nations which are Members of the WTO.

(b) Each of the following developing countries which are Members of the WTO shall be subject to the provisions which are applicable to other developing country Members according to paragraph 2(b) of Article 27 when GNP per capita has reached $1,000 per annum:[68] Bolivia, Cameroon, Congo, Côte

---

[68]   The inclusion of developing country Members in the list in paragraph (b) is based on the most recent data from the World Bank on GNP per capita.

d'Ivoire, Dominican Republic, Egypt, Ghana, Guatemala, Guyana, India, Indonesia, Kenya, Morocco, Nicaragua, Nigeria, Pakistan, Philippines, Senegal, Sri Lanka and Zimbabwe.

Appendix 4 List of cases

1. EU ANTI-DUMPING AND COUNTERVAILING CASES

Synthetic handbags from China, OJ 1997, L208, p. 31 (Chapter 4, Section 4.3; Chapter 8, Section 8.1)

Compact fluorescent lights from China, OJ 2001, L195, p. 8. (Chapter 4, Section 4.8)

Unbleached (grey) cotton fabrics from various countries (provisional duties) OJ 1996, L295, p. 3 (Chapter 4, Section 4.9; Chapter 8, Section 8.2)

Cellulose filament yarn from USA, OJ 2002, L251 p. 9 (Chapter 4, Sections 4.9 and 4.10; Chapter 8, Section 8.2; Chapter 10, Section 10.1.4)

Refined antimony trioxide from the People's Republic of China, OJ 1994, L176, p. 41 (Chapter 4, Section 4.11)

Methylamine from the German Democratic Republic and Romania, OJ 1982, L238 p. 35 (Chapter 4, Section 4.11).

Leather handbags from China, OJ 1997, L33 p. 11 and L208 p. 31 (Chapter 4, Section 4.11)

DRAMs from Japan, OJ 1990, L193, p. 1 (Chapter 4, Section 4.12)

CD-Rs from India, OJ 2003, L138, p. 1 (Chapter 4, Section 4.12)

Barium carbonate from China, OJ 2005, L189, p. 15 (Chapter 5, Section 5.7.1)

CD-Rs from Taiwan, OJ 2002 L160, p. 2 (Chapter 6, Section 6.3, footnote, Section 6.5)

Seamless tubes from Romania, OJ 1997, L141 p. 36 (provisional duties) (Chapter 6, Sections 6.3)

Gum Rosin from China, OJ 1994, L41 p. 50 (Chapter 8, Section 8.1)

Ring binder mechanisms from China and Malaysia, OJ 1997, L22 p. 1 (Chapter 8, Section 8.2)

Certain footwear from China and Taiwan, OJ 2006, L275 p. 1 (Chapter 8, Section 8.2)

PET film from India, OJ 1999, L316, p. 1 (countervailing duties) and OJ 2001, L227 p. 1 (anti-dumping duties) (Chapter 10, Section 10.2)

2. EU COURT CASES (EUROPEAN COURT OF JUSTICE AND COURT OF FIRST INSTANCE)

Calcium metal from Russia and China, Case C-358/89, *Extramet Industrie S.A.* v. *Council,* [1992] ECR I-3813 (Chapter 4, Section 4.7)

Stainless steel bright bars from India, Case T-58/99, *Mukand Ltd and Others* v. *Council,* [2001] ECR II-2521 (Chapter 4, Section 4.7)

Paint brushes from China, Case C-16/90, *Nölle* v. *Hauptzollamt Bremen-Freihafen,* [1991] ECR I-5163 (Chapter 5, Section 5.7.1)

Mini-ball bearings from Japan, Case 240/84, *NTN Toyo Bearing Co., Ltd.* v. *Council,* [1987] ECR 1809 (Chapter 6, Sections 6.1, 6.5.1)

CD-Rs from Taiwan, Case T-274/02, *Ritek Corp and Prodisc Technology Inc* v. *Council,* Judgment of 24 October 2006 (Chapter 6, Section 6.8)

Seamless tubes from Romania, Case C-76/00P, *Petrotub SA and Republica SA* v. *Council,* [2003] ECR I-79 (Chapter 6, Sections 6.2, 6.5, 6.5.1)

3. WTO PANEL AND APPELLATE BODY CASES

Australia — Subsidies Provided to Producers and Exporters of Automotive Leather (Complainant: United States), Panel WT/DS126/R, 25 May 1999 (Chapter 3, Section 3.5, footnote)

European Communities — Anti-Dumping Duties on Imports of Cotton-type Bed Linen from India (Complainant: India), Panel WT/DS141/R, 30 October 2000; Appellate Body, WT/DS141/AB/R, 1 March 2001 (Chapter 6, Section 6.8)

European Communities – Anti-Dumping Duties on Malleable Cast Iron Tube or Pipe Fittings from Brazil (Complainant: Brazil), Panel WT/DS219/R, 7 March 2003 (Chapter 6, Section 6.8)

United States – Countervailing Measures concerning certain products from the European Communities (Complainant: European Communities), Appellate Body WT/DS212/AB/R, 9 December 2002 (Chapter 7, Section 7.7)

United States – Imposition of Countervailing Duties on Certain Hot-Rolled Lead and Bismuth Carbon Steel Products Originating in the United Kingdom (Complainant: European Communities), Appellate Body WT/DS138/AB/R, 10 May 2000 (Chapter 7, Section 7.7)

United States — Laws, Regulations and Methodology for Calculating Dumping Margins (Zeroing) (Complainant: European Communities), Panel WT/DS294/R, 31 October 2005; Appellate Body WT/DS294/AB/R, 31 March 2006 (Chapter 6, Section 6.8)

United States – Measures Relating to Zeroing and Sunset Reviews (Complainant: Japan and Others), Appellate Body WT/DS 322/AB/R, 9 January 2007 (Chapter 6, Section 6.8)

Index